Chris Cook is Head of the Department of History, Philosophy and European Studies at the Polytechnic of North London. He was educated at St. Catharine's College, Cambridge, where he took first-class honors in history. After research at Nuffield College, Oxford, he was subsequently Lecturer in Politics at Magdalen College, Oxford, before moving to the London School of Economics as Senior Research Officer.

His many previous publications include (with co-editors) *Sources in British Political History, 1900–51*; *British Historical Facts, 1830–1900*; *The Decade of Disillusion*; *By-Elections in British Politics*; *The Atlas of Modern British History, 1700–1970*; *Crisis and Controversy: Essays in Honor of A. J. P. Taylor*; *Post-War Britain*; *The Slump*; and *A Short History of the Liberal Party, 1900–84*. He is a Fellow of the Royal Historical Society.

John Paxton is editor of *The Statesman's Year-Book*. He has written many books on European affairs, including *The Developing Common Market*; *A Dictionary of the European Communities*; and *Companion to Russian History*. His other works include *The Statesman's Year-Book World Gazetteer*; *Calendar of Creative Man* (with Sheila Fairfield); and *Everyman's Dictionary of Abbreviations*.

EUROPEAN POLITICAL FACTS, 1918–84

EUROPEAN
POLITICAL FACTS,
1918–84

CHRIS COOK
and
JOHN PAXTON

Facts On File Publications
New York, New York ● Oxford, England

First edition (*European Political Facts. 1918–73*) 1975
New edition (*European Political Facts. 1918–84*) 1986

Published in the United Kingdom by
The Macmillan Press Ltd

First published in the United States by
Facts on File, Inc.
460 Park Avenue South
New York, New York 10016

Printed in Hong Kong

Library of Congress Cataloging in Publication Data
Cook, Chris, 1945–
European political facts. 1918–84.
Includes index.
1. Europe–Politics and government–1918–1945–
Handbooks, manuals, etc. 2. Europe–Politics and
government–1945–   –Handbooks, manuals, etc.
3. International agencies–Handbooks, manuals, etc.
I. Paxton, John. II. Title.
JN12.C643   1986   320.94'02'02   85–10162
ISBN 0–8160–1301–2

CONTENTS

PREFACE

As European countries move closer together for political, economic, social and cultural co-operation, there is an increasing need for readily accessible facts concerning the recent history of these countries. We have made this our prime aim in compiling *European Political Facts, 1918–84*.

Our coverage is from the Atlantic to the Urals and in adopting this broad, outward-looking concept of Europe we have, naturally, encountered considerable editorial difficulties. The general aim is comparability between countries. This was not always easy to achieve and in some cases impossible, particularly for comparisons between 'East' and 'West' Europe.

1918 is a watershed between an old and a new Europe and the editors felt that this was a realistic starting point although some facts are given for earlier years where these are pertinent. Space naturally limits the data which can be presented for 35 countries covering a span of 66 years.

We are grateful to many people and organizations for their help and advice. In the first place we should like to acknowledge our debt to David Butler, who was a pathfinder with his highly successful *British Political Facts*.

Gratitude also goes to Sheila Fairfield and Dione Daffin for hours of work digging for facts; to Brian Hunter for tremendous help on eastern European countries; and to Stephen Brooks.

We have to thank Penny White for excellent typing and sharp eyes for inconsistencies. We must also thank Sue Warren, Len Jones and Alison Johnson for their very great help with proof reading.

But some error and inconsistency can still appear in a work of this kind and the editors are solely responsible. We do ask readers to alert us if they spot errors, and constructive and informed criticism will be welcome for future editions.

Chris Cook
John Paxton

1 INTERNATIONAL ORGANIZATIONS

THE UNITED NATIONS

The United Nations is an association of states which have pledged themselves, through signing the Charter, to maintain international peace and security and to co-operate in establishing political, economic and social conditions under which this task can be securely achieved. Nothing contained in the Charter authorizes the organization to intervene in matters which are essentially within the domestic jurisdiction of any state.

The United Nations Charter originated from proposals agreed upon at discussions held at Dumbarton Oaks (Washington, DC) between the USSR, US and UK from 21 Aug to 28 Sep, and between US, UK and China from 29 Sep to 7 Oct 44. These proposals were laid before the United Nations Conference on International Organization, held at San Francisco from 25 Apr to 26 June 45, and (after amendments had been made to the original proposals) the Charter of the United Nations was signed on 26 June 45 by the delegates of 50 countries. Ratification of all the signatures had been received by 31 Dec 45.

The United Nations formally came into existence on 24 Oct 45, with the deposit of the requisite number of ratifications of the Charter with the US Department of State. The official languages of the United Nations are Chinese, English, French, Russian and Spanish; the working languages are English, French and (in the General Assembly) Spanish and Russian.

The headquarters of the United Nations is in New York City, USA.

Membership. Membership is open to all peace-loving states whose admission will be effected by the General Assembly upon recommendation of the Security Council.

The Principal Organs of the United Nations are: 1. The General Assembly 2. The security Council 3. The Economic and Social Council 4. The Trusteeship Council 5. The International Court of Justice 6. The Secretariat.

1. The General Assembly consists of all the members of the United Nations. Each member is entitled to be represented at its meetings by five delegates and five alternate delegates, but has only one vote. The General Assembly meets regularly once a year, commencing on the 3rd Tuesday in September; the session normally lasts until mid-December and is resumed for some weeks in the new year if this is required. Special sessions may be convoked by the Secretary-General if requested by the Security Council, by a majority of the members of the United Nations or by one member concurred with by the majority of the members. The General Assembly elects its President for each session.

The first regular session was held in London from 10 Jan to 14 Feb and in New York from 23 Oct to 16 Dec 46.

Sixteen special sessions have been held in the period 1947–81.

The work of the General Assembly is divided between six Main Committees and the Special Political Committee, on each of which every member has the right to be represented by one delegate. I. Political Security. II. Economic and Financial. III. Social, Humanitarian and Cultural. IV. Trust and Non-Self-Governing Territories. V. Administrative and Budgetary. VI. Legal.

In addition there is a General Committee charged with the task of co-ordinating the proceedings of the Assembly and its Committees; and a Credentials Committee which verifies the credentials of the delegates. The General Committee consists of 25 members, comprising the President of the General Assembly, its 17 Vice-Presidents and the Chairmen of the seven Main Committees. The Credentials Committee consists of nine members, elected at the beginning of each session of the General Assembly. The Assembly has two standing committees – an Advisory Committee on Administrative and Budgetary Questions and a Committee on Contributions. The General Assembly establishes subsidiary and *ad hoc* bodies when necessary to deal with specific matters.

The General Assembly may discuss any matters within the scope of the Charter, and with the exception of any situation or dispute on the agenda of the Security Council, may make recommendations on any such questions or matters. For decisions on important questions a two-thirds majority is required, on other questions a simple majority of members present and voting. In addition, the Assembly at its fifth session, in 1950, decided that if the Security Council, because of lack of unanimity of the permanent members, fails to exercise its primary responsibility for the maintenance of international peace and security in any case where there appears to be a threat to the peace, breach of the peace or act of aggression, the General Assembly shall consider the matter immediately with a view to making appropriate recommendations to members for collective measures, including in the case of a breach of the peace or act of aggression the use of armed force when necessary, to maintain or restore international peace and security.

The General Assembly receives and considers reports from the other organs of the United Nations, including the Security Council. The Secretary-General makes an annual report to it on the work of the organization.

2. The Security Council consists of 15 members, each of which has one representative and one vote. There are five permanent and ten non-permanent members elected for a two-year term by a two-thirds majority of the General Assembly. Retiring members are not eligible for immediate re-election. Any other member of the United Nations will be invited to participate without vote in the discussion of questions specially affecting its interests.

The Security Council bears the primary responsibility for the maintenance of peace and security. It is also responsible for the functions of the UN in trust territories classed as 'strategic areas'. Decisions on procedural questions are made by an affirmative vote of nine members. On all other matters the affirmative vote of nine members must include the concurring votes of all permanent members (in practice, however, an abstention by a permanent member is not considered a veto), subject to the provision that when the Security Council is considering methods for the peaceful settlement of a dispute, parties to the dispute abstain from voting.

For the maintenance of international peace and security the Security Council can, in accordance with special agreements to be concluded, call on armed forces, assistance and facilities of the member states. It is assisted by a Military Staff Committee consisting of the Chiefs of Staff of the permanent members of the Security Council or their representatives.

The Presidency of the Security Council is held for one month in rotation by the member states in the English alphabetical order of their names.

The Security Council functions continuously. Its members are permanently represented at the seat of the organization, but it may meet at any place that will best facilitate its work.

The Council has two standing committees, of Experts and on the Admission of New Members. In addition, from time to time, it establishes *ad hoc* committees and commissions such as the Truce Supervision Organization in Palestine. It has also appointed a Representative for India and Pakistan.

Permanent Members: China, France, USSR, UK, USA.

3. The Economic and Social Council is responsible under the General Assembly for carrying out the functions of the United Nations with regard to international economic, social, cultural, educational, health and related matters. By Nov 77, 15 specialized inter-governmental agencies working in these fields had been brought into relationship with the United Nations. The Economic and Social Council may also make arrangements for consultation with international non-governmental organizations and, after consultation with the member concerned, with national organizations; by Sep 78, 231 non-governmental organizations had been granted consultative status and a further 534 were on the register.

The Economic and Social Council consists of 54 member states elected by a two-thirds majority of the General Assembly. Nine are elected each year for a three-year term. Retiring members are eligible for immediate re-election. Each member has one vote. Decisions are made by a majority of the members present and voting.

The Council nominally holds two sessions a year, and special sessions may be held if required. The President is elected for one year and is eligible for immediate re-election.

The Economic and Social Council has the following commissions:

Regional Economic Commissions: ECE (Economic Commission for Europe); ECAFE (Economic Commission for Asia and the Far East. Bangkok); ECLA (Economic Commission for Latin America. Santiago, Chile); ECA (Economic Commission for Africa. Addis Ababa). These Commissions have been established to enable the nations of the major regions of the world to co-operate on common problems and also to produce economic information.

(1) Six Functional Statistical Commissions with sub-commission on Statistical Sampling; (2) Commission on Human Rights, with sub-commission on Prevention of Discrimination and Protection of Minorities; (3) Social Development Commission; (4) Commission on the Status of Women; (5) Commission on Narcotic Drugs; (6) Population Commission; (7–10) Four regional Economic Commissions for Europe, Asia and the Far East, Latin America, Africa.

The Economic and Social Council has the following standing committees: The Economic Committee, Social Committee, Co-ordination Committee, Committee on Non-Governmental Organizations, Interim Committee on Programme of Conferences, Committee for Industrial Development, Advisory Committee on the Application of Science and Technology to Development, Committee on Housing, Building and Planning.

Other special bodies are the Permanent Central Opium Board, the Drug Supervisory Body, the Interim Co-ordinating Committee for International Commodity Arrangements and the Administrative Committee on Co-ordination to ensure (1) the most effective implementation of the agreements entered into between the United Nations and the specialized agencies and (2) co-ordination of activities.

4. The Trusteeship Council. The Charter provides for an international trusteeship system to safeguard the interests of the inhabitants of territories which are not yet fully self-governing and which may be placed thereunder by individual trusteeship agreements. These are called trust territories.

The Trusteeship Council consists of one member administering trust territories: USA: the permanent members of the Security Council that are not administering trust territories: China, France, USSR and UK. Decisions of the Council are made by a majority of the members present and voting, each member having one vote. The Council holds one regular session each year, and special sessions if required.

5. The International Court of Justice was created by an international treaty, the State of the Court, which forms an integral part of the United Nations Charter. All members of the United Nations are *ipso facto* parties to the Statute of the Court.

The Court is composed of independent judges, elected regardless of their nationality, who possess the qualifications required in their countries for appointment to the highest judicial offices, or are jurisconsuls of recognized competence in international law. There are 15 judges, no two of whom may be nationals of the same state. They are elected by the Security Council and the General Assembly of the United Nations sitting independently. Candidates are chosen from a list of persons nominated by the national groups in the Permanent Court of Arbitration established by Hague Conventions of 1899 and 1907. In the case of members of the United Nations not represented in the Permanent Court of Arbitration, candidates are nominated by national groups appointed for the purpose by their governments. The judges are elected for a nine-year term and are eligible for immediate re-election. When engaged on business of the Court, they enjoy diplomatic privileges and immunities.

The Court elects its own President and Vice-Presidents for three years and remains permanently in session, except for judicial vacations. The full court of 15 judges normally sits, but a quorum of nine judges is sufficient to constitute the Court. It may form chambers of three or more judges for dealing with particular categories of cases, and forms annually a chamber of five judges to hear and determine, at the request of the parties, cases by summary procedures.

Competence and Jurisdiction. Only states may be parties in cases before the Court, which is open to the states parties to its Statute. The conditions under which the Court will be open to other states are laid down by the Security Council. The Court exercises its jurisdiction in all cases which the parties refer to it and in all matters provided for in the Charter, or in treaties and conventions in force. Disputes concerning the jurisdiction of the Court are settled by the Court's own decision.

The Court may apply in its decision: (a) international conventions; (b) international custom; (c) the general principles of law recognized by civilized nations; and (d) as subsidiary means for the determination of the rules of law, judicial decisions and the teachings of highly qualified publicists. If the parties agree, the Court may decide a case *ex aequo et bono*. The Court may also give

5

an advisory opinion on any legal question to any organ of the United Nations or its agencies.

Procedure. The official languages of the Court are French and English. At the request of any party the Court will authorize the use of another language by this party. All questions are decided by a majority of the judges present. If the votes are equal, the President has a casting vote. The judgment is final and without appeal, but a revision may be applied for within ten years from the date of the judgment on the ground of a new decisive factor. Unless otherwise decided by the Court, each party bears its own costs.

Judges. The judges of the Court are elected by the Security Council and the General Assembly.

'National' Judges. If there is no judge on the bench of the nationality of the parties to the dispute, each party has the right to choose a judge. Such judges shall take part in the decision on terms of complete equality with their colleagues.

The Court has its seat at The Hague, but may sit and exercise its functions elsewhere whenever it considers this desirable. The expenses of the Court are borne by the United Nations.

6. The Secretariat is composed of the Secretary-General, who is the chief administrative officer of the organization, and an international staff appointed by him under regulations established by the General Assembly. However, the Secretary-General, the High Commissioner for Refugees and the Managing Director of the Fund are appointed by the General Assembly.

The Secretary-General acts as chief administrative officer in all meetings of the General Assembly, the Security Council, the Economic and Social Council and the Trusteeship Council.

Secretaries-General:

Trygve Lie (Norway)	1 Feb 46–10 Apr 53
Dag Hammarskjöld (Sweden)	10 Apr 53–17 Sep 61
U Thant (Burma)	
[Acting Secretary-General 1961–2]	3 Nov 61–31 Dec 71
Kurt Waldheim (Austria)	1 Jan 72–31 Dec 81
Javier Perez de Cuellar (Peru)	1 Jan 82–

The Secretary-General is assisted by Under-Secretaries-General and Assistant Secretaries-General.

THE LEAGUE OF NATIONS

The League of Nations formally came into existence on 10 Jan 20, through the coming into force at that date of the Treaty of Versailles. The two official languages of the League were English and French. The seat of the League was Geneva, Switzerland.

The League of Nations was an association of states which had pledged themselves, through signing the Covenant (*i.e.* the constitution of the League) not to go to war before submitting their disputes with each other, or states not members of the League, to arbitration or enquiry and a delay of from three to nine months. Furthermore, any state violating this pledge was automatically in a state of outlawry with the other states, which were bound to sever all economic and political relations with the defaulting state.

Secretaries-General of the League:

Sir Eric Drummond [E of Perth] (Britain)	1919–32
Joseph Avenol (France)	1933–40

On Joseph Avenol's resignation, 26 July 40, Sean Lester (Irish Republic) became Acting Secretary-General.

Membership. The following European States joined the League on the dates given below:

Albania[1]	16 Dec 20
Belgium	10 Jan 20
Bulgaria	16 Dec 20
Czechoslovakia	10 Jan 20
Denmark	8 Mar 20
Estonia[1]	22 Sep 21
Finland	16 Dec 20
France	10 Jan 20
Germany	8 Sep 26
Greece	30 Mar 20
Hungary	18 Sep 22
Irish Free State	10 Sep 23
Italy	10 Jan 20
Latvia[1]	22 Sep 21
Lithuania[1]	22 Sep 21
Luxembourg	16 Dec 20
Netherlands	9 Mar 20

[1] Made declarations putting the protection of their national minorities under League auspices as a condition of their entry into the League.

Norway	5 Mar 20
Poland	10 Jan 20
Portugal	8 Apr 20
Romania	8 Apr 20
Spain	10 Jan 20
Sweden	9 Mar 20
Switzerland	8 Mar 20
Turkey	18 July 32
USSR	18 Sep 34
UK	10 Jan 20
Yugoslavia	10 Feb 20

The following European states withdrew from the League: Spain on 8 Sep 26, Germany on 21 Oct 33, Italy on 11 Dec 37, and Hungary on 11 Apr 39, announced their withdrawal from the League; according to Art. 1, par. 3, of the Covenant the notice of withdrawal only came into force two years after it had been given. On 22 Mar 28, Spain resolved to continue a member of the League.

Austria ceased to be a member after her annexation by Germany in Mar 38.

The League was formally dissolved in 1946, but in practice it had not met since 1939.

THE ORGANS OF THE LEAGUE

The Primary Organs of the League were: 1. The Council, 2. The Assembly, 3. The Secretariat, 4. The Permanent Court of International Justice (at The Hague).

1. The Council was originally composed of four permanent members (the British Empire, France, Italy and Japan) and four non-permanent members to be elected every year by a majority of the Assembly. The first non-permanent members, appointed by the Peace Conference and named in the Covenant before the first Assembly met, were Belgium, Brazil, Greece and Spain. With the approval of the majority of the Assembly, the Council was able to appoint new permanent and non-permanent members. At the Assembly of Sep 26 Germany was admitted to the League and given a permanent seat on the Council. At the same time the number of non-permanent seats, already increased to six in 1922, was further increased to nine, the period of office to be three years. In order to institute the new system of rotation, three were elected for one year, three for two years, and three for three years, so that at all subsequent Assemblies three members retired instead of nine at once. Furthermore, the rule was established that a retiring member was ineligible for re-election for three years unless specially declared re-eligible. The number of members elected after being declared re-eligible could not exceed three. Hitherto the only states to secure a declaration of re-eligibility had been Poland and Spain. Both countries applied for re-eligibility in 1937, but neither of them obtained the necessary majority for re-election during the 18th Assembly, Sep 37. China re-entered the Council in 1936 as a result of such a declaration. Owing to complaints that a number of members of the League were in practice unable to enter the Council, a tenth non-permanent seat was created for three years in 1933, and in 1936 this seat was continued in existence for another three years and an eleventh non-permanent seat created for three years (*i.e.* till 1939). Any member of the League not represented on the Council was invited to send a representative to sit on it at any meetings at which matters especially affecting it were being discussed. A similar invitation could be extended to states not members of the League.

The Council met on the 3rd Monday in January, the 2nd Monday in May, and just before and after the Assembly in September.

2. The Assembly. Every state member of the League was entitled to be represented by a delegation to the Assembly composed of not more than three delegates and three substitute delegates, but it had only one vote. It met at the seat of the League (Geneva) on the second or, in certain circumstances, the first Monday in September. It could meet at other places than Geneva; extraordinary sessions could be called to deal with urgent matters.

The President was elected at the first meeting of the session, and held office for the duration of the session.

The Assembly divided itself into the following seven principal committees, on each of which every state member of the League had the right to be represented by one delegate:

I. Juridical.
II. Technical Organizations.
III. Disarmament.
IV. Budget and Staff.
V. Social Questions.
VI. Political Questions and admission of New Members.
VII. As an experiment, the General Committee of the 19th Assembly decided to set up a Seventh Committee to deal with questions of Health, Opium and Intellectual Co-operation.

The decisions of the Assembly had to be voted unanimously, except where the Covenant or the Peace Treaties provided otherwise. As a general principle decisions on questions of procedure were voted by majority, or in some cases by a two-thirds majority.

3. The Secretariat was a permanent organ composed of the Secretary-General and a number of officials selected from among citizens of all member states and from the United States of America. The Secretary-General, who took office in July 33, was M. Joseph Avenol (France). The other officials were appointed by the Secretary-General with the approval of the Council.

The Under-Secretaries-General as from 1 Feb 37 were:

> Sean Lester (Ireland) Deputy Secretary-General
> F. Walters (UK)
> Vladimir Sokoline (USSR) as from 20 Feb 37
> Podesta Costa (Argentine) as from Jan 38

4. Permanent Court of International Justice. The Permanent Court at The Hague was created by an international treaty, the Statute of the Court, which was drafted in 1920 by a committee appointed by the Council of the League of Nations and revised in 1929 with amendments which came into force in 1936. The revised Statutes adopted at the 10th Assembly provided for 15 judges for the Court, and stipulated that the Court should remain permanently in Session except for such holidays as it may decide. The judges were elected jointly by the Council and the Assembly of the League for a term of nine years.

On the dissolution of the League of Nations and the establishment of the United Nations Organization, the Court was superseded by the International Court of Justice.

The Secondary Organs of the League were:

(a) The Technical Organizations
    1. Economic and Financial
    2. Health
    3. Communications and Transit
(b) Advisory Committees
    1. Military, Naval and Air Commission
    2. Commission of Enquiry for European Union
    3. Mandates Commission
    4. Opium Committee
    5. Social Committee
    6. Committee of Experts on Slavery
(c) Committees of Intellectual Co-operation
(d) International Institutes
    1. Institute of Intellectual Co-operation (Paris)
    2. Institute of Private Law (Rome)
(e) Administrative Organization High Commissioner for Free City of Danzig

INTERNATIONAL LABOUR ORGANIZATION

The ILO was constituted in 1919 as an autonomous organization of the League of Nations. Its aim is to improve labour conditions through international action. Membership of the League carried with it membership of the Organization. When the League was dissolved the Organization was recognized as a specialized agency of the UN.

At its inception the ILO consisted of the International Labour Conference, meeting at least once a year, and the International Labour Office controlled by a governing body composed of 16 Government representatives, 8 employers' representatives and 8 workers' representatives. The decision of the Conference took the form of Draft Conventions or Recommendations. A draft Convention obliged the state concerned to approach the competent authority and ask for action. If action was taken, the member state was obliged to communicate the formal ratification of the Convention to the Secretary-General of the League. A Recommendation, if acted upon, did not require formal ratification, but the Secretary-General was informed of the action taken.

The ILO held 24 sessions between 1919 and 1939, adopted 63 Draft Conventions and 56 Recommendations; 134 ratifications were recommended to the competent authorities for action, 51 were authorized by the competent authorities, 837 were actually deposited with the Secretary-General of the League.

The following bodies assisted the work of the ILO:

The Joint Maritime Commission
The Correspondence Committee on Social Insurance
The Permanent Agricultural Committee
The Correspondence Committee on Industrial Hygiene
The Committee of Experts on Native Labour
The Committee of Experts on the Application of Conventions
The Advisory Committee on Salaried Employees
The Correspondence Committee on Accident Prevention
The Correspondence Committee on Women's Work
The Committee of Statistical Experts
The Advisory Committee on Management
The Advisory Committee of Correspondents on Workers' Spare Time
The Correspondence Committee on Unemployment Insurance and Placing
The Migration Committee
The Committee of Experts on Safety in Coalmines
The Committee of Experts on Rights of Performers as regards Broadcasting
The International Tripartite Committee on the Textile Industry.

11

EUROPEAN TRADE UNION CONFEDERATION

The ETUC was formally established in Feb 73 with some 29m. members from 14 EEC and EFTA countries (Austria, Belgium, Denmark, Finland, France, Federal Republic of Germany, Iceland, Italy, Luxembourg, Netherlands, Norway, Sweden, Switzerland, UK) and the proscribed *Unión General de Trabajadores* of Spain. Membership in 1984 was 43m. from 34 centres in 20 countries.

INTERNATIONAL CONFEDERATION OF FREE TRADE UNIONS

The ICFTU was founded in London in 1949. The amended constitution provides for co-operation with the UN and the ILO and for regional organizations to promote trade unionism, especially in developing countries.

The Congress of the Confederation meets every three years and elects the Executive Board of 29 members nominated on an area basis for a three-year period; the Board meets at least twice a year. There are joint committees with the International Trade Secretariat. In 1984 there was a membership of about 83m. from 135 affiliated organizations in 95 countries.

WORLD FEDERATION OF TRADE UNIONS

The WFTU was established in 1945, representing trade-union organizations in more than 50 countries, Communist and non-Communist (excluding Germany and Japan). In Jan 1949 the British, Netherlands and US trade unions withdrew from WFTU, and by 1951 all non-Communist unions had left, as had the Yugoslavian Federation.

The Congress meets every four years. In between, the governing body is the General Council of 134 members which meets once a year at least. In between meetings of the General Council WFTU is controlled by the Bureau, consisting of the President, the General Secretary and members from different continents, the total number being decided at each Congress. The Bureau is elected by the General Council.

Main member groups in 1983: Soviet All-Union Central Council of Trade Unions, 107m.; German Democratic Republic Free German Trade Union Federation, 8m.; Czechoslovak Central Council of Trade Unions, 6m.; Romanian General Confederation of Labour, 6.4m.; the Hungarian Central Council of Trade Unions, 4.5m.; French Confederation of Labour, 2m.

WORLD CONFEDERATION OF LABOUR

The International Federation of Christian Trade Unions was established in 1920 as a mainly Catholic organization; it ceased to exist in 1940 through Fascist and Nazi suppression, most of its members being Italian or German. It was reconstituted in 1945 and renamed World Confederation of Labour in 1968. Its policy is based on the papal encyclicals *Rerum novarum* (1891) and *Quadragesino anno* (1931), but it claims some Protestant members in Europe.

The Christian International is federative, leaving wide discretion to the autonomy of its constituent unions. Its governing body is Congress, which meets every three years. The General Council, meeting at least once a year, is composed according to the proportion of membership of Congress. Congress elects the Executive Committee of at least 12 members which appoints the Secretary-General.

The total membership in 1983 was 14m. in about 90 countries. The largest group is the Confederation of Christian Trade Unions of Belgium with a membership of 1.1m.

ORGANIZATION FOR ECONOMIC CO-OPERATION AND DEVELOPMENT (OECD)

On 30 Sep 61 the Organization for European Economic Co-operation (OEEC) was replaced by the Organization for Economic Co-operation and Development. The change of title marks the Organization's altered status and functions: with the accession of Canada and USA as full members it ceased to be a purely European body; while at the same time it added development aid to the list of its other activities. The member countries are now Australia, Austria, Belgium, Canada, Denmark, Finland, France, Federal Republic of Germany, Greece, Iceland, Ireland, Italy, Japan, Luxembourg, the Netherlands, Norway, Portugal, Spain, Sweden, Switzerland, Turkey, UK and USA. New Zealand and Yugoslavia participate in certain of the Organization's activities and have been given special status for these associations.

The aims of the reconstituted Organization, as defined in the convention signed on 14 Dec 60, are as follows: (a) to achieve the highest sustainable economic growth and employment and a rising standard of living in member countries, while maintaining financial stability, and thus to contribute to the development of the world economy; (b) to contribute to sound economic expansion in member as well as non-member countries in the process of economic development; and (c) to contribute to the expansion of world trade

13

on a multilateral, non-discriminatory basis in accordance with international obligations. Responsibility for the achievement of these aims has been vested in the Economic Policy Committee, the Development Aid Committee and the Trade Committee. The second of these is made up of representatives of all the 16 principal capital-exporting member countries, together with the Commission of the European Communities. Other committees deal with economic and development review; the environment; technical co-operation; payments; invisible transactions; insurance; fiscal matters; agriculture; fisheries; education; science policy; manpower and social affairs; energy, industry, gas, tourism, maritime transport, etc. Two of the purely European aspects of OEEC have been retained: the European Nuclear Energy Agency and the European Monetary Agreement with its Board of Management.

An OECD Development Centre began work in 1963. In 1968 a Centre for Educational Research and Innovation was set up.

NORTH ATLANTIC TREATY ORGANIZATION (NATO)

On 28 Apr 48 the Canadian Secretary of State for External Affairs broached the idea of a 'security league' of the free nations, in extension of the Brussels Treaty of 17 Mar 48. The United States Senate, on 11 June, recommended 'the association of the United States with such regional and other collective arrangements as are based on continuous self-help and mutual aid, and as affect its national security'. Detailed proposals were subsequently worked out between the Brussels Treaty powers, the USA and Canada.

On 4 Apr 49 the foreign ministers of Belgium, Canada, Denmark, France, Iceland, Italy, Luxembourg, the Netherlands, Norway, Portugal, the UK and the USA met in Washington and signed a treaty, the first article of which read as follows:

> The parties undertake, as set forth in the Charter of the United Nations, to settle any international disputes in which they may be involved by peaceful means in such a manner that international peace and security and justice are not endangered, and to refrain in their international relations from the threat or use of force in any manner inconsistent with the purposes of the United Nations.

The Treaty came into force on 24 Aug 49. Greece and Turkey were admitted as parties to the Treaty in 1951 (effective Feb 52), the Federal Republic of Germany in Oct 54 (effective 5 May 55).

As reorganized by the Council at its session in Lisbon in Feb 52, the structure of NATO is as follows:

14

The *Council*, the principal body of the organization, 'charged with the responsibility of considering all matters concerning the implementation of the provisions of the Treaty', incorporates the Council and the Defence Committee originally envisaged. The Council is a Council of Governments, on which NATO nations are normally represented by their Minister for Foreign Affairs and/or the Minister of Defence, or by other competent Ministers, especially those responsible for financial and economic affairs. The Council normally meets at ministerial level two or three times a year.

Each member government appoints a *Permanent Representative* to represent it on the Council when its ministerial representatives are not present. Each Permanent Representative also heads a national delegation of advisers and experts. The Permanent Representatives meet once or twice a week and can be called together at short notice at any time.

In carrying out its role, the Council is assisted by a number of committees, some of a permanent nature, some temporary. Like the Council, the membership of each committee is made up of national representatives. They study questions submitted to them by the Council for recommendation. The work of the committees has a direct bearing on the activities of the International Secretariat.

The Political Committee, charged with preparing the political agenda for the Council, dates from 1957 as does the Economic Committee, which studies and reports to the Council on economic issues of special interest to the Alliance. In 1963 a Defence Planning Committee was established as the civilian co-ordinating body for the defence plans of member countries. Since France's withdrawal from NATO military organizations, this committee is composed of the Permanent Representatives of the 14 countries which take part in NATO's integrated common defence. Like the Council, it also meets at ministerial level. And at the Ministerial meeting in Dec 66 two bodies for nuclear planning were established: the Nuclear Defence Affairs Committee and a Nuclear Planning Group of 7–8 members.

Among other important committees are: the Science Committee and the Infrastructure Committee, whose varied tasks are directly linked to fundamental and applied research; the Senior Civil Emergency Planning Committee; the Committee for European Airspace Co-ordination; the Committee for Pipelines; the Committee for Information and Cultural Relations; and the Civil and Military Budget Committees, who carefully supervise the expenditures of NATO funds for the maintenance of the International Secretariat and military headquarters. In Nov 69 the Council established a Committee on the Challenges of Modern Society to consider problems of the human environment. This new committee examines methods of improving the exchange of views and experience among the Allied countries in the task of creating a better environment for their societies.

15

More recently, the old Armaments Committee has been replaced by the Conference of National Armaments Directors.

Headquarters: 1110 Brussels, Belgium.

Secretary-General: Lord Carrington (UK), appointed Jun 84.

The Secretary-General takes the chair at all Council meetings, except at the opening and closing of Ministerial sessions, when he gives way to the Council President. The office of President is held annually by the Foreign Minister of one of the Treaty countries.

The *Military Committee* is composed of the Chiefs of Staff or their representatives of all the member countries except France, which in 1966 withdrew from the Military Committee while remaining a member of the Council. (Iceland, having no military establishment, may be represented by a civilian.) It meets at Chiefs of Staff level two or three times a year as required, but remains in permanent session at the level of military representatives and is assisted by an integrated *international military staff*. It provides general policy guidance of a military nature to the Council.

In Dec 50 the Council approved the establishment of an integrated force for the defence of Western Europe under a Supreme Headquarters Allied Powers, Europe (SHAPE). General Eisenhower was the first Supreme Allied Commander Europe (SACEUR); he was succeeded by Generals Ridgway (1 June 52), Alfred M. Gruenther (11 July 53), Lauris Norstad (20 Nov 56), Lyman L. Lemnitzer (1 Jan 63) and Andrew J. Goodpaster (1 July 69); Deputies: Field-Marshal Lord Montgomery, 1950–8; Gen Sir Richard Gale, 1958–60; Gen. Sir Hugh Stockwell, GCB, KBE, DSO, 1960–3; Marshal of the Royal Air Force Sir Thomas Pike, GCB, CBE, DFC, 1964–7; Gen Sir Robert Bray, KCB, CBE, DSO, 1967–70; Gen Sir Desmond Fitzpatrick, DSO, MBE, MC, 1970–.

The *European Command* covers the land area from the North Cape to the Mediterranean and from the Atlantic to the eastern border of Turkey, excluding the UK and Portugal, the defence of which does not fall under any one major NATO Command.

The *Atlantic Command* extends from the North Pole to the Tropic of Cancer and from the coastal waters of North America to those of Europe and Africa, but excludes the Channel and the British Isles. The Supreme Allied Commander Atlantic (SACLANT), Adm Charles K. Duncan (USN), is an operational rather than an administrative commander, and, unlike SACEUR, has no forces permanently attached to his command in peace-time.

The *Channel Command* covers the English Channel and the southern North Sea. The Allied C-in-C Channel is Adm Sir Edward Ashanore.

The *Canada–US Regional Planning Group*, which covers the North American area, develops and recommends to the Military Committee plans for the defence of this area. It meets alternately in Washington and Ottawa.

WESTERN EUROPEAN UNION

On 17 Mar 48 a 50-year treaty 'for collaboration in economic, social and cultural matters and for collective self-defence' was signed in Brussels by the Foreign Ministers of the UK, France, the Netherlands, Belgium and Luxembourg.

On 20 Dec 50 the Western Union defence organization was merged with the North Atlantic Treaty command.

After the rejection by France of the European Defence Community on 30 Aug 54 a conference was held in London from 28 Sep to 3 Oct 54, attended by Belgium, Canada, France, Federal Germany, Italy, the Netherlands, Luxembourg, the UK and the USA, at which it was decided to invite the Federal Republic of Germany and Italy to accede to the Brussels Treaty, to end the occupation of Western Germany and to invite the latter to accede to the North Atlantic Treaty; the Federal Republic agreed that it would voluntarily limit its arms production, and provision was made for the setting up of an agency to control the armaments of the seven Brussels Treaty powers; the UK undertook not to withdraw from the Continent her four divisions and the Tactical Air Force assigned to the Supreme Allied Commander against the wishes of a majority, *i.e.* four, of the Brussels Treaty powers, except in the event of an acute overseas emergency.

At a Conference of Ministers held in Paris from 20 to 23 Oct 54 these decisions were put into effect. The Union was formally inaugurated on 6 May 55.

The *Council of WEU* consists of the Foreign Ministers of the seven powers or their representatives. An *Assembly*, composed of the WEU delegates to the Consultative Assembly of the Council of Europe, meets twice a year, usually in Paris. An *Agency for the Control of Armaments* and a *Standing Armaments Committee* have been set up in Paris. The social and cultural activities were transferred to the Council of Europe on 1 June 60.

COUNCIL OF EUROPE

In 1948 the 'Congress of Europe', bringing together at The Hague nearly 1000 influential Europeans from 26 countries, called for the creation of a united Europe, including a European Assembly. This proposal, examined first by the Ministerial Council of the Brussels Treaty Organization, then by a conference of ambassadors, was at the origin of the Council of Europe. The Statute of the Council was signed at London on 5 May 49 and came into force two months later. The founder members were Belgium, Denmark, France, Ireland, Italy, Luxembourg, the Netherlands, Norway, Sweden and the United Kingdom.

Turkey and Greece joined in 1949, Iceland in 1950, the Federal Republic of Germany in 1951 (having been an associate since 1950), Austria in 1956, Cyprus in 1961, Switzerland in 1963, Malta in 1965.

Membership is limited to European states which 'accept the principles of the rule of law and of the enjoyment by all persons within (their) jurisdiction of human rights and fundamental freedoms'. The Statute provides for both withdrawal (Art 7) and suspension (Arts 8 and 9). Greece withdrew from the Council in Dec 69.

Structure. Under the Statute two organs were set up: an inter-governmental *Committee of* (Foreign) *Ministers* with powers of decision and of recommendation to governments, and an inter-parliamentary deliberative body, the *Consultative Assembly* – both of which are served by the Secretariat. In addition, a large number of committees of experts have been established, two of them, the Council for Cultural Co-operation and the Committee on Legal Co-operation, having a measure of autonomy; on municipal matters the Committee of Ministers receive recommendations from the European Local Authorities Conference.

The Committee of Ministers meets usually twice a year, their deputies ten times a year.

The Consultative Assembly normally consists of 170 persons elected or appointed by their national parliaments (Austria 6, Belgium 7, Cyprus 3, Denmark 5, France 18, Federal Republic of Germany 18, Greece 7, Iceland 3, Ireland 4, Italy 18, Liechtenstein 2, Luxembourg 3, Malta 3, Netherlands 7, Norway 5, Portugal 7, Spain 12, Sweden 6, Switzerland 6, Turkey 12, UK 18); it meets for three-week-long sessions every year. For domestic reasons Cyprus is not at present represented in the Assembly. The work of the Assembly is prepared by parliamentary committees.

The *Joint Committee*, consisting of the Committee of Ministers and representatives of the Assembly, harmonizes relations between the two organs.

Under the European Convention of 1950 a special structure has been established for the protection of human rights. A *European Commission* investigates alleged violations of the Convention submitted to it either by states or, in some cases, by individuals. Its findings can then be examined by the *European Court of Human Rights* (set up in 1959), whose obligatory jurisdiction has been recognized by 11 states, or by the Committee of Ministers, empowered to take binding decisions by two-thirds majority vote.

For questions of national refugees and over-population, a Special Representative has been appointed, responsible to the governments collectively.

Aims and Achievements. Art 1 of the Statute states that the Council's aim is 'to achieve a greater unity between its members for the purpose of safeguarding and realizing the ideals and principles which are their common heritage and facilitating their economic and social progress'; 'this aim shall be pursued . . . by discussion of questions of common concern and by agreements and common action'. The only limitation is provided by Art 1 (d), which excludes 'matters relating to national defence'.

It has been the task of the Assembly to propose action to bring European countries closer together, to keep under constant review the progress made and to voice the views of European public opinion on the main political and economic questions of the day. The Ministers' role is to translate the Assembly's recommendations into action, particularly as regards lowering the barriers between the European countries, harmonizing their legislation or introducing where possible common European laws, abolishing discrimination on grounds of nationality and undertaking certain tasks on a joint European basis.

In May 1966 the Committee of Ministers approved a programme, designed to streamline the activities of the Council of Europe. It comprises projects for co-operation between member governments in economic, legal, social, public health, environmental and educational and scientific matters; and is to be reviewed every year.

About 115 conventions have been concluded, covering such matters as social security, patents, extradition, medical treatment, training of nurses, equivalence of degrees and diplomas, innkeepers' liability, compulsory motor insurance, the protection of television broadcasts, adoption of children, transportation of animals and *au pair* replacement. A *Social Charter* sets out the social and economic rights which all member governments agree to guarantee to their citizens.

The official languages are English and French.

Headquarters: Maison de l'Europe, Strasbourg, France.

EUROPEAN COMMUNITIES

In May 50, Belgium, France, the Federal Republic of Germany, Italy, Luxembourg and the Netherlands started negotiations with the aim of ensuring continual peace by a merging of their essential interests. The negotiations culminated in the signing in 1951 of the Treaty of Paris creating the European Coal and Steel Community (ECSC). After it was found impossible to create European Communities covering Defence and Foreign Affairs, two more communities with the aims of gradually integrating the economies of the six nations and of moving towards closer political unity, the European Economic Community (EEC) and the European Atomic Energy Community (EAEC or Euratom) were created in 1957 by the signing of the Treaties of Rome.

19

On 30 June 70 membership negotiations began between the Six and the United Kingdom, Denmark, Ireland and Norway. On 22 Jan 72 those four countries signed a Treaty of Accession, although this was rejected by Norway in a referendum in Nov 72. On 1 Jan 73 the United Kingdom, Denmark and Ireland became full members. On 28 May 79 the Greek Treaty of Accession was signed, and Greece joined the Community on 1 Jan 81. Negotiations for accession were in progress in 1984 with Spain and Portugal.

In a consultative referendum held on 24 Feb 82, Greenlanders voted by 12 615 to 11 180 to withdraw from the European Community and this was achieved in 1985.

The institutional arrangements of the Communities provide an independent executive with powers of proposal (the Commission), various consultative bodies, and a decision-making body drawn from the governments (the Council). Until 1967 the three Communities were completely distinct, although they shared some non-decision-making bodies: from that date the executives were merged in the European Commission, and the decision-taking bodies in the Council. The institutions and organs of the Communities are as follows:

The *Commission* consists of 14 members appointed by the member states to serve for 4 years; the President and Vice-Presidents are appointed initially for 2 years, but are generally re-appointed for the rest of their term. The Commission acts independently of any country in the interests of the Community as a whole, with as its mandate the implementation and guardianship of the Treaties. In this it has the right of initiative (putting proposals to the Council for action); and execution (once the Council has decided); and can take the other institutions or individual countries before the Court of Justice should any of these renege upon their responsibilities.

The **Council of Ministers** consists of Ministers from the 10 national governments and represents the national as opposed to the Community interests. It is the body which has the power of decision in the Community. Under the Treaties many of its decisions are taken to be by qualified majority vote; since the 'Luxembourg Compromise' of 1966 majority voting has been used for minor matters only.

The **European Parliament** consists of 434 members elected by the ten national members. Elections were held in June 84, and France, the Federal Republic of Germany, Italy and the United Kingdom each returned 81 members; the Netherlands 25, Belgium and Greece 24, Denmark 16, Ireland 15, and Luxembourg 6. The Socialists remained the largest single group with 130 seats. *See* also page 131.

The Parliament has a right to be consulted on a wide range of legislative proposals, and forms one arm of the Communities' Budgetary Authority.

The **Court of Justice** is composed of eleven judges and five advocates general, is responsible for the adjudication of disputes arising out of the application of the treaties, and its findings are enforceable in all member countries.

President: Robert Lecourt.

Address: 12, rue de la Côte-d'Eich, Luxembourg.

The **Economic and Social Committee**, common to the EEC and EURATOM, has an advisory role and consists of 156 representatives, employers, trade unions, consumers, etc. The **Consultative Committee**, of 84 members, performs a similar role for the ECSC.

The **Court of Auditors** was established by a Treaty signed on 22 July 75 which took effect on 1 June 77. It consists of 10 members, and replaced the former **Audit Board**. It audits all income and current and past expenditure of the European Communities.

EUROPEAN FREE TRADE ASSOCIATION (EFTA)

The European Free Trade Association has six member countries: Austria, Iceland, Norway, Portugal, Sweden and Switzerland. A seventh country, Finland, is an associate member. The Stockholm Convention establishing the Association entered into force on 3 May 60 and Finland became associated on 27 Mar 61. Iceland joined EFTA on 1 Mar 70 and was immediately granted duty-free entry for industrial goods exported to EFTA countries, while being given ten years to abolish her own existing protective duties. Two founder members of EFTA, the United Kingdom and Denmark, left EFTA on 31 Dec 72 to join the EEC.

When the Association was created it had three objectives: to achieve free trade in industrial products between member countries, to assist in the creation of a single market embracing the countries of Western Europe, and to contribute to the expansion of world trade in general.

The first objective was achieved on 31 Dec 66, when virtually all inter-EFTA tariffs were removed. This was 3 years earlier than originally planned. Finland removed her remaining EFTA tariffs a year later on 31 Dec 67 and Iceland removed her tariffs on 31 Dec 79.

The fulfilment of the second aim was secured in 1972. On 22 Jan 72 the UK and Denmark signed the Treaty of Accession to the EEC whereby they became members of the enlarged Community from 1 Jan 73. On 22 July 72, five other EFTA countries, Austria, Iceland, Portugal, Sweden and Switzerland signed Free Trade Agreements with the enlarged EEC. A similar agreement negotiated with Finland was signed on 5 Oct 73. Norway, whose intention of joining the EEC was reversed following a referendum, signed a similar agreement on 14 May 73. Through these agreements virtually complete free trade in industrial goods was achieved in 16 Western European countries from July 77. The free trade agreements apply also to Greece since its accession to the EEC on 1 Jan 81. A multilateral free trade agreement between the EFTA countries and Spain, a candidate for EEC membership, came into force on 1 May 80 and the first tariff cuts were applied on 1 June 80.

The third objective was to contribute to the expansion of world trade. More than half EFTA trade is with the EEC.

EFTA tariff treatment applies to those industrial products which are of EFTA origin, and these are traded freely between member countries. Each EFTA country remains free, however, to impose its own rates of duty on products entering from outside EFTA or the EEC.

Generally, agricultural products do not come under the provisions for free trade, but bilateral agreements have been negotiated to increase trade in these products.

The operation of the Convention is the responsibility of a Council assisted by a small secretariat. Each EFTA country holds the chairmanship of the Council for six months.

THE WARSAW PACT

On 14 May 55 the USSR, Albania, Bulgaria, Czechoslovakia, the German Democratic Republic, Hungary, Poland and Romania signed, in Warsaw, a 20-year treaty of friendship and collaboration, after the USSR had (on 7 May) annulled the 20-year treaties of alliance with the UK (1942) and France (1944).

The main provisions of the Treaty are as follows:

Article 4. In case of armed aggression in Europe against one or several States party to the pact by a State or group of States, each State member of the pact . . . will afford to the State or States which are the object of such aggression immediate assistance . . . These measures will cease as soon as the Security Council takes measures necessary for establishing and preserving international peace and security.

Article 5. The contracting Powers agree to set up a joint command of their armed forces to be allotted by agreement between the Powers, at the disposal of this command and used on the basis of jointly established principles. They will also take over agreed measures necessary to strengthen their defences.

Article 9. The present treaty is open to other States, irrespective of their social or Government regime, who declare their readiness to abide by the terms of the treaty in order to safeguard peace and security of the peoples.

Article 11. In the event of a system of collective security being set up in Europe and a pact to this effect being signed – to which each party to this treaty will direct its efforts – the present treaty will lapse from the day such a collective security treaty comes into force.

In 1981 (estimate) the armed forces of the Warsaw Pact countries totalled 4.82m., including 3.71m. Russians, compared with 4.99m. NATO forces.

Marshal Grechko was from July 60 to Apr 67 C.-in-C. of the united Armed Forces with headquarters in Moscow. He was succeeded by Marshal I. I. Yakubovsky in 1967 and by Marshal V. G. Kulikov in Jan 77.

In 1962 Albania was no longer invited to the Warsaw Pact meetings but was not formally expelled.

Two Soviet divisions are stationed in Poland, 20 divisions in German Democratic Republic, four divisions in Hungary and five in Czechoslovakia.

COUNCIL FOR MUTUAL ECONOMIC ASSISTANCE

Membership. Founder members, in 1949, were USSR, Bulgaria, Czecho-slovakia, Hungary, Poland, Romania. Later admissions were Albania (1949; ceased participation 1961), Cuba (1972), German Democratic Republic (1950), Mongolia (1962). Since 1964 Yugoslavia has enjoyed associated status with limited participation. Observers are China, North Korea, North Vietnam.

The Charter consists of a preamble and 17 articles.

Extracts from the *Charter*:

Article 1 *Aims and Principles*: '(1) The purpose of the Council is to facilitate, by uniting and coordinating the efforts of its member countries, the planned development of the national economy, acceleration of economic and technical progress in these countries, a rise in the level of industrialization in countries with less developed industries, uninterrupted growth of labour productivity and a steady advance of the welfare of the peoples. (2) The Council is based on the principles of the sovereign equality of all member countries.'

Article 2 *Membership* 'open to other countries which subscribe to the purposes and principles of the Council'.

Article 3 *Functions and Powers* to (a) 'organize all-round . . . cooperation of member countries in the most rational use of natural resources and acceleration of the development of their productive forces' (b) 'foster the improvement of the international socialist division of labour by coordinating national economic development plans, and the specialization and cooperation of production in member countries' (d) to 'assist in . . . carrying out joint measures for the development of industry and agriculture . . . transport . . .

23

principal capital investments . . . [and] trade'.

Article 4 *Recommendations and Decisions* '. . . shall be adopted only with the consent of the interested member countries'.

The Structure. The supreme authority is the *Session* of all members held (usually annually) in members' capitals in rotation. All members must be present, and decisions must be unanimous. The *Executive Committee* is made up of one representative from each member state of deputy premier rank. It meets at least once every three months and has a *Bureau for Common Questions of Economic Planning*.

The administrative organ is the *Secretariat*.

The *Secretariat*: Prospekt Kalinina, 56, Moscow, G-205.

The *Secretary*: N. V. Faddeev.

There is a *Committee for Co-operation in the Field of Planning* and a *Committee for Scientific and Technical Co-operation*.

There are *Permanent Commissions* on Economic Questions; Statistics; Foreign Trade; Currency and Finance; Electricity; Peaceful Uses of Atomic Energy; Geology; Coal Industry; Oil and Gas Industry; Chemical Industry; Iron and Steel Industry; Non-Ferrous Metals Industry; Engineering Industry; Radio Engineering and Electronics Industries; Light Industry; Food Industry; Agriculture; Construction; Transport; Posts and Telecommunications; Standardization. There is an *Institute of Standardization* and two *Standing Conferences* of Water Conservation Authorities, and of Freight and Shipping Organizations. The latter has a Chartering Co-ordination Bureau.

The *International Bank for Economic Co-operation* was founded in 1963 with a capital of 300m. roubles and started operating on 1 Jan 64. It undertakes multilateral settlements in 'transferable roubles' (*i.e.* used for intra *Comecon* clearing accounts only) and advances credits to finance trading and other operations. The transferable rouble is a unit of account: gold content 0.987412 grammes.

The *International Investments Bank* was founded in 1970 and went into operation on 1 Jan 71 with a capital of 1000m. roubles (70% transferable and 30% convertible or in gold). In 1971 it financed 16 engineering, transport and chemical projects.

Stages of Development: COMECON was founded in Jan 49, partly in response to such Western initiatives as the Marshall Plan, and ostensibly to promote economic development through the joint utilization and co-ordination of resources. In its early years, however, member states were dominated by the Stalinist drive to autarky and the Council remained a façade functioning merely as a registration agency for bilateral foreign trade and credit agreements. The mid-1950s brought the first attempts to reduce the parallelism in member states' economies, and the Council began to function as a discussion centre for long-term plan co-ordination, a process perhaps hastened by the signature of the Treaty of Rome in 1957.

In 1962 Khrushchev, with the support of the more industrialized members (Czechoslovakia, East Germany, Poland) attempted to convert COMECON from a trade organization into a supra-national authority under which member states' economies would be integrated according to the 'international socialist division of labour'.

Integration plans failed at this stage, partly owing to domestic developments in the USSR (dismissal of Khrushchev), and partly owing to the obstructionist attitude of Romania, who objected to the status of non-industrialized raw-material producer.

In the aftermath of the USSR's invasion of Czechoslovakia renewed Soviet pressure in 1969 for integration encountered rather less intransigence. Romania refused to adhere to the International Investments Bank when it was first mooted in 1970 but joined eventually in 1971. Her trade within COMECON was scheduled to increase after 1972. Hungary and Poland propounded a view that a free trade area with preferential tariffs should be formed and individual currencies should ultimately be made convertible.

Present Trends: The *Comprehensive Programme* foresees increased international co-operation with no lessening of respect for national sovereignty. No supra-national authority is envisaged.

Long-term plans are to be co-ordinated and capital investments harmonized. An additional form of trade is envisaged in non-quota goods which need not be balanced bilaterally but counted in total trade for clearing purposes. Standardization and specialization of production have begun. Long-term aims include the establishment of arbitration organs with powers to settle disputes, and strengthening the transferable rouble to full convertibility.

OTHER EUROPEAN ORGANIZATIONS

	founded
Economic Commission for Europe (ECE)	1947
Brussels Treaty Organization	1948
Danube Commission	1949
Inter-governmental Committee for European Migration	1952
Nordic Council	1952
European Conference of Ministers of Transport (ECMT)	1953
European Organization of Nuclear Research (CERN)	1953
European Civil Aviation Conference (CEAC)	1955
European Nuclear Energy Agency (ENEA)	1957

	founded
Benelux Economic Union	1958
European Conference of Postal and Telecommunications Administrations (CEPT)	1959
European Organization for the Safety of Air Navigation (EUROCONTROL)	1963
European Space Agency (ESA)	1975

2 HEADS OF STATE

ALBANIA

Declared independent 1912, invaded by Austria in 1916. Italian C.-in-C. in Albania proclaims independence again on 3 June 17. A provisional republican government ruled until 1921, followed by government under a Council of Regents until Jan 25, when Albania was proclaimed a Republic.

PRESIDENT

Ahmed Beg Zogu   31 Jan 25–30 Aug 28

Albania was proclaimed a monarchy on 1 Sep 28 and the President became King Zog I.

KING

Zog I, m. Countess Geraldine Apponyi   1 Sep 28–13 Apr 49
                                   (formally deposed *in absentia* 2 Jan 46)
Victor Emmanuel III of Italy (*see* Italy)   14 Apr 39–30 Nov 43
                                   (reigned following Italian invasion until
                                   Italian cabinet nullified his Albanian title)
Between 1 Dec 43 and 1 Dec 45 there were provisional governments with no head of state. The Republic was proclaimed 12 Jan 46.

PRESIDENT

Dr Omer Nishani   13 Jan 46–24 July 53
Maj.-Gen. Haxhi Lleshi   24 July 53–22 Nov 82
Ramiz Alia   22 Nov 82–

The President is a nominal Head of State; power is held by the First Secretary of the Central Committee: Enver Hoxha.

AUSTRIA

The Republic was proclaimed on 12 Nov 18.

PRESIDENT

Dr X. Seits   12 Nov 18–9 Nov 20
(President of the National Assembly and stood in for a head of state)

Dr M. Hainisch	9 Dec 20–4 Dec 28
Dr W. Miklas	5 Dec 28–13 Mar 38

Austria was incorporated into the German Reich on 12 Mar 38. For 1938–45 *see* Germany. A provisional government was installed on liberation, 28 Apr 45.

PRESIDENT

Dr K. Renner	20 Dec 45–31 Dec 50
Dr T. Körner	27 May 51–4 Jan 57
Dr A. Schárf	5 May 57–28 Feb 65
Dr F. Jonas	23 May 65–23 Apr 74 (died)
Dr B. Kreisky	24 Apr 74–8 July 74 (interim)
Dr R. Kirchschläger	8 July 74–

BELGIUM

KING

Albert, m. Elizabeth of Bavaria, succeeded his uncle
Leopold II   17 Dec 09–17 Feb 34
Leopold III, m. (i) Astrid of Sweden (ii) Mlle Lilian Baels,
succeeded his father   23 Feb 34–20 Sep 44
Regency   21 Sep 44–21 July 50
Leopold III   22 July 50–16 July 51 (abdic.)
Baudouin, m. Fabiola de Mora y Aragón,
succeeded his father   17 July 51–

BULGARIA

KING

Ferdinand (elected), m. (i) Marie Louise of Parma
(ii) Eleonore of Reuss Köstritz   7 July 87–4 Oct 18 (abdic.)
Boris III, m. Giovanña of Savoy,
succeeded his father   4 Oct 18–28 Aug 43
Simeon II, succeeded his father   28 Aug 43–8 Sep 46

On 8 Sep 46 a plebiscite ended the monarchy and established a Republic, which was proclaimed on 15 Sep, but had no head of state until the new constitution came into force on 4 Dec 47.

PRESIDENT (Chairman of the Praesidium)

Dr M. Nctchcv	9 Dec 47–27 May 50
Gen. G. Damianov	27 May 50–27 Nov 58
D. Ganev	30 Nov 58–20 Apr 64
G. Traikov	23 Apr 64–7 July 71
T. Zhivok	7 July 71–

CYPRUS

From 1918 until 1959 Cyprus was a British dependency; for heads of state *see* United Kingdom. An independent Republic came into being on 16 Aug 60, the President having been previously elected.

PRESIDENT

Archbishop Makarios	14 Dec 59–3 Aug 77 (died)
Spyros Kyprianou	3 Aug 77–

Nicos Sampson assumed the Presidency on the temporary overthrow of Archbishop Makarios; he was succeeded by Glafkos Clerides on 23 July 74 until 7 Dec 74.
A Turkish Cypriot Federated State with Rauf Denktash as President was proclaimed 13 Feb 75.

CZECHOSLOVAKIA

An independent state was founded on 14 Nov 18, formed from four provinces of the Austrian Empire: Bohemia, Moravia, Silesia, Slovakia. (Hungarian Slovakia and Ruthenia joined the Czechoslovak state in 1920.)

PRESIDENT

Tomas G. Masaryk	14 Nov 18–13 Dec 35
Dr Edvard Beneš	18 Dec 35–4 Oct 38
Dr Emil Hácha	1 Dec 38–1 June 45

Dr Beneš continued as President of the Czech government in exile after Czechoslovakia was proclaimed a German protectorate on 16 Mar 39. He returned to Prague in 1945. (Slovakia: *see* separate entry.)

PRESIDENT

Dr Edvard Beneš	2 June 45–7 June 48
K. Gottwald	14 June 48–14 Mar 53

A. Zápotecký	21 Mar 53–13 Nov 57
A. Novotný	19 Nov 57–22 Mar 68
Gen. Ludvik Svoboda	30 Mar 68–27 May 75
Dr Gustáv Husák	29 May 75–

DENMARK

KING

Christian X, m. Alexandrine of Mecklenburg, succeeded his father
   Frederick VIII   14 May 12–20 Apr 47
Frederick IX, m. Ingrid of Sweden,
   succeeded his father   20 Apr 47–14 Jan 72

QUEEN

Margrethe II, m. Henri de Morpezat,
   succeeded her father   14 Jan 72–

ESTONIA

Proclaimed an independent state 24 Feb 18. The constitution came into force on 20 Dec 20, with a provisional government in power. On formation of the cabinet in 1923 the Prime Minister was given powers of head of state.

PRIME MINISTER AND HEAD OF THE STATE

I. Kukk	25 Nov 23–15 Dec 24
M. Jaakson	16 Dec 24–14 Dec 25
J. Teemant	15 Dec 25–8 Dec 27
M. Toenisson	9 Dec 27–3 Dec 28
A. Rei	4 Dec 28–8 July 29
O. Strandmann	9 July 29–11 Feb 31
C. Paets	12 Feb 31–20 Feb 32
J. Teemant	21 Feb 32–31 Oct 32
C. Paets	1 Nov 32–26 Apr 33

A new constitution, setting up the office of President, was adopted on 3 Oct 34. Constantin Paets was appointed President.
The USSR incorporated Estonia as a member on 7 Aug 40.

FINLAND

Proclaimed independent on 6 Dec 17, and a Regent installed. Republican constitution came into force on 14 June 19.

PRESIDENT

Prof K. J. Ståhlberg	1 Aug 19–15 Feb 25
Dr L. Relander	16 Feb 25–15 Feb 31
Dr P. E. Svinhufvud	16 Feb 31–14 Feb 37
K. Kallio	15 Feb 37–30 Nov 40
Dr R. Ryti	19 Dec 40–4 Aug 44
Field-Marshal Mannerheim	4 Aug 44–9 Mar 45
J. Paasikivi	9 Mar 45–15 Feb 56
Dr U. Kekkonen	15 Feb 56–26 Jan 82
Dr M. Koivisto	26 Jan 82–

FRANCE

PRESIDENT OF THE REPUBLIC

R. Poincaré	17 Jan 13–17 Jan 20
P. Deschanel	17 Jan 20–23 Sep 20
A. Millerand	23 Sep 20–10 June 24
G. Doumergue	13 June 24–31 May 31
P. Doumer	31 May 31–7 May 32
A. Lebrun	10 May 32–11 July 40

Marshal Pétain on 11 July 40 took over the powers of President and added them to his own as Prime Minister. He then appointed a Chief of State.

CHIEF OF STATE

Adm. Darlan	10 Feb 41–16 Nov 42
P. Laval	17 Nov 42–12 May 45 (left France)

A Government of National Unity was formed on 1 Dec 45, with Gen. Charles de Gaulle as head of state. He resigned on 2 Feb 46. A new constitution came into force on 24 Dec 46 (Fourth Republic).

PRESIDENT OF THE REPUBLIC

V. Auriol	16 Jan 47–23 Dec 53
R. Coty	24 Dec 53–5 Oct 58

A new constitution came into force on 5 Oct 58 (Fifth Republic).

PRESIDENT OF THE REPUBLIC

Gen. C. de Gaulle	8 Jan 59–28 Apr 69
A. Poher	28 Apr 69–20 June 69 (interim)
G. Pompidou	20 June 69–2 Apr 74
A. Poher	2 Apr 74–27 May 74 (interim)
V. Giscard d'Estaing	27 May 74–21 May 81
F. Mitterand	21 May 81–

GEORGIA

Proclaimed an independent state 26 May 18.

PRESIDENT

N. Jordania	26 May 18–

Georgia was occupied by Soviet forces in 1921, and became a member of the USSR.

GERMANY

The Republic was proclaimed on the abdication of Kaiser Wilhelm II, on 9 Nov 18.

PRESIDENT

Friedrich Ebert	11 Feb 19–28 Feb 25
P. von Hindenburg	26 Apr 25–2 Aug 34

CHANCELLOR AND FÜHRER

Adolf Hitler	2 Aug 34–30 Apr 45
Adm. C. Doenitz	30 Apr 45–5 June 45

All power was transferred to the Allied Control Council on the surrender of Germany at the end of World War II on 5 June 45. The constitution of the Federal Republic of Germany came into force on 21 Sep 49.

PRESIDENT

Dr T. Heuss	12 Sep 49–1 July 59
Dr H. Lübke	1 July 59–30 June 69
Dr G. Heinemann	1 July 69–30 June 74
W. Scheel	1 July 74–30 June 79
K. Carstens	1 July 79–

The constitution of the German Democratic Republic came into force on 7 Oct 49.

PRESIDENT

Wilhelm Pieck   11 Oct 49–7 Sep 60

The office of President was replaced by the Council of State on 12 Sep 60.

CHAIRMAN OF THE COUNCIL OF STATE

Walter Ulbricht	12 Sep 60–1 Aug 73
Willi Stoph	3 Oct 73–29 Oct 76
E. Honecker	29 Oct 76–

GREECE

KING

Alexandros, succeeded on the expulsion of his father,
  Konstantinos   12 June 17–25 Oct 20
Konstantinos XII, m. Sophia of Prussia. Recalled by
  plebiscite to succeed his son   5 Dec 20–27 Sep 22 (abdic.)
Gëorgios II, m. Elizabeth of Romania, succeeded
  his father   27 Sep 22–18 Dec 23 (expelled)
A Republic was established by plebiscite on 13 Apr 24.

PROVISIONAL PRESIDENT

Adm. Konduriotis   20 Dec 23–18 Mar 26

DICTATOR

Gen. Pangalos   18 Mar 26–22 Aug 26

PROVISIONAL PRESIDENT (reappointed)

Adm. Konduriotis   4 Dec 26–14 Dec 29

PRESIDENT

A. Zaimis   14 Dec 29–3 Nov 35

By a plebiscite on 3 Nov 35 the Republic ended and the monarchy was restored.

KING

Gëorgios II, returned   25 Nov 35–1 Apr 47
Paul I, m. Frederika Louise of Brunswick,

succeeded his brother   1 Apr 47–6 Mar 64
Konstantinos XIII, m. Anne-Marie of Denmark,
 succeeded his father   6 Mar 64–1 June 73

The King handed over his powers to a Regent on 13 Dec 67 and left Greece.
The monarchy was declared abolished on 1 June 73.

PROVISIONAL PRESIDENT

G. Papadopoulos   1 June 73–25 Nov 73

PRESIDENT

Lieut.-Gen. P. Ghizikis   25 Nov 73–14 Dec 74 (resigned)
M. Stassinopoulos   18 Dec 74–20 June 75 (interim)
K. Tsatsos   20 June 75–12 May 80 (resigned)
K. Karamanlis   15 May 80–

HUNGARY

An independent Republic was proclaimed on 16 Nov 18.

PROVISIONAL PRESIDENT

Count M. Károlyi   16 Nov 18–22 Mar 19

The Soviet Hungarian Republic was proclaimed by Béla Kun's government
on 22 Mar 19, and was followed by a counter-revolutionary régime under
Admiral Horthy. In Jun 20 Hungary was proclaimed a monarchy.

REGENT

Adm. M. von Nagybánya Horthy   1 Mar 20–16 Oct 45

A Regency Council was appointed after Horthy's resignation and ruled until
the setting up of the Provisional National Government on 24 Dec 45. A new
republican constitution came into force on 1 Feb 46.

PRESIDENT

Dr Z. Tildy   1 Feb 46–30 July 48
A. Szakasits   3 Aug 48–24 Apr 50
S. Rónai   8 May 50–1 Aug 52

CHAIRMAN OF THE PRAESIDIUM

I. M. Dobi   1 Aug 52–14 Apr 67

CHAIRMAN OF THE PRESIDING COUNCIL

P. Losonczi   14 Apr 67–

ICELAND

A sovereign state came into being on 1 Dec 18, still acknowledging the Danish King as head.

KING

Christian X (see Denmark)   1 Dec 18–24 May 44

The link with the crown was ended and a republic came into being on 17 June 44. ·

PRESIDENT

Sveinn Björnssen   17 June 44–24 Jan 52
Ásgeir Ásgeirsson   1 July 52–1 Aug 68
Kristján Eldjárn   1 Aug 68–1 Aug 80
Vigdis Finnbogadóttir   1 Aug 80–

IRELAND

By the Irish Free State Agreement Act of 1922 Ireland obtained the status of a self-governing Dominion, still recognizing the British sovereign as head of state.

KING

George V (see United Kingdom)
Edward VIII (see United Kingdom)
George VI (see United Kingdom)

The constitution of the Irish Free State as an independent sovereign state came into force on 29 Dec 37.

PRESIDENT

Dubhglas de hIde (Dr Douglas Hyde)   25 June 38–24 June 45
S. T. Ó Ceallaigh (S. T. O'Kelly)   25 June 45–24 June 59
Éamon de Valéra   25 June 59–24 June 73
Erskine Childers   25 June 74–17 Nov 74
Cearbhall Ó Dalaigh   3 Dec 74–22 Oct 76
Dr Patrick Hillery   3 Dec 76–

ITALY

KING

Victor Emmanual III, m. Elena of Montenegro,
  succeeded his father Umberto   29 July 00–9 May 46 (abdic.)
Umberto II, succeeded his father   9 May 46–13 June 46 (abdic.)

(On 30 Mar 38 King Victor Emmanual gave unlimited powers to Benito
Mussolini to hold in time of war and in the name of the King. Mussolini
resigned these powers on 25 July 43.)
A Republic was proclaimed on 18 June 46.

PRESIDENT

L. Einaudi	10 May 48–29 Apr 44
G. Gronchi	29 Apr 55–6 May 62
A. Segni	6 May 62–28 Dec 64
G. Saragat	28 Dec 64–29 Dec 71
G. Leone	29 Dec 71–15 June 78
A. Fanfani	15 June 78–8 July 78
A. Pertini	9 July 78–

LATVIA

Proclaimed a sovereign state on 18 Nov 18.

PRESIDENT

J. Tschakste	18 Nov 18–8 Apr 27
G. Zemgals	8 Apr 27–8 Apr 30
A. Kviesis	9 Apr 30–11 Apr 36
K. Ulmanis	12 Apr 36–21 July 40

The USSR agreed to accept Latvia on 6 Aug 40.

LIECHTENSTEIN

PRINCE

John II, succeeded his father   12 Nov 58–11 Feb 29
Francis I, succeeded his brother   11 Feb 29–25 Aug 38
Francis Joseph II, m. Countess Gina von Wilczek,
  succeeded his great-uncle   25 Aug 38–

LITHUANIA

Proclaimed an independent state 16 Feb 18
Constituent assembly elected an acting president on 15 Apr 20.

ACTING PRESIDENT
A. Stulginskis   15 Apr 20–8 June 26

PRESIDENT
Dr Grinius   8 June 26–19 Dec 26
M. Smetona   19 Dec 26–30 June 40

On 21 July 40 Lithuania voted to become a member of the USSR.

LUXEMBOURG

GRAND-DUCHESS
Marie-Adelaide, succeeded her father
   Grand Duke Willem   26 June 12–15 Jan 19 (abdic.)
Charlotte, m. Felix of Bourbon Parma, succeeded
   her sister   15 Jan 19–12 Nov 64 (abdic.)

GRAND DUKE
Jean, m. Joséphine Charlotte of Belgium,
   succeeded his mother   12 Nov 64–

MALTA

Until 1974 Malta was a member of the Commonwealth acknowledging the British sovereign as head of state. A Republic was established on 13 Dec 74 with a president.

PRESIDENT
Sir A. Marno   13 Dec 74–27 Dec 76
A. Buttigieg   27 Dec 76–16 Feb 82
A. Barbara   16 Feb 82–

MONACO

PRINCE

Albert, m. (i) Lady Mary Douglas Hamilton, (ii) Alice, Dowager Duchess de Richelieu, succeeded his father	10 Sep 1889–26 June 22
Louis II, succeeded his father	26 June 22–9 May 49
Rainier III, m. Miss Grace Kelly, succeeded his grandfather	9 May 49–

THE NETHERLANDS

QUEEN

Wilhelmina, m. Henry of Mecklenburg Schwerin, succeeded her father	23 Nov 1890–4 Sep 48 (abdic.)
Juliana, m. Bernhard of Lippe-Besterfeld, succeeded her mother	4 Nov 48–30 Apr 80 (abdic.)
Beatrix, m. Claus von Amsberg, succeeded her mother	1 May 80–

NORWAY

KING

Haakon VII, formerly Prince Carl of Denmark, m. Maud of Great Britain, elected to the throne	18 Nov 05–21 Sep 57
Olav V, m. Märtha of Sweden, succeeded his father	21 Sep 57–

POLAND

Independent state proclaimed on 5 Nov 18.

PRESIDENT

J. Pilsudski	11 Nov 18–9 Dec 22
Gabriel Narutowicz	9 Dec 22–16 Dec 22 (assassinated)

S. Wojciechowski	20 Dec 22–15 May 26
I. Moscicki	1 Jun 26–29 Mar 39

On 29 Mar 39 the German occupation of Poland began.

PRESIDENT, HEAD OF THE POLISH GOVERNMENT IN EXILE

W. Raczkiewicz	30 Sep 39–28 June 45

PRESIDENT

Boleslaw Bierut	28 June 45–21 July 52

On 22 July 52 a new constitution replaced the office of President with a Council of State.

CHAIRMAN OF THE COUNCIL OF STATE

A. Zawadski	20 Nov 52–7 Aug 64
E. Ochab	12 Aug 64–8 Apr 68
Marshal M. Spychalski	10 Apr 68–23 Dec 70
J. Cyrankiewicz	23 Dec 70–28 Mar 72
H. Jabloński	28 Mar 72–

PORTUGAL

PRESIDENT

Dr S. Paes	28 Apr 18–14 Dec 18 (assassinated)
João Antunes	16 Dec 18–5 Oct 19
Dr A. de Almeida	5 Oct 19–5 Oct 23
M. T. Gomes	5 Oct 23–11 Dec 25
Dr B. L. Machado Guimarâes	11 Dec 25–1 June 26

A provisional government was in power from 1 June 26 until 29 Nov 26.

PRESIDENT

Marshal A. O. F. Carmona	29 Nov 26–18 Apr 51
Marshal F. H. C. Lopes	22 July 51–9 Aug 58
Rear-Adm. A. de D. R. Tomás	9 Aug 58–25 Apr 74
Gen. Antonio de Spinola	15 May 74–30 Sep 74
Gen. Francisco da Costa Gomes	30 Sep 74–27 June 76
Gen. Antonio R. Eanes	14 July 76–

ROMANIA

KING

Ferdinand I, m. Marie of Saxe-Coburg and Gotha,
   succeeded his uncle   11 Oct 14–21 July 27
Mihai (Michael) I, succeeded his grandfather since his father
   Carol had renounced his rights   21 July 27–8 June 30
Carol II, m. Helen of Greece, succeeded his son by
   act of parliament   8 June 30–6 Sep 40 (abdic.)
Mihai I, proclaimed on abdication of his father
                           6 Sep 40–30 Dec 47 (abdic.)

As a result of a plebiscite a Republic was established and the King abdicated.

PRESIDENT OF THE PRAESIDIUM

C. I. Parhon	13 Apr 48–23 Jan 52
Dr P. Groza	2 June 52–7 Jan 58
I. G. Maurer	11 Jan 58–21 Mar 61
G. Gheorghiu-Dej	21 Mar 61–19 Mar 65
C. Stoica	22 Mar 65–9 Dec 67
N. Ceauçescu	9 Dec 67–

SAN MARINO

No titular head of state; co-regents are annually elected.

SLOVAKIA

Declared an independent country 14 Mar 39.

PRESIDENT

Dr J. Tiso   26 Oct 39–1 Apr 45

Slovakia was re-incorporated with Czechoslovakia in Apr 45.

SPAIN

KING

Alphonso XIII, m. Victoria Eugenie Battenberg,
   succeeded his father at his birth   17 May 1886–14 Apr 31 (abdic.)

A Republic proclaimed on 14 Apr 31.

PRESIDENT

N. A. Zamora y Torres	10 Dec 31–7 Apr 36
M. Azaña	10 May 36–4 Mar 39

CHIEF OF THE SPANISH STATE

Gen. Francisco Franco	9 Aug 39–20 Nov 75

Prince Juan Carlos de Borbòn y Borbòn, grandson of Alphonso XIII, was sworn in as successor to the Chief of State in July 1969.

KING

Juan Carlos, I. m. Sophia of Greece	22 Nov 75–

SWEDEN

KING

Gustaf V, m. Victoria of Baden, succeeded his father
  Oscar II   8 Dec 07–29 Oct 50
Gustaf IV Adolf, m. (i) Margaret Victoria of Connaught,
  (ii) Lady Louise Mountbatten, succeeded his father 29 Oct 50–16 Sep 73
Carl XVI Gustaf, succeeded his grandfather   16 Sep 73–

SWITZERLAND

PRESIDENTS (elected for an annual term)

1918	Dr F. Ludwig	1930	Dr Jean M. Musy
1919	Gustave Ador	1931	Dr Henri Häberlin
1920	Giuseppe Motta	1932	Dr Giuseppe Motta
1921	Edmund Schulthess	1933	Dr Edmund Schulthess
1922	Dr Robert Haab	1934	Dr Marcel Pilet-Golaz
1923	Karl Scheurer	1935	Rudolf Minger
1924	Dr Ernest Chuard	1936	Dr Albert Meyer
1925	Dr Jean M. Musy	1937	Dr Giuseppe Motta
1926	Henri Häberlin	1938	Dr Johannes Baumann
1927	Giuseppe Motta	1939	Philipp Etter
1928	Edmund Schulthess	1940	Dr Marcel Pilet-Golaz
1929	Dr Robert Haab	1941	Dr Ernst Wetter

41

1942 Philipp Etter
1943 Enrico Celio
1944 Walter Stampfi
1945 Eduard von Steiger
1946 Karl Kobelt
1947
1948 Enrico Celio
1949 Ernst Nobs
1950 Max Petitpierre
1951 Eduard von Steiger
1952 Karl Kobelt
1953 Philipp Etter
1954 Rudolphe Rubattel
1955 Max Petitpierre
1956 Markus Feldmann
1957 Hans Streuli
1958 Thomas Holenstein
1959 Paul Chaudet
1960 Max Petitpierre
1961 Friedrich Trangott Wahlen
1962 Paul Chaudet
1963 Willy Spühler

1964 Ludwig von Moos
1965 Hanspeter Tschudi
1966 Hans Schattner
1967 Roger Bonvin
1968 Willy Spühler
1969 Ludwig von Moos
1970 Hanspeter Tschudi
1971 Rudolf Guägi
1972 Nello Celio
1973 Roger Bonvin
1974 Ernst Brugger
1975 Pierre Graber
1976 Rudolf Gnägi
1977 Kurt Furgler
1978 Willi Ritschard
1979 Hans Hürlimann
1980 Georges-André Chevallaz
1981 Kurt Furgler
1982 Fritz Honegger
1983 Pierre Aubert
1984 Léon Schlumpf

TURKEY

SULTAN

Mohammed V, succeeded his brother	27 Apr 09–3 July 18
Mohammed VI, succeeded his brother	3 July 18–1 Nov 22

The office of Sultan was abolished on 1 Nov 22 and only that of Caliph (held by the Sultans) retained, to be filled by election from the Osman princes.

CALIPH

Prince Abdul Medjid	17 Nov 22–2 Mar 24

A republic was proclaimed on 29 Oct 23.

PRESIDENT

M. Kemal Atatürk	29 Oct 23–10 Nov 38
I. Inönü	11 Nov 38–21 May 50

C. Bayar	22 May 50–27 May 60
C. Gursel	26 Oct 61–27 Mai 66
Cevdet Sunay	28 Mar 66–28 Mar 73
Fahri Korutürk	6 Apr 73–6 Apr 80
Ihsan Sabri Caglayangil	6 Apr 80–12 Sep 80
Gen. Kenan Evren	12 Sep 80–

USSR

Constitution for the Federal Republic adopted on 10 July 18, by a government which took office on 8 Nov 17.

PRESIDENT OF THE COUNCIL OF PEOPLE'S COMMISSARS

V. I. Ulianov-Lenin	8 Nov 17–29 Dec 22

A new constitution of 30 Dec 22 replaced this office by a Central Executive Committee with four chairmen.
A new constitution came into force on 5 Dec 36 establishing the office of Chairman of the Praesidium of the Supreme Soviet of the USSR, as head of state.

CHAIRMAN

M. I. Kalinin	5 Dec 36–27 July 46
N. M. Shvernik	19 Mar 46–6 Mar 53
Marshal K. E. Voroshilov	6 Mar 53 7 May 60
L. I. Brezhnev	7 May 60–15 July 64
A. I. Mikoyan	15 July 64–9 Dec 65
N. V. Podgorny	9 Dec 65–16 June 77
L. I. Brezhnev	16 June 77–10 Nov 82
Y. V. Andropov	16 June 83–9 Feb 84
K. V. Chernenko	11 Apr 84–10 Mar 85

UNITED KINGDOM

KING

George V, m. Victoria Mary of Teck, succeeded his father	
Edward VII	6 May 10–20 Jan 36
Edward VIII, succeeded his father	20 Jan 36–10 Dec 36 (abdic.)

George VI, m. Lady Elizabeth Bowes-Lyon, succeeded on the
abdication of his brother   10 Dec 36–6 Feb 52

QUEEN

Elizabeth II, m. Philip of Greece, succeeded her
father   6 Feb 52–

VATICAN

SUPREME PONTIFF

Benedict XV	3 Sep 14–22 Jan 22
Pius XI	6 Mar 22–13 Feb 39
Pius XII	2 Mar 39–9 Oct 58
John XXIII	28 Oct 58–3 June 63
Paul VI	21 June 63–6 Aug 78
John Paul I	26 Aug 78–28 Sep 78
John Paul II	16 Oct 78–

YUGOSLAVIA

The state was founded on 29 Dec 18 as the Serb, Croat and Slovene State
(Montenegro joined on 1 March 21). The name was changed to Yugoslavia on
3 Oct 29.

KING

Peter I, m. Zorka of Montenegro, elected king   2 June 03–6 Aug 21
Alexander I, m. Marie of Romania, succeeded his
father   6 Aug 21–9 Oct 34 (assassinated)
Peter II, succeeded his father   9 Oct 34–29 Nov 45 (abdic.)

On 29 Nov 45 King Peter abdicated and a Republic was proclaimed.

PRESIDENT OF THE PRESIDIUM

Dr I. Ribar   2 Dec 45–13 Jan 53

PRESIDENT OF THE REPUBLIC

Marshal J. Broz-Tito   14 Jan 53–4 May 80

HEAD OF THE COLLECTIVE PRESIDENCY

L. Kolisevski	4 May 80–15 May 80
C. Mijatovic	15 May 80–15 May 81
S. Krajger	15 May 81–15 May 82
P. Stambolić	15 May 82–15 May 83
M. Spiljak	15 May 83–

3 PARLIAMENTS

ALBANIA

From 1920 until the Italian invasion Albania had a parliamentary system of government with a single elected chamber, but neither under the Republic nor under the monarchy did this function effectively. Under the Republic formed in 1946 there has been one chamber, the People's Assembly, elected on universal suffrage of all over 18, and sitting for a four-year term. The Assembly elects its Presidium and Council of Ministers. The Chairman of the Presidium is also the head of the state, and the Chairman of the Council of Ministers the Prime Minister. The Assembly, the Council and the Presidium operate on the Soviet pattern; the Assembly sits for short sessions, the Presidium more or less permanently, although the Assembly must meet twice a year. The Assembly has one member for each 8000 voters. The Presidium has a chairman and three deputy chairmen, a secretary and ten members. The initiation and passing of legislation, and the exercise of legislative and executive power is the same as in the Soviet Union.

AUSTRIA

On 12 Nov 18 the Austrian members of the Austro-Hungarian imperial Reichsrat, having constituted themselves the German National Assembly, declared that Austria was a Republic. The following January a Constituent Assembly was elected as supreme authority for the purposes of framing a new constitution which came into operation in Nov 20. The Assembly had one chamber and was elected on universal adult suffrage. The new constitution provided for a bi-cameral federal legislature. The National Council was elected by proportional representation for four years, and could be adjourned only by its own decision. It could be summoned immediately on the request of at least a quarter of its members, or of the government. The Federal Council was elected by the Provincial Diets, having representatives from each province who sat for the length of term of their Diet. The Federal Council could initiate bills through the government; a bill passed by the National Council would be passed to the Federal Council and, if amended by them, reconsidered by the National Council and passable by a majority in that house. The Federal Council had no power to amend estimates.

The President was elected by both houses in joint session, for four years; his

46

duties were mainly ceremonial and symbolic and all acts of government were the responsibility of ministers. The ministers were elected by the National Council on a motion submitted by its Principal Committee, and were not allowed to continue as Council members, if they were, or to become Council members while in office. Legislature and Executive were widely separate. The government suspended parliament in 1933 and in 1934 dissolved the Socialist Party; after strong reaction a new constitution, with socialist leanings, was brought in in 1935, but parliament worked with increasing difficulty until the integration with Germany in 1938, when it virtually ceased to operate.

A constitution similar to that of 1920 was restored in 1945. The state has now a Nationalrat with deputies elected on the original suffrage and a Bundesrat of deputies elected by the Provincial Diets. Bills must pass both houses. In 1984 the Nationalrat had 183 deputies and the Bundesrat 58; of the latter there may be not more than 12 members for any one Province, and not less than three. Bundesrat members are not necessarily members of the Provincial Diets, but they must be eligible to be so; they are elected for varying terms, whereas Nationalrat members sit for four years, two regular sessions being convened each year in spring and autumn. An extraordinary session may be held if the government or one-third of the members of either house demand it.

Bills must pass both houses; they may be initiated by either house or by the government but must be presented in the National Council. There is provision also for the popular initiative; every proposal signed by 200 000 Länder voters or half the voters in each of the three Länder must be submitted to the National Council. The National Council may also request a referendum on a bill which it has assented to. All bills go secondly to the Federal Council which may object to them within eight weeks; the bill becomes law if the National Council reaffirms it with half its members present.

BELGIUM

Belgium is a constitutional monarchy with two legislative chambers, the Chamber of Representatives and the Senate. The King shares legislative powers with the two chambers and exercises the executive power in conjunction with his ministers; he may not act alone. He appoints ministers from among members of parliament, and sanctions laws. The chamber of Representatives consists of 212 members – the maximum number is one for every 40 000 inhabitants – elected on proportional representation for four-year terms. Members must be at least 25. The Senate members must be at least 40 and are elected as follows: one member for every 200 000 inhabitants, elected by the provincial councils on proportional representation; half the number of Chamber deputies elected by the same electorate. Since 1965 there

47

have been 106 directly-elected members and 48 provincial members. Constitutionally the Chamber and the Senate have equal powers; bills may be introduced in both houses and must pass both before being signed by the King. Traditionally the legislature possessed considerable control over the cabinet, since all legislation passes through a strong committee system in both houses. In the years between the two world wars particularly this provided stability when political life was disrupted by Fleming-Walloon or Catholic-Protestant differences.

In Oct 21 the length of service for members of the Senate was reduced from eight years to four, and the franchise was extended to all men over 21, together with women who were war-widows or war-sufferers. Before 1921 there was a system of plural votes on grounds of property or income. The franchise was extended to women in 1948.

Senate and Chamber meet annually in October (November until 1921) and must sit for at least forty days. The government, through the King, has power to dissolve either chamber separately or both chambers at once. In the latter case a new election must take place within forty days and a meeting of the Chambers within two months; no adjournment for longer than one month may be made without the consent of both Chambers.

Money bills originate in the Chamber of Representatives. There is also a strong subsidiary body – the Court of Accounts – with members appointed by the Chamber with authority to control all treasury work and all provision for revenue and expenditure. By an Act 23 Dec 46 a Council of State was also set up, with separate sections for legislation and administration on constitutional matters.

BULGARIA

The constitution of 1879 was still in operation in 1918, after amendment in 1911. The legislature was a single chamber, the National Assembly (Sobranje). Members were elected by universal manhood suffrage; one member for every 20 000 inhabitants. All literate men over 30 were eligible to sit, except for soldiers, clergy and those deprived of civil rights. The term was four years, but the Assembly could be dissolved at any time by the King, and elections held within two months. There was a second, but not permanent, chamber, the Grand Sobranje; this had twice the membership of the Sobranje but was elected only for special purposes. It sat to decide questions on territory, changes to the constitution or the succession to the throne. Both houses were elected on proportional representation. Laws passed by the National Assembly required the assent of the King, who might himself initiate legislation through his ministers. After 1911 the King might also make treaties with foreign powers without having the Assembly's consent; he might also issue regulations and take emergency measures in time of danger, although it was the cabinet who assumed responsibility for such measures. Cabinet members were chosen by the King. They were required to countersign royal acts and were responsible both to the King and to the Assembly.

In Oct 37 an electoral law fixed the number of Sobranje members at 160 (it had previously had 227) and the size of constituencies to at least 20 000 electors, comprising all men and all married women over 21.

A Republic was proclaimed in Sep 46 and a new constitution drawn up in Dec 47 which was replaced, but not significantly altered, by a new one in 1971; it provides for a parliament on the Russian model, except that there is only one assembly, as before, consisting of deputies elected by secret, direct and universal suffrage of all inhabitants over 18, one deputy for every 30 000 – later every 20 000 – inhabitants. The Assembly elected its Presidium of chairman, two deputy chairmen, secretary and 15 members; this is the most powerful organ of the state. There is also a Council of Ministers elected by the National Assembly. The relation of the three bodies to each other is on the Russian pattern.

CYPRUS

An independent Republic was set up in 1960 with a unicameral parliament, the House of Representatives. The House had 50 members, 35 Greek and 15 Turkish, who were directly elected within their respective communities. The communities also had their own Communal Chambers, to which certain domestic issues were reserved. The franchise was universal and the term for members five years. Greek members elected a Greek President of the House, Turkish members a Turkish Vice-President. The Prime Minister and Council of Ministers were appointed by the President of the Republic. In practice the office of President and Prime Minister were combined.

In Dec 63 the Turkish members ceased to attend parliament. On 13 Feb 75 a Turkish Cypriot Federated State was formed, having its own legislative assembly and executive council.

CZECHOSLOVAKIA

The constitution of the Republic was put into operation in 1920. It provided for a two-chamber parliament, the National Parliament, which consisted of a Chamber of Deputies and a Senate, elected on proportional representation by all citizens over 21. The Chamber was elected for six years and had 300 deputies; the Senate sat for eight years and had 150 members. Legislation might be introduced by the government or by either of the chambers. Bills passed by the deputies were passed to the Senate for consideration. A bill rejected by the Senate could still become law if passed again with an absolute majority by the deputies. If the Senate rejected it by a three-quarters majority then it required a three-fifths majority to pass in the Chamber. A bill initiated in the Senate died if it was dismissed twice by an absolute majority in the Chamber. Bills relating to money and defence could only be initiated by the deputies. The legislature had no strong control over the government; if the National Parliament rejected a government bill the government could still decide (unanimously) to put the bill to a referendum, provided it was not an amendment to the constitution.

The President (Dr Masaryk) was in fact elected for life, but the constitution provided that in future the President would be elected by the National Parliament for a seven-year term. His election would need the attendance of an absolute majority of the parliament and a three-fifths majority of votes. He was to be head of state, but the government would be responsible for the exercise of his powers. He could not declare war without parliamentary approval. He could dissolve both chambers, but not during the last six months of his presidency. He might return a bill to parliament with his observations on it, when it could only be carried if an absolute majority of all members adhered to it.

The parliament did not operate effectively after Czechoslovakia became a German Protectorate in 1939.

A new constitution of June 48 provided for a single-chamber National Assembly with 300 members elected for six years. In 1953 a Presidium on the Soviet model was set up, with a Chairman (Prime Minister) and ten deputies; later in the same year the number of deputies was reduced to four and the Presidium considerably reduced in power. In 1969 the state became a federation; the new Federal Assembly consists of the Chamber of Nations, with 75 Czech and 75 Slovak delegates elected by the National Councils of the Czechs and Slovaks, and the Chamber of the People which has 200 deputies elected by national suffrage.

The Federal Assembly has overall responsibility for constitutional and foreign affairs, defence and the federal economy. Other matters fall to the National Councils; the Czech has 200 deputies and the Slovak 150. Since 1971 all Deputies, federal and national, have been elected for a five-year term.

DENMARK

The constitutional Charter of 1915 provided that the legislative power should be held by the King and the Rigsdag (parliament) jointly, and that the executive power be held by the King and exercised through his ministers, although he could not declare war or sign a peace treaty without parliament's consent. There were two chambers: the Folketing (lower house) had 149 members, 117 of them elected by proportional representation and 31 additional seats divided among parties who had insufficient votes to win any. It sat for a four-year term but might be dissolved by the King. There was no specific ruling that the ministers who formed the King's Council of State and who were appointed and dismissed by him, were responsible to the Folketing in the parliamentary sense. The King normally presided over the Council of State; he had the right to object to its decisions and to re-introduce the matter at a future meeting. In his absence the Prime Minister presided. The Landsting had 78 members indirectly elected and sat for a term of eight years; those members elected in the Landsting electoral districts sat for four years, when there was a further election for half of their number; members elected by the former Landsting sat for the whole eight years; there were 56 members elected in the districts and 19 by the Landsting. Parliament was obliged to meet annually in October. Ministers had access to both houses but could only vote in the chamber of which they were members.

The constitutional Charter of June 1953 abolished the Landsting. The Folketing remained with 179 members, 135 of them elected in the districts, and 40 additional seats. The Council of State continued to operate as a cabinet, ministers being individually and collectively responsible to the Folketing for their actions. The legislative power is still the joint prerogative of the Queen and the Folketing, and the executive power is still vested in the Queen acting through her ministers. The cabinet is only called the Council of State when the Queen is presiding.

Any member may initiate a bill. Bills are approved or not after three readings. If one-third of members request it, a bill that has been passed may be subject to a referendum. A bill that is to be subject to referendum may be withdrawn within five weeks of its being passed. The referendum is held and its result acted upon in accordance with the Prime Minister's decision. Since 1978 the franchise, formerly of men and women over 21, has been extended to those over 18 years.

ESTONIA

The Constitutional Assembly of 1918 formulated a constitution which came into force in 1920. This provided for a republican state with a State Assembly elected by all citizens over 25, by proportional representation, and sitting for three years.

The Assembly had 100 members, and elected its own chairman and officers from among them. The Assembly appointed a government responsible to it and consisting of the head of state and his ministers. The executive prepared the budget and submitted it to the Assembly for approval. Bills passed in the

Assembly might remain unpromulgated for two months if one-third of the Assembly demanded it; within that period a referendum could be demanded, or the bill's adoption recommended, by 25 000 citizens entitled to vote.

A second constitution was framed in 1934 and a third in 1938, when the main changes were made. A President was to be popularly elected for a term of six years. Parliament had two chambers, the first having 80 members directly elected by the national electorate for a five-year term. The second – the State Council – had 40 members all over 40 years of age and elected by organizations and public bodies. The Prime Minister, no longer head of state, was chosen by the President and formed his own cabinet which was responsible to parliament. He did not automatically resign on a vote of no confidence; it was the President's decision whether the cabinet should be dismissed or parliament dissolved. Since 1940 Estonia has been a constituent republic of the USSR.

FINLAND

The constitutional law of 1919 provided for a republican state with a President and a single-chamber parliament. The President is elected indirectly for a six-year term. He ratifies or withholds consent to new law, dissolves the Diet and orders new elections and conducts foreign affairs. In all this he must act through his ministers, who are individually and collectively responsible to the Diet, and must take all his decisions in meetings of the cabinet. He has a strong veto power on legislation, and if he does not give the necessary approval within three months the bill dies. In this event, if the new Diet accepts the bill exactly as it was after new elections, it becomes valid without his assent.

Every citizen over 18 may vote and every citizen over 20 may be elected to the Diet, which has 200 members and is elected by proportional representation for a four-year term (originally a three-year term). The house meets annually for at least 120 days after which it determines the date of its own rising. The President, as embodying the supreme executive power, initiates legislation by introducing bills into the Diet; the Diet with the President has power to propose a new law or to repeal or amend an existing one. New bills are drafted by the Council of State (cabinet), and may be passed for opinion to the Supreme Court or Supreme Administrative Court. Bills adopted by the house are submitted to the President. The Council of State has no fixed size but consists of as many ministers as are necessary, and always includes a Chancellor of Justice and a deputy who have the right to assist at all sessions of the Council of State and of tribunals and public departments, with free access to their minutes. These may not be members of the Diet. There is a strong system of Diet committees which must be constituted within five days of the opening of a session. Standing committees are the Committees on Fundamental Laws, Laws, Foreign Affairs, Finance and a Bank Committee. The Grand Committee must also be established within the same period, having 45 members elected by the Diet. No member of the government may be a committee member. The Grand Committee serves as a body to consider bills which have had their first reading and previously been passed to one of the specialist committees for opinion. The opinion of the Grand Committee is heard at the second reading.

FRANCE

The Third Republic kept the constitution of 1875 until it ended in 1940. This provided for two chambers, a Chamber of Deputies and a Senate. The Chamber of 26 members was elected for four years by manhood suffrage on proportional representation. The Senate had 314 members elected for nine years, one third retiring every three. Both houses assembled annually in January, and were obliged to remain in session for at least five months of the twelve. Bills could be presented in both houses either by the government or by private members, except financial bills which were solely the concern of the deputies. There was also a Council of State presided over by the Minister of Justice and other members all appointed by the President. It gave opinion on any question of administration put to it by the government.

The President was a symbolic head of state, theoretically with many powers but in practice not exercising them. He had the right to dissolve the Chamber, but did not use it after 1877; the suspensory veto over acts of parliament was never used. His role in lawmaking and the determination of policy was controlled by the cabinet.

The government's executive power lay with the ministers who were not necessarily members of either house and were chosen by the President in conjunction with the Prime Minister. They were responsible to both houses and were obliged to countersign (individually) every act of the President. Political dissension between many small parties made for weakness in the executive which had on several occasions to be offset by a grant of special powers made by parliament to the ministers. Special powers to proceed by decree for budgetary and taxation measures were granted in 1926; special powers were also granted in 1934, 1935, 1937 and 1938 and over a hundred decrees issued. Similarly ministers seldom felt strong enough to ask for a dissolution and election on the defeat of a measure; they normally resigned. Between 1870 and 1934 France had 88 ministries with an average life of less than nine months.

The constitution for the Fourth Republic was submitted to the vote in 1946. The Senate was replaced by the Council of the Republic as a purely advisory body, the Chamber by the National Assembly as the legislative body. The executive had limited power to dissolve parliament, and popular sovereignty was invested in the referendum. In 1954, by a constitutional amendment, the Council of the Republic had some power restored to it as a delaying body, with power to hold up National Assembly action in public matters for 108 days. It could also initiate bills and pass them to the National Assembly. The Assembly then had 627 members, 544 of them from Metropolitan France, elected all at the same time for a five-year term. The position of the President was similar to that under the Third Republic, except that the President of the Council of Ministers (Prime Minister) had taken over some of his powers, principally the power to propose legislation to parliament and to issue edicts to supplement the law. The programme of the cabinet had to be approved by public vote by an absolute majority of the National Assembly before the Council of Ministers could be appointed. Once appointed they were responsible to the Assembly but not to the Council of the Republic. The Prime Minister in theory had considerable powers; he assured the execution of all national laws, directed the armed forces and appointed most civil and military officials. In practice, however, he spent much of his time trying to maintain a cohesive executive when no one party was ever strong enough to govern alone.

Under the Fifth Republic the President is head of the government as well as head of state. He can dissolve parliament, negotiate treaties and deal with emergencies without counter-signature. He appoints (rather than formally nominating) the Prime Minister. He is indirectly elected for a seven-year term, but there is no bar to re-election. He may submit matters to the Constitutional Council for opinion, ask parliament to reconsider bills, give ruling on proposals to submit bills to referendum. Before acting outright in an emergency he must consult both executive and legislature, but he is not bound to their advice. Nor is he bound to accept the resignation of the government if the National Assembly has caused it to resign.

The Constitutional Council is appointed for nine years, one-third of its members retiring every three years. The National Assembly now has 491 members directly elected for five years (474 from Metropolitan France) and neither the Prime Minister nor any of the cabinet are allowed to hold seats in it. The Council of the Republic continues as the Senate, and all bills go to it. The Senate has 305 members (287 from Metropolitan France), indirectly elected for nine years, one-third retiring every three years. Both houses sit for about five months of the year, one session beginning in October, and the second in April. Sessions are shorter than before, the number of private members' bills is considerably fewer – an average of 2000 a year under the Fourth Republic, 200 a year under the fifth – and the programme of the National Assembly is determined by the government and not by the house.

GERMANY

In Jan 19 a National Assembly was elected by proportional representation, the franchise being of all over 20. This assembly elected the first President of the

Republic in Feb 19, and laid down that future presidents were to be elected by direct vote, for seven years. A constitution was promulgated on 11 Aug 19 by which a new federal republic was provided with a bicameral federal parliament, to be responsible for defence, foreign relations, tax, customs and railways. The upper house (Reichsrat) had 55 members representing the component states and each member had an individual vote. All bills had to be approved by the Reichsrat before being introduced into the lower house (Reichstag). Members of the Reichstag were elected by proportional representation on a franchise of all over 20, for a four-year term. There was a cabinet appointed by the President but requiring the confidence of the Reichstag.

The President initiated orders and decrees, although they had still to be countersigned, appointed all national officials, decided the sessions and dissolutions of the Reichstag and ordered referenda. Without consulting the government or the legislature he could, in time of danger, suspend the national authorities and appoint a national commissioner in their place, employ the armed forces and suspend certain fundamental rights. By 1932 his emergency powers had been used 233 times, the Reichstag having the right to repeal any measures taken when the emergency was over.

By the law of 14 July 33 all political parties except the National Socialist German Workers' Party were declared illegal; the Reichstag did not operate normally from that date. Its meetings became shorter until they were limited to sessions of two or three days, and it met infrequently. It remained virtually dead until 1949.

Note: The constitution of 1919 provided for popular election of the president, but Paul von Hindenburg was the only president so elected. President Ebert was elected by the Constituent Assembly itself, and Adolf Hitler assumed the Presidency by incorporating it with his own office of Chancellor.

GERMAN DEMOCRATIC REPUBLIC

In 1948 the Soviet-occupied zone of Germany had a People's Council: this was converted into a People's Chamber in 1949 and on 7 Oct 49 the Chamber enacted a constitution for the Democratic Republic. A new constitution was approved by referendum on 6 Apr 68.

The Chamber has 500 deputies who are directly elected for four years. It assures the enforcement of its own laws and decisions and lays down the principles to which the Council of State, the Council of Ministers, the National Defence Council, the Supreme Court and the Procurator General should adhere. No one can limit the rights of the Chamber. It can hold plebiscites, declare a state of defence when necessary, and approve and terminates state treaties. In between its sessions it authorizes the Council of State to fulfil all tasks resulting from the Chamber's laws and decisions. The

Council is elected for four years. It deals with bills to be submitted to the Chamber and submits them for discussion by the Chamber's committees; it convenes the Chamber either on request or on its own initiative; it issues decrees and decisions with the force of law; it has power to interpret existing law; it issues the writs for elections; its Chairman represents the Republic in international relations. (The Council was formed to replace the office of President abolished in 1960.) The Council is an organ of the Chamber and responsible to it.

The Council of Ministers is also an organ of the Chamber and elected by it. Its Chairman is proposed to the Chamber by the Chairman of the Council of State. It functions collectively in the exercise of executive power; from within its ranks it appoints a Presidium; the Chairman of the Council is also the Chairman of the Presidium. The Chamber reaches decisions by majority vote. Bills may be presented by the deputies of the parties or mass organizations represented, by the committees of the Chamber, the Council of State, the Council of Ministers or by the Confederation of Free German Trade Unions. The bill's conformity with the constitution is examined by the Council of State; the bill is then discussed in committee and comments submitted to the Chamber in plenary session. Drafts of basic laws, prior to their being passed, are submitted to the electorate for discussion.

The Chamber can be dissolved before the end of its electoral term only on its own decision taken on a two-thirds majority. After the end of an electoral term the Council of Ministers and the Council of State continue their work until the new Chamber elects new Councils.

FEDERAL REPUBLIC OF GERMANY

A Constituent Assembly met in 1948 and devised a Basic Law which was approved by the parliaments of the separate states of the federation and came into force in 1949 as the first constitution of the Federal Republic. Parliament consists of the Federal Council (Bundesrat) which is composed of members of governments of the Länder.

The Bundestag has 49 members and 22 non-voting members for Berlin. Elections for a new Bundestag take place in the last three months of its term, or in the case of its dissolution after not more than 60 days. The new house meets not more than 30 days after election. The President of the Bundestag may convene the house at any time and must do so if asked by one-third of its members or by the Federal President or Federal Chancellor.

Meetings are public, but the public may be excluded. Members of the Bundesrat or of the government have free access to the Bundestag meetings and committee meetings and must be heard at any time; the same is true of

Bundestag members at meetings of the Bundesrat, and either house may demand the presence of any member of the Federal Government.

The governments of the Länder appoint and recall those of their members who make up the Bundesrat, or they may appoint other members to represent them. Each Land has at least three votes; Länder with over 2m. inhabitants have four, those with over 6m. have five. Each Land has as many members as it has votes, and the votes may only be given as a block. The government has an obligation to keep the Bundesrat informed of the conduct of Federal affairs.

Bills are introduced in the Bundestag either by the government or by members of either house. Government bills go to the Bundesrat first, and the house must give an opinion within three weeks. A bill adopted in the Bundestag then goes to the Bundesrat, which may within two weeks demand a joint committee to consider it. Bills altering or adding to the constitution require Bundesrat approval before they may be passed; such bills need a two-thirds majority in both houses. For other bills the Bundesrat has a power of veto, but even then a veto adopted by a majority of Bundesrat votes may be rejected by a majority of Bundestag votes. There is provision for a state of legislative emergency for a bill which the Bundestag has rejected despite the government declaring it urgent, or a bill which has been put forward with a request for a vote of confidence.

The Federal Chancellor is elected by the Bundestag on the proposal of the Federal President. Ministers are appointed and dismissed by the President on the Chancellor's proposal. The Chancellor determines and assumes responsibility for general policy, and within that policy the ministers run their own departments on their own responsibility. The President is elected by indirect vote for a five-year term; immediate re-election is allowed once. His orders and instructions require countersignature by the Chancellor or by a minister.

GREECE

The constitution of 1911 continued in force until 1925 when it was replaced temporarily by a new one; this was abandoned in 1935 and the original reinstated although some parts of the second constitution were substituted for some of the original clauses later in the year. The constitution of 1952 further amended that of 1911, and remained in force until 1968 when a new one was adopted after a referendum. In 1973 the Monarchy ended and a Republic came into being, with a President as head of state. The 1952 constitution was reintroduced in modified form in 1974, and a new one was promulgated in 1975. All constitutions except the 1925 have provided for a single-chamber parliament, the House of Representatives. This has been the sole or joint source of legislation except during periods of rule by military junta (1967–73, 1973–4).

The House had at least 150 members elected by direct universal suffrage for four years. It met annually in October for each regular session, which had to be for at least three months. It sat in public but the public could be excluded, if the majority of members so decided. It shared with the King or his Regent the legislative power and the right of proposing laws; this second right the King or the Regent exercised through his ministers. Their countersignature was necessary for all his acts, and through them his executive power was exercised. If no minister consented to sign the decrees dismissing an entire ministry and appointing a new one, they could be signed by the President of the new ministry whom the King had appointed. He could suspend the work of a session once only; he could dissolve the house, but the decree of dissolution had to include the convocation of the electors within 45 days and of the new house within three months. He had no power to delay the operation of the law. A bill was at first accompanied by an explanatory report and sent to a committee of the house; it was brought in for discussion when the committee had reported, or when the time allowed for such report has elapsed. No proposal was considered accepted unless it had been discussed and voted on twice at separate sittings. A bill could be passed in one sitting provided the committee to which it was submitted had agreed, and provided less than twenty representatives objected before the close of the debate, Ministers had free access to debates and could demand a hearing at any time; they voted only if they were members. They were individually responsible to the House, and no order from the King could release them from their responsibility.

The 1925 Republican constitution provided for a Senate as well as a Chamber of Representatives, and a President. The President was elected for five years by both houses in joint session. The Chamber had between 200 and 300 directly elected members and the Senate 120 members indirectly elected. The ministers were responsible to both houses for the actions of the executive, *i.e.* the President. Bills could be introduced by members of both houses and by the government; the Senate had power to delay legislation but the Chamber could pass a bill by majority vote over the Senate's opposition after three months or earlier at a joint session if the Senate requested one. The budget was initiated in the Chamber and the Senate was obliged to pronounce on it within one month. The President required ministerial countersignature for all his acts.

The unicameral parliament provided by other constitutions had members directly elected by universal adult suffrage, for four years. Under the monarchy there were at least 150 members, under the presidency, at least 200.

The House shares with the President the legislative power and the right to propose laws; this second right the President exercises through his ministers. Their countersignature is necessary for all his acts, and through them his executive power is exercised. He has no power to delay the operation of the law. Ministers have free access to debates and may demand a hearing at any

58

time; they vote only if they are members. They are individually responsible to the House.

HUNGARY

The first permanent Parliament set up after the end of the Austro-Hungarian monarchy was the National Assembly of 1920. The head of the state was Admiral Horthy who held the title of Regent; he had power of suspensive veto over laws passed by the Assembly and power to dissolve the house provided a newly elected Assembly met within 90 days. When the Assembly ended in 1922 a law was passed by government decree (*i.e.* by the Regent's ministers) making the 200 seats in rural constituencies subject to open and not secret voting. Men over 24 who had completed the course at elementary school, and women over 30 with certain qualifications received the vote. The government's supporters were returned in strength, but the working of parliament became disorderly and difficult. In 1924 the government was granted extraordinary powers for a two-year period of reconstruction.

In 1926 a second chamber was formed, comprising male members of the former reigning house, elected representatives of hereditary members of the former Upper House, about 50 members elected by town and county municipalities, about 31 members as religious representatives, about 40 members elected by institutions and organizations and some life members appointed by the head of the state. It ceased functioning after 1944. In 1937 the Regent was made no longer responsible to parliament. In 1938 the number of deputies in the Assembly was increased from 245 to 260. The Assembly proclaimed a Republic in 1946. In 1949 a further – Communist – constitution was set up with parliament electing a Presidium on the Soviet model; the Presidium is in continual session and has power to dissolve government bodies and to annul legislation. The Assembly has 352 deputies, and since 1967 more than one candidate has been allowed to stand for election in each constituency provided they supported the policies of the Patriotic Front and received 30% of the votes cast at pre-election nominations. Members were elected for four years until 1975, when the term was changed to five years. The Assembly also elects a Council of Ministers with a chairman as Prime Minister. The relationship between Assembly, Council and Presidium is on the Soviet model.

ICELAND

The constitution in force in 1918 was based on the Charter of 1874. Executive power belonged to the King (who was King of both Denmark and Iceland as two separate sovereign states) and was exercised through ministers responsible to him and to parliament (the Althing). The legislative power rested conjointly with the Althing and the King. The Althing had 40 members, 34 of them elected by universal suffrage in constituencies and the remaining 6 elected for the whole country on proportional representation. The 34 sat for 6 years, the rest for 12. The Althing had an Upper House of 14 members – *i.e.* the 6 described above and 8 others elected by the whole Althing from among the 34. The remaining 26 members formed the Lower House. The Althing met every other year in July, and could not sit for longer than four weeks without royal sanction. Ministers had free access to both houses, but could only vote in the house of which they were members. Budget bills had to be introduced in the Lower House, but all other bills could be introduced in either. If the houses could not agree on a bill they assembled in common sitting and the decision was by a two-thirds majority except in the case of a budget bill, for which a simple majority was enough.

In the Charter of 1920 and its amendments of 1934 some alterations were made to the composition of the Althing: the number of members had not to exceed 49, of whom 38 were elected from the constituencies, each electing candidates by simple majority except for the capital which elected 6 on proportional representation. Not more than 11 supplementary seats were distributed among parties having insufficient seats in proportion to their electors. The Upper House was composed of one-third of Althing members elected by both houses in common sitting. The Althing met every year. The electoral law of 1959 provided for an Althing of 60 members, of whom 49 were elected in 8 constituencies by proportional representation, with 11 supplementary members chosen as before. The republic was proclaimed in 1944 and a President elected to exercise executive power through the ministers. He serves for four years.

IRELAND

There are two houses in the Irish parliament, the House of Representatives (Dáil) and the Senate. The House had 166 members in 1984 elected by universal adult suffrage. The Senate has 60 members of whom 11 are nominated by the Prime Minister, 6 elected by the universities and 43 elected by a college from representatives of the public services and interests. The President is elected for a seven-year term and may be re-elected for consecutive terms. The constitution in force is that of 1937. The constitution formed by Dáil Eireann in 1919 was a temporary one, not intended as a permanent basis for a fully operating government. It provided for a chairman for the Dáil, a Prime Minister and other ministers; it defined the competence of the Dáil and made provision for audit and budgeting. The constitution of the Irish Free

State in 1922 provided for a constitutional monarchy with responsible government by a cabinet of ministers. In order to restrict the power of the executive there was also provision for referendum and popular initiative, and for the direct election by the Dáil of ministers who were not Dáil members or members of the cabinet. All these measures, however, had lapsed or been removed within five years.

Note: The 1937 constitution did not declare a Republic. It provided instead for a continuation of the arrangements made at the abdication of Edward VIII, when the mention of the Crown was removed from the previous constitution and an ordinary statute (The Executive Authority (External Relations) Act) put in its place to provide an organ for the state in the conduct of its external affairs. In 1948 it was therefore possible to create the Republic by ordinary legislation and not by changing the constitution. The President appoints the Prime Minister on the nomination of the Dáil, and the other ministers on the nomination of the Prime Minister, with the previous approval of the Dáil. The Prime Minister holds office until he chooses to resign, in which case the government is deemed also to have resigned, until he loses majority support or until he himself secures dissolution by asking the President. Appointment to the government is distinct from appointment to a department. Members of the government may include members of the Senate (but in practice have only done so twice). There is provision for ministers without portfolio.

Bills are proposed mainly by the government in planned legislative programmes. There is provision for private members' bills, but few are initiated. The Senate has power to delay legislation while the Dáil reconsiders its previous decision. Bills can be discussed at parliamentary party meetings either between their preparation and presentation to the house, or between presentation and second reading.

There may be no amendment to the constitution without a referendum, though this was possible before 1930.

ITALY

Italy is a Republic, with a President and a parliament consisting of a Chamber of Deputies and a Senate. The Chamber is elected for five years by direct and universal suffrage with one deputy for every 80 000 inhabitants. The Senate is elected for six years with at least six senators for each Region – one for every 200 000 inhabitants – except for the Valle d'Aosta which has only one. The President can nominate five senators for life, and may himself become a senator for life upon retiring from the Presidency.

Parliament may be dissolved by the President. A cabinet need resign only on a motivated motion of censure.

61

A joint session of Chamber and Senate is needed to elect a President, with an additional three delegates from each Regional Council (one from the Valle d'Aosta). The presidential term is seven years.

The Republic was established in 1946, following a referendum on 2 June and the consequent abdication of King Umberto II on 13 June. The republican constitution came into force on 1 Jan 48.

The constitution prior to 1948 was an expansion of the Statuto fondamentale del Regno of 1848. The executive power belonged to the sovereign and was exercised through responsible ministers; legislative power rested in King and parliament, which consisted of a Senate and a lower chamber. This latter was the Chamber of Deputies until 1938; it was elected by universal adult male suffrage for five years with one deputy for every 71 000 of the population. The King had power to dissolve it at any time provided he ordered new elections and convoked a new meeting within four months. In 1938 the Chamber was replaced by the Chamber of Fasci and Corporations which had first met in 1929. Membership of this consisted of the Duce and the members of the Grand Fascist Council, a third body whose approval was needed for all constitutional measures and which consisted of original members of the Fascist Party on its coming to power, who were appointed for an indefinite period, ministers and other dignitaries appointed for the duration of their terms of office and other members appointed for three years by the Duce. The Duce as Prime Minister was responsible to the King.

Suffrage in 1919 was by proportional representation. In 1923 this was replaced by a system of election in fifteen constituencies, with two-thirds of seats allotted to whichever party gained at least 25% of total votes. In 1925 there was a further alteration introducing single-member constituencies, by-elections and suffrage for all over 25. Parliament, however, did not function normally after the Fascist ministry took power in 1922, as the Fascists were the only effective party.

LATVIA

The constitution came into force in 1922 and provided for a republican state with a single house of parliament (the Saeima). The house had 100 representatives directly elected on universal adult suffrage by proportional representation for a term of three years. The house elected the state President by absolute majority for a three-year term. The President chose the Prime Minister, who appointed the cabinet. The cabinet was responsible to the house. The President had the right to dissolve parliament only after the proposal to dissolve it had been voted on and confirmed by the electorate. If he did not obtain this confirmation he was obliged to resign. In 1934 the parliament was disbanded and a government set up which combined executive and legislative power in the former Council of Ministers. This government was led by the former Prime Minister Karlis Ulmanis. He combined his office with that of President in 1936. Since 1940 Latvia has been a constituent republic of the USSR.

LIECHTENSTEIN

The constitution of 1921 provides for a Diet of 15 members in one house, elected on universal suffrage and proportional representation. They sit for four years. The Prince convokes, closes and dissolves the Diet, and may adjourn it for three months provided the adjournment is announced before the full Diet. Convocation may be demanded by 400 citizens, and dissolution decided by plebiscite on the demand of 600. The Diet supervises the entire administration of the state. Bills may be initiated by the Diet, the Prince acting through the government, and the citizens (400 or three communes). To be valid a law must be passed by an absolute majority of at least two-thirds of members. If the Diet rejects a bill submitted to it by popular initiative, it is obliged to submit the bill to referendum, when it can be passed by the citizens even if the Diet disagrees. The government is appointed by the Prince with the approval of the Diet; he acts through them, but all his actions must be countersigned and it is his ministers who are responsible.

LITHUANIA

The constitution was adopted in 1922 and provided for a single-chamber parliament elected for three years by universal suffrage and proportional representation. Elections for a new house had to take place before the expiration of the previous term. The President of the Republic was elected by parliament for three years and by absolute majority; he could run for two successive terms but no third term without a break. He appointed the Prime Minister, and confirmed the ministers chosen by him, and also appointed the State Comptrollers (with auditing powers), but all bodies appointed could only function with the confidence of the house. He had power to return a bill to the house for reconsideration within twenty-one days of the passage; but was then bound to accept it if it was passed again by an absolute majority. His power of delay could be cancelled by a declaration of urgency by the house. He presided at and took part in cabinet meetings.

Any amendment to the constitution could be brought forward by the house, the government, or 50 000 citizens, but needed a three-fifths majority of the total number of deputies for adoption. After that a referendum could be demanded on it. Ministers had individual and collective responsibility.

63

In 1926 the democratic system was brought to an end by political confusion. Further constitutional changes were made in 1928 and 1938 on authoritarian lines. By 1938 a dictatorship had been established and the house was no longer operating normally. In 1940 Lithuania became a constituent republic of the USSR.

LUXEMBOURG

The constitution of 1868 was amended in 1919, 1948 and 1956. In 1919 it was decided that sovereign power was vested in the people and that deputies to the single Chamber of Deputies were to be elected on universal suffrage by the list system of proportional representation. The Chamber of Deputies had 48 members in 1919. They were elected for a six-year term, half of them being re-elected every three years. The head of state shared legislative power with the Chamber and exercised the executive power through the cabinet. The constitution allowed the sovereign to organize the government. The sovereign also chose the 15 members of the permanent Council of State who served for life. The Council discussed proposed legislation and was obliged to give an opinion on any matter referred to it by the sovereign or the representatives of the law.

In 1956 the term of office for deputies was altered to five years.

The Grand Duke names and dismisses the government, which must consist of at least three members who may not be members of the Chamber, and who are responsible collectively and individually.

Bills are passed after two readings with an interval of three months approved by an absolute majority.

MONACO

The constitution of 1911 lasted until 1959; it provided for a National Council of 18 members elected for a five-year term by 30 delegates of municipalities and 21 electors chosen by adult male suffrage. Legislative power was exercised by the Prince and the Council, executive power by a Minister of State and a three-member Council of Government under the Prince.

In 1959 the Prince suspended this constitution and dissolved the National Council, which was then revived in 1962 as a directly elected body with a five-year term. Executive power is still vested in the Prince, the Minister of State who represents him, and the Council. The Minister directs all administration and presides over the Council with the casting vote. The Council consists of three members named by the Prince (members for the Interior, Finance and Public Works). The Council takes its decisions after deliberation and prepares

64

drafts and ordinances for the Prince's consideration. Legislative power is vested in the Prince and the National Council. The Assembly of the National Council chooses a Bureau, with President and Vice-President. The Assembly sits for two sessions a year, each of 15 days at most; the Prince may convoke and dissolve it. He communicates with the assembly through the Minister of State, who, together with the councillors, may attend at his own wish and must attend when asked. The initiative rests with the Prince, but the National Council may submit draft proposals to him and ask him to initiate them. The National Council controls the budget, which is submitted to it by the Council, and has sole right to levy direct taxation.

THE NETHERLANDS

The parliament consists of two chambers. The Upper House has had 75 members since 1956, prior to which it had 50. They are elected by members of the Provincial States. The Second Chamber has had 150 deputies since 1956 (100 before that) and they are directly elected on universal suffrage and proportional representation. The Second Chamber shares legislative power with the sovereign, who has power to dissolve both chambers provided elections take place within 40 days and the new house or houses be convoked within three months.

The Upper House is elected for six years, and half the members retire every three years. The Lower House members are elected for four years.

Bills are proposed either by the Sovereign, acting through responsible ministers, or by a member of the Lower House. The Upper House has power only to approve or reject them without amendment; the houses must ultimately agree. Ministers and Secretaries of State attend sessions of both houses either at their own or parliament's wish, but they may not be members of either house. The constitution can only be revised if the bill for its revision is passed and confirmed again by a second parliament after the dissolution of the first.

The constitutional amendments of 1922 provided that the Upper House should be elected for six years and not for nine as formerly. Until 1922 the right to declare war and to conclude and ratify treaties with foreign powers was a royal power, exercised in conjunction with the cabinet. Since then, the exercise of these powers has depended on previous parliamentary sanction. The constitution allows considerable royal initiative, but in practice the operation of the cabinet system has set this aside. There is also a Council of State of not more than 16 members which sits as an advisory body on all legislative matters and is consulted by the Crown, the government or parliament.

NORWAY

Norway's constitution dates from 1814; although there have been amendments since, the nature of the Storting (Parliament) is virtually the same as then provided. The state is a constitutional monarchy; in default of male heirs the King proposes a successor to parliament which have the right to select another. The King also has power of veto which may be exercised twice; a bill which passes three parliaments formed by three elections becomes law without his assent.

Parliament assembles in October every year for a session of no fixed duration. Once the house is assembled it divides in two by electing one-quarter of its members to form the Lagting or Upper House; the remaining three-quarters forming the Odelsting or Lower House. There is a president nominated for each house and for the joint house. Most questions are decided by the joint house, but legislation must be considered by both houses separately. If they disagree, then the bill must be decided by parliament as a whole and the decision taken on a two-thirds majority (of voters, not of total membership). The same majority is needed for constitutional amendments.

The executive is represented by the Crown acting through the Prime Minister and cabinet of 14 ministers. The ministers attend sessions of parliament and take part in discussions, but they do not vote. They do initiate bills.

There is a strong committee system through which all proposed legislation must pass before submission to the house. All bills are proposed in the Odelsting, and if accepted are sent to the Lagting. The Lagting may either approve a bill as it stands or reject it as it stands and give its reasons. If rejected it is returned to the Odelsting which will send it once more, either in an amended or original form, to the Lagting. If still rejected the joint session must take place to pass it.

The Crown has no power of dissolution, nor can it summon parliament to meet. The dates of meeting are decided by parliament itself. Election is direct, by all citizens over 20 and by proportional representation. The 150 members are elected for a three-year term.

POLAND

The constitution of the Republic came into operation in 1920. The legislature consisted of a Diet and a Senate. Diet members were elected on universal suffrage for a five-year term. The Senate was elected on universal suffrage of all citizens over 30 and by proportional representation in the provincial districts. It sat also for five years.

National minorities represented 20% of Diet membership.

The Diet had the power of initiating legislation, and had to submit every bill it passed to the Senate. The Senate was obliged to refer a bill back within 30 days if it was suggesting amendments; otherwise the bill was promulgated. If the Diet accepted the Senate's amendments by a simple majority or rejected them by a majority of eleven-twentieths, the bill was passed in the form it left the Diet for the second time.

A President was elected by parliament as a whole for a term of seven years. His position was largely symbolic and his actions required the consent of parliament. He might dissolve the Diet if he had the consent of the Senate, but the Senate in so consenting determined its own dissolution. He exercised the executive power through a council of ministers responsible to the Diet.

There was also a Supreme Court of Control which made independent and judicious survey of the government's provincial administration. Its president was a minister, not a member of the Council of Ministers but responsible to the Diet.

The constitution could only be amended by a two-thirds majority of at least half the number of deputies and senators fixed by law. It might be revised once every 25 years by simple majority of a joint session.

The constitution of 1935 made radical changes in the office of President and the composition of the houses. The working of the original Diet was frequently disrupted by party differences; now there were to be no political parties in the Diet or the Senate. The Senate was to have one-third of its 96 Senators nominated by the President of the Republic and the remaining two-thirds elected by colleges.

The President was chosen by referendum from two candidates, one elected by the two houses together and the other nominated by the retiring President. He could now exercise without countersignature his right to nominate and dismiss the Prime Minister and the Inspector-General of the armed forces, to nominate judges and senators, and to dissolve the Diet and the Senate before the end of their term. If the Diet and the Senate demanded the dismissal of a minister or of the cabinet, the President might concur or dissolve the houses.

The present constitution was adopted in 1952. There is now one chamber which sits for four years and is elected by all citizens over 18. It elects, on the Russian pattern, a Council of Ministers with a Chairman as Prime Minister, and a Council of State composed of a Chairman, a Secretary and 14 members, which sits in almost permanent session and exercises the power of a Presidium.

PORTUGAL

By the republican constitution of 1911, legislative power was given to a Congress with a Chamber of Deputies and a Senate. There were 164 deputies elected for three years by male suffrage. The Senate had 71 members elected by electoral colleges formed from the Municipal Councils, and sat for six years with half the number retiring every three years. The Chamber of Deputies had priority in the discussion of financial bills, bills promoted by the government and of those relating to the armed forces. The Senate might amend or reject, but both houses had to agree, by joint session if necessary, before a bill could be promulgated by the President.

The President was elected by joint session of both houses for a four-year term. He had no power of veto but did have power of dissolution after consulting the cabinet. The cabinet was responsible for his acts. For the period of the first constitution the cabinet was extremely weak owing to differences between numerous small parties. Its power to advise dissolution was used frequently and both houses were dissolved for long periods.

The constitution of 1933 remained in force until 1974. It provided for a President directly elected by citizens with literacy or financial qualifications. The National Assembly was to have one chamber with 90 deputies elected for four years by direct suffrage. There was to be a Privy Council of ten members to assist the President. In practice one party took over the National Assembly and has retained control. In 1959 the constitution was amended to provide for indirect election of the President by an electoral college made up of members of the National Assembly and of the Corporative Chamber. On 25 Apr 74 the Government was overthrown and a Junta of National Salvation installed. The dissolution of the National Assembly and of the Council of State followed.

A new constitution was adopted in 1976 and revised in 1982. The President was now elected by popular vote for a five-year term. He was to appoint the Prime Minister and, on the latter's recommendation, the other ministers. A new National Assembly was provided with 250 members, still elected by direct vote for a four-year term. In 1982 the effective ruling junta was abolished and replaced by a Council of State and a Constitutional Tribunal.

ROMANIA

The constitution of 1866 continued in force with amendments until 1923. It provided for a monarchy acting through responsible ministers, and a two-chamber parliament. The Chamber of Deputies was elected by three classes of electors whose franchise depended on property and educational qualifications. The Senate was elected by two classes with property qualifications higher than those required for electors to the Chamber. By the 1923 constitution the King's powers were defined as those of a constitutional monarch, sharing legislative power with the Chamber and the Senate. All three had the right of initiating measures.

The Chamber of Deputies was elected in universal suffrage by all over 21, by proportional representation and compulsory ballot. The Senate was composed of elected and *ex officio* members, some elected on a similar system to members of the Chamber, some by electoral colleges of local councillors with one senator for each Department (the largest local government unit), and some by members of Chambers of Commerce, institutes of Agriculture and Commerce etc., and by the universities. The *ex officio* members included church officials, members of learned institutions, former political and parliamentary figures. All bills, initiated by either the chamber or the King, passed before a Legislative Council which gave help in drafting and co-ordinating measures. It was consulted in all cases except those concerning the budget. The King had power of suspensive veto. A constitution was adopted in 1938 which introduced Senate members nominated by the King, equal in number to those elected. Senators sat for nine years and deputies for six, and the election of deputies was now by all citizens of 30 years and over engaged in manual work, agriculture, commerce, industry or intellectual work. Senators were elected by the same professions, but the age limit was 40. In 1939 the Principal Council and the Grand Council were instituted, to elect eight representatives from each of three classes – agriculturists, free professions and workers. The Principal Council would have executive power and the Grand Council would be an advisory body. By that time the parliament had been in dissolution for over a year, having been dissolved in December 1937. In December 1947 the state became a republic. A new constitution was passed in 1948 providing for one chamber, the Grand National Assembly, which is elected by all over 18 years, for four years with one deputy for every 40 000 inhabitants. This body sits in short sessions twice a year. It elects a Presidium which sits almost permanently and to which its legislative powers are delegated. The Presidium has a chairman, who is head of state, four vice-chairmen, a secretary and 22 members. There is also a Council of Ministers, but all ministerial policies are shaped by deliberative collegiate bodies of which the minister is chairman. The Council of Ministers and the Presidium (or Council of State) relate to the Assembly as on the Russian pattern. In 1972 the National Assembly's term was changed from four years to five.

SPAIN

Spain was a constitutional monarchy until the system was virtually set aside by the military *coup d'état* under General Primo de Rivera in 1923. The constitution had provided for legislative power being exercised by the parliament of two chambers and the King; both chambers were equal in authority, and ministers were responsible to them. Parliamentary life was frequently disrupted and always weakened by political confusion, and no single strong authority emerged.

The military and civil dictatorships which followed abolished the parliament temporarily together with the post of Prime Minister and other Ministries except War and Foreign Affairs. In 1925 a civilian cabinet was restored, but the parliament was still in dissolution.

The constitution of 1931 provided a single-chamber parliament, Congress, and republican state under a President. The Congress was elected for four years by universal suffrage on proportional representation. Electors and deputies had to be over 23. Executive power was held by the head of state, through a Council of Ministers headed by a Prime Minister whom he appointed. There was a Council of the Realm of 16 members, of whom 10 were elected by the Cortes (parliament), and a National Council which was partly elected and partly appointed. The Cortes consisted of members of the government; national councillors; presidents of the supreme court of justice, the council of the realm, the supreme military tribunal, the court of exchequer and the national economic council; 150 representatives of trade unions; representatives of municipalities and provincial councils elected by their respective corporations; 100 deputies (2 from each province) elected by the heads of families; 30 representatives of universities, learned societies, chambers of commerce. Its function was to prepare and pass laws, working through commissions and through plenary session. The Commissions were arranged and appointed by the President of the Cortes in agreement with the government. President and government also arranged the agenda. Laws once passed were sent to the head of state who might within one month return them to the Cortes for fresh deliberation.

A new constitution came into force in 1978, establishing a parliamentary monarchy. The new Cortes was bicameral. The upper house or Senate had 208 senators, 4 each for the 47 peninsular provinces and others elected by the insular provinces, Ceuta and Melilla and the autonomous communities. The lower house or Congress of Deputies had 300–400 members, elected by proportional representation. Suffrage for both houses is universal and direct; the term of both houses is four years. Executive power is vested in the Prime Minister, who is elected by the Congress, and his cabinet.

SWEDEN

The constitution in force in 1918 was that of 1809, under which executive power lay with the King who exercised it through the Council of State with the Prime Minister at its head. All members of the Council of State were responsible for the acts of the government. The ministries prepared bills for the Diet, issued general directives and made higher appointments but did not as a rule take individual administrative decisions. This was done by central boards, whose organization depended on the appropriations granted by the Diet. The King in Council might ask the advice of the boards, but was not bound to follow it. All members of the Council of State were also members of parliament.

Until 1971 there were two chambers of the legislature, the Upper and Lower Houses. The Upper House had members elected by proportional representation, candidates being chosen on property or income qualifications. They sat for eight years and were elected by members of county councils, the electors of Stockholm and five other large towns. The Lower House had 230 members elected by proportional representation. In 1921 women were given the franchise like men at the age of 23. Also in 1921 the two houses gained the right to appoint their own speakers, with an elected substitute to take his place if necessary. Formerly speakers were appointed by the king. In the same year the King's prerogative of consulting a private committee on important questions of foreign relations was modified; a Foreign Affairs Committee was set up consisting of 16 members from each house and appointed by the parliament, and the King was bound to take its advice. All foreign agreements of importance were submitted to parliament for ratification.

Bills passed by the houses passed through a strong committee system which provided opinion on all except finance bills. If the houses disagreed on any bill, the matter would go to each house separately; the houses would then sit together and decide by majority. Both houses had equal powers in framing laws.

Since 1971 the Diet has consisted of one chamber. It has 350 members directly elected by universal suffrage for three years. All over 19 have the vote, and proportional representation is used in 28 constituencies from which 310 members are elected. The remaining 40 seats are distributed to parties receiving at least 4% of votes.

In 1975 a new constitution made parliament the central organ of government, in which the King no longer has any powers.

SWITZERLAND

The constitution is that of 1874, and under it the highest authority is vested in the electorate. This consisted of all male citizens over 20 until 1971 when the franchise was extended to women. The electorate has power through referendum to vote on amendments to or revision of the constitution. Referenda are also held on laws and international treaties if 30 000 voters or eight cantons request them, and the electorate can also initiate constitutional amendments if 50 000 voters support the initiative. The legislature consists of two chambers, the Council of States and the National Council. The Council of States has 46 members chosen and paid by the 23 cantons; election procedures depend on which canton they represent. The National Council has 200 councillors directly elected for four years in proportion to the population of the cantons, with at least one member for each canton or half-canton. Members are paid not by the cantons but from federal funds.

Laws to be submitted to popular vote must have been agreed by both chambers. The chief executive authority lies with the Bundesrat or Federal Council. It has seven members elected from seven different cantons by a joint session of both chambers. It sits for a four-year term. The members must not hold any other office in the cantons or the Confederation. The President of the Federal Council is the President of the Confederation. He and his vice-president are first magistrates of the state. They are elected by a Federal Assembly for one year only. The seven members of the Council act as ministers and heads of the seven administrative departments.

Bills can be introduced in parliament by a member, by either of the houses or by the Federal Council.

TURKEY

In Apr 20 the Grand National Assembly declared itself the sole sovereign representative of the nation, and repudiated the authority of the Sultan and the old parliament at Constantinople. The Assembly consisted of one chamber and every citizen over 18 voted for its members, who had to be at least 30. Members sat for two years then (from 1924) for four years. The house sat annually and could not be in recess for more than four months of the year. Special sessions could be convened at the request of one-fifth of the members, the President of the Council or the President of the Republic. The Assembly was responsible for preparing, framing and passing laws, concluding conventions and treaties of peace, making declarations of war, examining and ratifying laws presented to it by the Commission on the Budget, coining money and administering punishment and pardon. A law passed by the Assembly was passed to the President of the Republic. He might return it for further consideration within ten days, but the Assembly could override his objections and re-vote the law. On bills concerning the budget or the constitution there was no power of veto. The President was elected by the Assembly for its own term, and might be re-elected. All his acts required countersignature by the President of the Council and the minister concerned. The President appointed the President of the Council (Prime Minister) who in turn designated members of his council from among members of the Assembly. Within a week of his appointment he was obliged to offer a programme and ask for a vote of confidence. Ministers were collectively and individually responsible to the Assembly.

There was also a Council of State from among suitably qualified men by the Assembly. This gave advice on legislation.

In 1934 the age for the franchise was altered to 23 and the age for deputies to 31.

In 1937 the principles of the Republican People's Party were incorporated into the constitution; from then on only this party was active in parliament, although there were independent members. Opposition parties came into being again in 1945. The Grand National Assembly was dissolved by the military *coup d'état* of 1960.

The constitution of 1961 provided for a seven-year term for the President, who might not be re-elected. He was elected by joint session of two houses, the National Assembly and the Senate, which had 150 members directly elected, 15 nominated by the President and 18 life senators. Laws were only initiated by the Assembly and the Council of Ministers. Bills were debated first in the Assembly and then referred to the Senate. If the houses did not agree on the bill, the decision was made by a joint committee which prepared another draft for submission to the Assembly. The Assembly then accepted either this draft or the one previously passed to the Senate, or the one amended by the Senate. If the Senate had amended by absolute majority, the Assembly could only revert to its unamended draft, also by absolute majority. Any bill which the Assembly rejected but the Senate adopted was returned to the Assembly for review.

In Sep 80 the Assembly was dissolved and power passed to a National Security Council. A new constitution was drafted and came into force in 1982. All who were members of parliament on 1 Jan 80 were banned from political life for five years. The new Assembly was to have 400 members sitting for a four-year term. A deputy could be expelled, and prevented from standing again for his new party, if he changed sides. The Assembly could also force the resignation of the Council of Ministers by a vote of no confidence. The President was to be elected by a two-thirds majority of the Assembly. He would appoint the Prime Minister, who would then appoint a cabinet. Presidential decrees must be countersigned by the Prime Minister, who assumes responsibility for them. The President was to be advised by a 20-member State Consultative Council which he appointed himself.

USSR

The Union of Soviet Socialist Republics was formally constituted on 6 July 23. The central executive power was the Council of the Union together with the Council of Nationalities, the latter being composed of five representatives from each of the autonomous and Allied republics and one representative from each of the autonomous regions. The supreme authority, however, lay with the Central Executive Committee which was elected by the Congress of Soviets of the Union. This was the source of all legislation and its decrees and resolutions were sovereign. Between its sessions authority was exercised by the Presidium, which was self-electing and nearly identical in membership with the Presidium of the Russian Socialist Federal Soviet Republic. The Central

Executive Committee met infrequently and for short terms; the power of the Presidium was therefore considerable. By 1926 the Executive Committee numbered about 300 and met three times a year. The Presidium prepared the order of business and executed the resolutions passed, being itself in almost continuous session.

The Central Executive Committee also elected the Council of People's Commissars. Originally this had greater power than the Presidium and acted as a cabinet of ministers responsible for departments, but by 1923 its power as a body had been considerably weakened. The Presidium had power to ratify or to stay the executions of the Council's resolutions, to be a court of appeal for any Commissar against the Council as a whole, and to require quarterly reports of all proceedings and instructions of the Council.

A new constitution was formed on 5 Dec 36 and remained in force until 1977. Under it there existed the Council (or 'Soviet') of the Union and the Soviet of Nationalities, who still form the two chambers of the Supreme Soviet; their legislative rights are equal; they are elected for a term of four years, the Soviet of the Union by citizens of the USSR on the basis of one deputy for every 300 000 inhabitants, the Soviet of Nationalities by citizens voting by Union and Autonomous Republics, Autonomous Regions and National Areas. The latter Soviet has 32 deputies from each Union Republic, 11 from each Autonomous Republic, 5 from each Autonomous Region and 1 from each National area. The Council of Ministers (previously called People's Commissars) is appointed by the Supreme Soviet. It is the highest executive and administrative organ but has no legislative power. It executes laws already made and co-ordinates departmental administration. The Chairman of the Council is equivalent to a Prime Minister. It has two First Deputy Chairmen with no departmental responsibility, and four vice-chairmen of whom one has a departmental responsibility. It is itself responsible to the Supreme Soviet or to the Presidium when the Soviet is not in session.

The Presidium of the Supreme Soviet has 39 members including a chairman (the President of the USSR), 5 vice-chairmen (one from each union republic) 21 members and a secretary. It is the practice to elect the chairmen of the presidia of the Union Soviets from among the vice-chairmen. Members of the Council of Ministers may not be elected to the Presidium. The Presidium convenes the sessions of the Supreme Soviet, dissolves it in the event of a deadlock and arranges new elections. It has the power to conduct referenda, to rescind the decisions and orders of the Council of Ministers if they are not in accordance with the law and constitution. The Presidium itself is empowered to interpret the law and constitution. Ministers are appointed and removed by the Presidium, but normally at the instance of the Council of Ministers. The Presidium commands the armed forces and has the power to declare war.

The constitution of 1977 defined the separation of powers between the central government and the constituent republics with their own Supreme

Soviets, Councils of Ministers and Presidiums. The Law on Elections to the Supreme Soviet of the USSR, 1978, laid down procedures for choosing candidates, who stand either as Communists or as 'non-party' candidates, and are elected by universal adult suffrage and direct ballot, following a preliminary selection conference.

UNITED KINGDOM

Parliament has two houses, the House of Lords and the House of Commons. The Commons are elected directly by universal adult suffrage for a five-year term. In 1918 the franchise was for men over 21 and women over 30; it was extended to women over 21 in 1928, and in 1970 the voting age was lowered to 18 years. The Lords is composed of hereditary peers and peeresses, those on whom peerages have been conferred for life, 2 archbishops and 24 bishops.

No English or Scottish peer may sit in the Commons unless he has disclaimed his title for life; Irish peers may sit.

The executive power lies nominally with the Crown, but in fact is exercised through the cabinet of responsible ministers, headed by the Prime Minister who recommends the appointment of other ministers. Ministers are members of either house.

In 1918 the House of Lords was as it had been reorganized by the Parliament Act of 1911. Bills certified by the Speaker of the House of Commons as money bills were to receive the royal assent one month after being sent to the House of Lords, whether the Lords had approved them or not. Any other public bill (except for one extending the life of parliament) passed by the Commons in three successive sessions and rejected by the Lords was to receive the royal assent nevertheless, provided two years had elapsed between the second reading in the first session of the Commons and the third reading in the third session. The 1949 Parliament Act reduced the delaying powers of the upper house to two sessions and one year. In 1958 the parliamentary balance of the house was improved by the introduction of peerages given for life to men and women by the Sovereign on the advice of the Prime Minister. Opposition party leaders are able to convey their own recommendations for peerages through the Prime Minister to the Queen.

Parliament sits from September or October to the same time of the following year, with a summer recess beginning in July. During adjournments the Speaker or the Lord Chancellor may give notice of an earlier meeting if it is in the national interest. All sessions end by prorogation, and all bills not passed by then lapse. Bills (including private members' bills) may originate in either House unless they deal with finance or representation when they are introduced in the Commons. Until 1939 private members generally had precedence for bills and motions on some 22 days in each session, of which some 13 days would be Fridays and shorter than other working days. Since 1967 private members have had precedence on 20 Fridays in each session. The United Kingdom has no written constitution.

YUGOSLAVIA

The Republic was established in 1945, with a President in place of the King. The constitution framed in 1953 provided for a parliament of two houses, the Federal Council and the Council of Producers, the latter being composed of one deputy for every 70 000 of the active population – that is, all engaged in production, transport and commerce. The houses sat separately except for joint sessions to elect officers, including the President of the Republic.

In 1963 a new Federal Assembly was established, with five chambers: Federal, Economic, Education and Culture, Social Welfare and Health, Organizational-Political. Each had 120 deputies and the Federal Chamber also had 70 members delegated by the six republics and two autonomous provinces; they sat as a Chamber of Nationalities. All members were elected for four years, half their number being renewed every two years; no one could be elected successively as a member of the same chamber or of the Federal Executive Council.

The Federal Chamber elected the Federal Executive Council from among its own members, to act as the Assembly's political executive organ; it consisted of a President, two Vice-Presidents and 14 members. The President of the Republic was elected by the Assembly in joint session of all its chambers.

In 1974 a new constitution set up a system of assemblies, based on work-place, employment or community, and at its apex a new bicameral legislature, the Assembly, consisting of the Federal Chamber and the Chamber of Republics and Provinces. The Federal Chamber has 30 delegates from self-managing organizations, communities and socio-political organizations from each Republic, and 20 from each Autonomous Province. The Chamber of Republics and Provinces has 12 from each Republican Assembly and 8 from each Provincial Assembly. The Federal Executive Council has a Chairman (prime minister), 14 members, 8 Federal Secretaries and 6 Chairmen of Federal Committees. The Republics are equally represented, with corresponding representation of the Autonomous Provinces. The prime minister is proposed by the President and elected by the Assembly, who also elect the other ministers at the proposal of the prime minister.

There is a State Presidency of eight members elected every five years; the annual President is Head of State.

The suffrage is for all over 18 years (16, if employed).

4 MINISTERS

ALBANIA

Turham Pasha was Prime Minister from 1918–20. S. Delvin, 1920 and in Dec 20 H. Prishtina was P.M. for a few days. P. Evangheli, July–Dec 21; X. Ypi, Dec 21–Dec 22. A. Zogu (later King Zog) Dec 22–Feb 24; S. Verlaci, Feb 24–June 24; F. Noli, Jun–Dec 24; K. Kotta, Dec 24–Mar 30.

Date of taking office	Prime Minister	Foreign Minister	Finance Minister
12 Jan 33	P. Evangheli	X. Vila	A. Dibra
In Apr 39 Italy invaded Albania and in June the office of Foreign Minister was abolished.			
12 Apr 39	S. Verlazi	X. Dino	
3 Dec 41	M. Kruja		
19 Jan 43	E. Libohova		
13 Feb 43	M. Bushati		
12 May 43	E. Libohova		
2 Dec 45	E. Hoxha	N. Miskane	
24 Mar 46		E. Hoxha	
		Gen. M. Shehu	
24 July 53		B. Shtylla	T. Jakova
20 July 54	Gen. M. Shehu		A. Kellezi
4 June 56			A. Verli
18 Mar 66		N. Nase	
29 Oct 74			L. Gogo
13 Nov 76			H. Toska
14 Jan 82	A. Çarçani		Q. Mihali
1 July 82		R. Mulile	

AUSTRIA

Date of taking office	Prime Minister	Foreign Minister	Finance Minister
12 Nov 18	Dr K. Renner	Dr K. Renner	R. Reisch
25 June 20	Dr M. Mayr	Dr M. Mayr	Dr F. Grimm
21 June 21	J. Schober	Baron Hennet	Dr A. Gurtler
31 May 22	Dr I. Seipel	Dr A. Grunberger	Dr V. Kienbock

AUSTRIA (*continued*)

Date of taking office	Prime Minister	Foreign Minister	Finance Minister
17 Nov 24	Dr K. Ramek	Dr H. Mataja	Dr J. Ahrer
15 Jan 26	Dr I. Seipel	Dr I. Seipel	Dr V. Kienbock
3 May 29	M. Streeruwitz		
26 Sep 29	J. Schober	J. Schober	O. Juch
25 Sep 30	M. Vaugoin		
3 Dec 30	O. Ender		
20 June 31	K. Buresch		
29 Jan 32		K. Buresch	E. Weidenhoffer
20 May 32	E. Dollfuss	E. Dollfuss	
10 May 33			K. Buresch
30 July 34	K. Schuschnigg	E. Berger-Waldenegg	
18 Oct 35			L. Draxler
3 Nov 36		G. Schmidt	H. Neumayer
13 Mar 38	A. Seyss Inquart	W. Wolf	
25 May 38			M. Fischbock

Note: The cabinet was limited in size after the union with the German Third Reich. The Foreign Ministry was carried on in Berlin by the German Foreign Minister. The Seyss Inquart cabinet was dissolved on the Allied occupation of Austria, and a provisional government under Dr K. Renner took office on 28 Apr 1945.

Date of taking office	Prime Minister	Foreign Minister	Finance Minister
18 Dec 45	Dr L. Figl	Dr L. Figl	G. Zimmerman
1 May 46		K. Gruber	
7 Nov 49			E. Margaretha
23 Jan 52			R. Kamitz
2 Apr 53	J. Raab		
25 Nov 53		L. Figl	
16 July 59		B. Kreisky	
9 June 60		E. Heilingsetzer	
11 Apr 61	A. Gorbach	B. Kreisky	J. Klaus
27 Mar 63			F. Korinek
2 Apr 64	J. Klaus		W. Schmitz
18 Apr 66		L. Toncic-Sorinj	
18 Jan 68		K. Waldheim	S. Koren
21 Apr 70	B. Kreisky	R. Kirschlager	H. Androsch
25 June 74		E. Bielka-Karttrev	
29 Oct 76		W. Pahr	
14 Jan 81			H. Satcher
24 May 83	F. Sinowatz	E. Lane	

BELGIUM

Date of taking office	Prime Minister	Foreign Minister	Finance Minister
21 Nov 18	L. Delacroix	P. Hyams	L. Delacroix
20 Nov 20	H. Carton de Wiart	H. Jaspar	G. Theunis
14 Dec 21	G. Theunis		
13 May 25	M. van de Vijvere		
17 June 25	Viscomte Poullet	E. Vandervelde	Baron Houtart
22 Nov 27		P. Hyams	
24 Nov 29	L. Delacroix		
6 June 31	J. Renkin	P. Hyams	
19 Feb 32			J. Renkin
23 Oct 32	Ct. de Brocqueville		H. Jaspar
12 June 34		H. Jaspar	M. Sap
25 Mar 35	P. van Zeeland	P. van Zeeland	M. L. Gérard
13 June 36		P. H. Spaak	H. de Man
24 Nov 37	P. E. Janson		
9 Mar 38			M. Merlot (ad interim)
1 May 38			M. Soudan
15 May 38	P. H. Spaak		M. L. Gérard
3 Dec 38			A. Jannsen
21 Jan 39		P. E. Janson	
20 Feb 39	H. Pierlot	E. Soudan	C. Gutt
18 Apr 39		H. Pierlot	
4 Sep 39		P. H. Spaak	
11 Feb 45	A. van Acker		G. Eyskens
31 Mar 46			F. de Vogel
19 Mar 47	P. H. Spaak		G. Eyskens
10 Aug 49	G. Eyskens	P. van Zeeland	H. Liebaert
8 June 50	J. Duvieusart		J. van Houtte
15 Aug 50	J. Pholien		
15 Jan 52	J. van Houtte		Baron Janssen
22 Apr 54	A. van Acker	P. H. Spaak	H. Liebaert
11 May 57		V. Larock	
25 June 58	G. Eyskens	P. Wigny	J. van Houtte
25 Apr 61	T. Lefevre	P. H. Spaak	A. Dequae
28 July 65	P. Harmel		G. Eyskens
20 Mar 66	P. van den Boeynants	P. Harmel	R. Henrion
18 June 68	G. Eyskens		Baron J. Snoy et d'Oppuers

BELGIUM (*continued*)

Date of taking office	Prime Minister	Foreign Minister	Finance Minister
20 Jan 72			A. Vlerick
22 Jan 73	E. Le Burton	R. van Elslande	W. de Clercq
25 Apr 74	L. Tindemans		
3 June 77		H. Simonet	G. Geens
20 Oct 78	V. Boeynants		
3 Apr 79	W. Martens		
18 May 80		C. -F. Nothomb	R. Henrion
30 June 80			P. Hatry
22 Oct 80			M. Eyskens
6 Apr 81	M. Eyskens		R. Vandeputte
17 Dec 81	W. Martens	L. Tindemans	W. de Clercq

BULGARIA

Date of taking office	Prime Minister	Foreign Minister	Finance Minister
14 Oct 19	A. S. Stamboliiski	A. S. Stamboliiski	R. Daskalov
11 Jan 22			M. Turlakov
10 Feb 23			P. Yanev

Note: Premier Stamboliiski was killed during the *coup d'état* of 9 June 23.

9 June 23	A. Tsankov	K. Kaltov	P. Todorov
1 Jan 25	A. Lyapchev	A. Burov	V. Mollov
12 Oct 31	N. Mushanov	N. Mushanov	S. Stefanov
19 May 34	K. Georgiev	K. Georgiev	P. Todorov (*coup d'état*)
24 May 34		K. Batalov	
22 Jan 35	Gen. P. Zlatev		M. Kalandarov (*coup d'état*)
21 Apr 35	P. M. Toshev	G. Kyoseivanov	M. Ryaskov (*coup d'état*)
23 Nov 35	G. Kyoseivanov		K. Gunev
38			D. Bozhilov
16 Feb 40	B. Filov	I. Popov	
11 Apr 42		B. Filov	
9 Sep 43	D. Bozhilov	S. Kirov	
10 Oct 43		D. Shishmanov	
1 June 44	I. Bagryanov	I. Bagryanov	D. Savov
12 June 44		P. Draganov	

BULGARIA (*continued*)

Date of taking office	Prime Minister	Foreign Minister	Finance Minister
2 Sep 44	K. Muraviev	P. Stainov	A. Girginov
9 Sep 44	K. Georgiev		P. Stoyanov
31 Mar 46		G. Kulishev	I. Stefanov
22 Nov 46	G. Dimitrov	K. Georgiev	
11 Dec 47		V. Kolarov	
21 July 49	V. Kolarov		
6 Aug 49		V. Poptomov	P. Kunin
8 Oct 49			K. Lazarov
1 Feb 50	V. Chervenkov		
27 May 50		M. Neichev	
17 Apr 56	A. Yugov		
18 Aug 56		K. Lukanov	
19 Nov 62	T. Zhivkov		
27 Nov 62		I. Bashev	D. Popov
8 July 71	S. Todorov		
16 Dec 71		P. Mladenov	
16 June 76			B. Belchev
16 June 81	G. Filipov		

CYPRUS

Cyprus was a British dependency until 1960, when it became an independent republic. Ministers were appointed in 1959, pending full independence.

Date of taking office	Prime Minister (or equivalent)	Foreign Minister	Finance Minister
5 Apr 59	Archbishop Makarios	Archbishop Makarios	R. Theocarous

In 1960 President Makarios combined the powers of President and Prime Minister, and held both.

22 Aug 60		S. Kyprianou	
1 July 62			R. Solomides
15 June 68			A. Patsalides
16 June 72		L. Christophides	
16 July 74		D. Dimitrou	
8 Aug 74		G. Clerides	
14 Jan 75		L. Christophides	

CYPRUS (continued)

Date of taking office	Prime Minister	Foreign Minister	Finance Minister

On the death of President Makarios in 1977 the succeeding President, Spyros Kyprianou, followed his practice regarding the post of Prime Minister.

Date of taking office	Prime Minister	Foreign Minister	Finance Minister
8 Mar 78		N. Rolandis	
1 Nov 79			A. Afxentiou
20 Apr 82			S. Vassiliou
22 Sep 83		G. Iacovou	

The Turkish Cypriot Federated State was proclaimed on 13 Feb 75 with Rauf Denktash as President. A constituent assembly was sworn in on 24 Feb 75 and elections were held on 20 June 76. A cabinet was appointed after N. Konuk had been appointed Prime Minister on 3 July 76.

The State declared itself independent on 15 Nov 83. A constituent assembly was set up, and an interim government took office:

N. Konuk	N. M. Ertekün	S. Cosar

CZECHOSLOVAKIA

Date of taking office	Prime Minister	Foreign Minister	Finance Minister
14 Nov 18	K. Kramař (provisional government)		
8 July 19	V. Tusar	E. Beneš	K. Sontag
15 Sep 20	J. Černý		M. Hanošek
26 Sep 21	E. Beneš		A. Novák
8 Oct 22	A. Švehla		T. Becka
18 Mar 26	J. Černý		K. Engliš
12 Oct 26	A Švehla		
13 Oct 27	Mgr. J. Šrámek		
1 Feb 29	J. Udrzal		B. Vlasek
8 Dec 29			K. Engliš
16 Apr 31			K. Trapl
29 Oct 32	M. Malypetr		
18 Dec 35		M. Hodža	
29 Feb 36	M. Hodža	K. Krofta	E. Franke
21 July 37			J. Kalfus
22 Sep 38	Gen. J. Syrový		
4 Oct 38		F. Chvalkovský	
30 Nov 38	R. Beran		

CZECHOSLOVAKIA (*continued*)

Date of taking office	Prime Minister	Foreign Minister	Finance Minister

Note: The Ministry of Foreign Affairs was dissolved by the Reich Protectorate, 18 Mar 39.

27 Apr 39	Gen. A. Eliáš		

Note: A government in exile was set up in London following the German invasion.

Date of taking office	Prime Minister	Foreign Minister	Finance Minister
24 July 40	Mgr. J. Šrámek	J. Masaryk	E. Outrata
27 Oct 41			L. Feierabend
6 Nov 45	Z. Fierlinger		V. Šrobár
2 July 46	K. Gottwald		J. Dolansky
15 June 48	A. Zápotocký	V. Clementis	
14 Mar 50	V. Široký		
31 Jan 53		V. David	
21 Mar 53		V. Široký	J. Kabes
15 Sep 53			J. Duris
22 Sep 63	J. Lenárt		R. Dvořák
11 Nov 65			B. Sucharda
1 Apr 68	O. Černík	J. Hajek	
19 Sep 68		O. Černík	

Note: On 31 Dec 68 Czechoslovakia became a federation, with separate governments for the Czech Socialist Republic and the Slovak Socialist Republic. Details below are for the central, federal, government:

1 Jan 69	O. Černík	J. Marko	B. Sucharda
3 Jan 71	L. Štrougal		R. Rohliček
9 Dec 71		B. Chňoupek	
14 Dec 73			L. Lér

DENMARK

Date of taking office	Prime Minister	Foreign Minister	Finance Minister
4 May 20	N. Neergard	E. Scavenius	N. Neergard
9 Oct 22		C. M. T. Cold	
23 Apr 24	T. Stauning	C. P. O. G. Moltke	C. V. Bramsnaes
29 Apr 29		P. Munch	
			H. P. Hansen
4 Nov 35			V. Buhl
		E. Scavenius	

DENMARK (continued)

Date of taking office	Prime Minister	Foreign Minister	Finance Minister
4 May 42	V. Buhl		
16 July 42			M. Andersen
9 Nov 42	E. Scavenius		J. Koefoed
8 Nov 45	K. Kristensen	G. Rasmussen	T. Kristensen
13 Nov 47	H. Hedtoft		H. C. Hansen
30 Oct 50	E. Erikson	O. B. Kraft	T. Kristensen
30 Sep 53	H. Hedtoft	H. C. Hansen	V. Kampmann
29 Jan 55	H. C. Hansen		
9 Oct 58		J. O. Krag	
19 Feb 60	V. Kampmann		
1 Mar 60			K. Philip
5 Sep 61			H. R. Knudsen
3 Sep 62	J. O. Krag	P. Haekkerup	
9 Nov 62			P. Hansen
24 Aug 65			H. Grünbaum
28 Nov 66		J. O. Krag	
1 Oct 67		H. Tabor	
1 Feb 68	H. T. I. Baunsgard	P. Hartling	P. Moller
17 Mar 71			E. Ninn-Hansen
9 Oct 71	J. O. Krag	K. B. Andersen	H. Grünbaum
5 Oct 72	A. Jørgensen		
19 Dec 73	P. Hartling	O. Guldberg	A. Andersen
13 Feb 75	A. Jørgensen	K. B. Andersen	K. Heinesen
30 Aug 78		H. Christophersen	
26 Oct 79		K. Olesen	S. Jakobsen
30 Dec 81			K. Heinesen
10 Sep 82	P. Schüter	U. Ellemann-Jensen	H. Christophersen

FINLAND

Date of taking office	Prime Minister	Foreign Minister	Finance Minister
26 Nov 18	L. Ingman	C. Enckell	
18 Apr 19	K. Castren		
18 Aug 19	J. Vennola		
15 Mar 20	M. Erich	E. R. W. Holsti	M. Wartiowaara
1 Mar 21	J. Vennola		R. Ryti
14 Nov 22	K. Kallio	J. Vennola	

FINLAND (continued)

Date of taking office	Prime Minister	Foreign Minister	Finance Minister
18 Jan 24	A. K. Kajander	C. Enckell	H. M. J. Relander
22 Nov 24	L. Ingman	H. Procopé	Y. Pulkkinen
1 Jan 26	K. Kallio	E. N. Setälä	K. Järvinen
13 Dec 26	V. Tanner	V. Voionmaa	A. Ryoma
27 Dec 28	O. Hantere	H. Procopé	H. M. J. Relander
16 Aug 29	K. Kallio		T. H. Reinekka
20 Mar 31	J. Sunila	M. Yrsjö-Koskinen	K. Järvinen
14 Dec 32	T. M. Kivimaki	A. V. Hackzell	H. J. M. Relander
12 Mar 37	A. K. Kajander	E. R. W. Holsti	V. Tanner
16 Nov 38		V. Voionmaa	
13 Dec 38		E. Erkko	
2 Dec 39	R. Ryti	V. Tanner	M. Pekkala
27 Mar 40		R. Witting	
4 Jan 41	J. W. Rangell		M. Pekkala and J. Koivosto (Joint Ministry)
May 42			V. Tanner
4 Mar 43	E. Linkomies	H. Ramsay	
8 Aug 44	A. Hackzell	C. Enckell	M. Hiltonen
21 Sep 44	U. Castren		
11 Nov 44	J. Paasikivi		M. Helo
9 Apr 45			S. Tuomija
25 Mar 46	M. Pekkala		R. Törngren
29 July 48	K. A. Fagerholm		O. Hiltunen
18 Mar 50	U. Kekkonen	A. Gartz	V. J. Sukselainen
17 Jan 51			O. Hiltunen
20 Sep 51		S. Tuomioja	V. J. Rantala
9 July 53		R. Törngren	
16 Nov 53	S. Tuomioja		T. Junnila
5 May 54	R. Törngren	U. Kekkonen	V. J. Sukselainen
20 Oct 54	U. Kekkonen	J. Virolainen	P. Tervo
17 Feb 56	K. A. Fagerholm	R. Törngren	A. Simonen
27 May 57	V. J. Sukselainen	J. Virolainen	N. Meinander
2 July 57			M. Miettunen
29 Nov 57	R. von Feiandt	P. J. Hynninen	L. Hietanen
26 Apr 58	R. Kuuskoski		M. I. O. Nurmela
29 Aug 58	K. A. Fagerholm	J. Virolainen	P. Hetemäki
13 Jan 59	V. J. Sukselainen	R. Törngren	W. Sarjala
19 June 59		A. Karjalainen	

FINLAND (continued)

Date of taking office	Prime Minister	Foreign Minister	Finance Minister
14 July 61	M. Miettunen		
13 Apr 62	A. Karjalainen		
18 Dec 63	R. R. Lehto	J. Hallama	E. J. Rekola
12 Sep 64	J. Virolainen	A. Karjalainen	E. Kaitila
27 May 66	K. R. Paasio		M. Koivisto
29 Dec 67			E. Raunio
22 Mar 68	M. Koivisto		
14 May 68	T. Aura	V. Leskinen	P. Hetemäki
15 July 70	A. Karjalainen		C. O. Tallgren
29 Oct 71	T. Aura	O. Mattila	P. Hetemäki
25 Feb 72	K. R. Paasio	K. Sorsa	M. Koivisto
4 Sep 72	K. Sorsa	A. Karjalainen	J. Virolainen
			E. Niskanen
13 June 75	K. Liinamaa	O. J. Mattila	H. Tuominen
			T. Varjas
30 Nov 75	M. Miettunen	K. Sorsa	P. Paavela
			V. Luukka
29 Sep 76		K. Korhonen	E. Rekola
			J. Loikkanen
17 May 77	K. Sorsa	P. Väyrynen	P. Paavela
			E. Rekola
25 May 79	M. Koivisto		A. Pekkala
			P. Työläjärvi
28 May 81			M. Forsman replaced
			P. Työläjärvi as 2nd
12 Feb 82	K. Sorsa		
17 Feb 82		P. Stenbäck	
1 Sep 82			J. Laine replaced
			M. Forsman as 2nd
6 May 83		P. Väyrynen	P. Vennamo replaced
			J. Laine as 2nd

FRANCE

Date of taking office	Prime Minister	Foreign Minister	Finance Minister
20 Jan 20	A. Millerand	A. Millerand	F. Marsal
20 Oct 20	M. Leygues		

FRANCE (*continued*)

Date of taking office	Prime Minister	Foreign Minister	Finance Minister
16 Jan 21	M. A. Briand	M. A. Briand	P. Doumer
15 Jan 22	R. Poincaré	R. Poincaré	M. de Lasteyrie
9 June 24	F. Marsal		
14 June 24	E. Herriot	E. Herriot	E. Clementel
16 May 25	M. Painlevé		
23 Nov 25	M. A. Briand		
23 Aug 26	R. Poincaré	M. A. Briand	R. Poincaré
11 Nov 28			H. Cheron
27 July 29	A. Briand		
2 Nov 29	A. Tardieu	A. Briand	P. Reynaud
13 Dec 30	M. Steeg		
27 Jan 31	P. Laval	A. Briand	P.-E. Flandin
14 Jan 32		P. Laval	
20 Feb 32	A. Tardieu	A. Tardieu	
3 June 32	E. Herriot	E. Herriot	M. Germain-Martin
18 Dec 32	J. Paul-Boncour	J. Paul-Boncour	H. Cheron
31 Jan 33	E. Daladier		G. Bonnet
26 Oct 33	A. Sarraut		
26 Nov 33	C. Chautemps		
30 Jan 34	E. Daladier	E. Daladier	F. Piétri
4 Feb 34			P. Marchandeau
9 Feb 34	G. Doumergue	Louis Barthou	M. Germain-Martin
13 Oct 34		P. Laval	
8 Nov 34	P.-E. Flandin		
1 June 35	F. Bouisson		J. Caillaux
7 June 35	P. Laval		
24 Jan 36	A. Sarraut	P.-E. Flandin	
5 June 36	L. Blum	Y. Delbos	V. Auriol
22 June 37	C. Chautemps		G. Bonnet
18 Jan 38			P. Marchandeau
13 Mar 38	L. Blum	J. Paul-Boncour	L. Blum
10 Apr 38	E. Daladier	G. Bonnet	P. Marchandeau
2 Nov 38			P. Reynaud
21 Mar 40	P. Reynaud	P. Reynaud	L. Lamoureux
18 May 40		E. Daladier	
5 June 40		P. Reynaud	Y. Bouthilier
16 June 40	Marshal P. Pétain	P. Baudouin	
24 Oct 40		P. Laval	
14 Dec 40		P.-E. Flandin	

87

FRANCE *(continued)*

Date of taking office	Prime Minister	Foreign Minister	Finance Minister
10 Feb 41		Adm. F. Darlan	
18 Apr 42	P. Laval	P. Laval	P. Cathala
10 Sep 44	Gen. C. de Gaulle	G. Bidault	R. Pleven
29 Jan 46	F. Gouin		A. Philip
24 June 46	G. Bidault		R. Schuman
16 Dec 46	L. Blum	L. Blum	A. Philip
22 Jan 47	P. Ramadier	G. Bidault	R. Schuman
24 Nov 47	R. Schuman		R. Mayer
26 July 48	A. Marie	R. Schuman	P. Reynaud
5 Sep 48	R. Schuman		C. Pineau
12 Sep 48	H. Queuille		H. Queuille
12 Jan 49			M. Petsche
28 Oct 49	G. Bidault		
2 July 50	H. Queuille		
12 July 50	R. Pleven		
10 Mar 51	H. Queuille		
11 Aug 51	R. Pleven		R. Mayer
20 Jan 52	E. Faure		E. Faure
8 Mar 52	A. Pinay		A. Pinay
8 Jan 53	R. Mayer	G. Bidault	M. Borgès-Mauoury
28 June 53	J. Laniel		E. Faure
19 June 54	P. Mendès-France	P. Mendès-France	E. Faure
23 Feb 55	E. Faure	A. Pinay	P. Pfimlin
31 Jan 56	G. Mollet	C. Pineau	P. Ramadier
5 Nov 57	F. Gaillard		P. Pfimlin
8 Jan 59	M. Debré	M. Couve de Murville	A. Pinay
May 59			M. Baumgartner
15 Apr 62	G. Pompidou		V. Giscard d'Estaing
9 Jan 66			M. Debré
12 July 68	M. Couve de Murville	M. Debré	F. Ortoli
22 June 69	J. Chaban-Delmas	M. Schumann	V. Giscard d'Estaing
6 July 72	P. Messmer		
5 Apr 73		M. Jobert	V. Giscard d'Estaing
27 May 74	J. Chirac		
28 May 74		J. Sauvagnargues	J.-P. Fourcade
17 Aug 76	R. Barre	L. de Guiringaud	R. Barre
30 Mar 77			R. Boulin
5 Apr 78			R. Monory
30 Nov 78		J. François-Poncet	

FRANCE *(continued)*

Date of taking office	Prime Minister	Foreign Minister	Finance Minister
21 May 81	P. Mauroy		
22 May 81		C. Cheysson	J. Delors
17 Jul 84	L. Fabius		
19 Jul 84			P. Beregovoy

GERMANY

Date of taking office	Prime Minister	Foreign Minister	Finance Minister
13 Feb 19	P. Scheidemann	V. von Brockdorff Rantzau	E. Schiffer
21 June 19	G. Bauer		M. Erzberger
28 Mar 20	H. Müller	Dr A. Köster	J. Wirth
25 June 20	C. Fehrenbach	W. Simons	
10 May 21	J. Wirth		A. Hermes
31 Jan 22		W. Rathenau	
22 Nov 22	W. Cuno	H. von Rosenberg	
13 Aug 23	G. Stresemann	G. Stresemann	
30 Nov 23	W. Marx		H. Luther
15 Jan 25	H. Luther		O. von Schleiben
19 Jan 26			H. Reinhold
17 May 26	W. Marx		H. Kohler
28 June 28	H. Müller		R. Hilferding
1 Apr 30	H. Brüning	J. Curtius	H. R. Dietrich
9 Oct 31		H. Brüning	

Note: The Brüning government was dismissed on 30 May 32.

Date of taking office	Prime Minister	Foreign Minister	Finance Minister
2 June 32	F. von Papen	K. von Neurath	L. E. Schwerin von Krosigk
4 Nov 32	K. von Schleicher		
30 Jan 33	A. Hitler		
5 Feb 38		J. von Ribbentrop	
30 Apr 45	C. Doenitz		

Note: Admiral Doenitz surrendered his powers to the allied occupation forces on 5 June 45.

FEDERAL REPUBLIC OF GERMANY

Date of taking office	Prime Minister	Foreign Minister	Finance Minister
20 Sep 49	K. Adenauer		F. Schäffer
13 Mar 51		K. Adenauer	
6 June 55		H. von Brentano	
24 Oct 57			F. Etzel
14 Nov 61		G. Schröder	H. Starke
11 Dec 62			R. Dahlgrün
17 Oct 63	L. Erhard		
1 Dec 66	K. Kiesinger	W. Brandt	F. J. Strauss
21 Oct 69	W. Brandt	W. Scheel	A. Möller
13 May 71			K. Schiller
7 Jul 72			H. Schmidt
16 May 74	H. Schmidt	H.-D. Genscher	H. Apel
3 Feb 78			H. Matthöfer
29 Apr 82			M. Lahnstein
1 Oct 82	H. Kohl		
4 Oct 82			G. Stoltenberg

GERMAN DEMOCRATIC REPUBLIC

Date of taking office	Prime Minister	Foreign Minister	Finance Minister
15 Nov 50	O. Grotewohl	G. Dertinger	H. Loch
15 Jan 53		A. Ackermann	
1 Oct 53		L. Bolz	
24 Nov 55			W. Rumpf
24 Sep 64	W. Stoph		
24 June 65		O. Winzer	
13 July 67			S. Bohm
3 Oct 73	H. Sindermann		
20 Jan 75		O. Fischer	
3 Nov 76	W. Stoph		
4 June 80			Dr W. Schmieder
26 June 81			E. Höfner

GREECE

Date of taking office	Prime Minister	Foreign Minister	Finance Minister
27 June 17	E. K. Venizelos	N. Politis	M. Negropontis
1 Apr 21	D. Gounaris	J. Baltazzi	M. Protopapadakis

GREECE (*continued*)

Date of taking office	Prime Minister	Foreign Minister	Finance Minister
26 Nov 22	Col. Gonotas	A. Alexandris	M. Kofinas
11 Mar 24	M. Papanastasiou	M. Papanastasiou	M. Papanastasiou
7 Oct 24	A. Michalakopoulos	A. Michalakopoulos	C. Gotsis
25 Oct 25	T. Rangalos	L. R. Canacaris	T. Rangalos
4 Dec 26	A. Zaimis	A. Michalakopoulos	C. Gotsis
19 July 28	E. Venizelos	A. Karapanos	G. Maris
23 Dec 30		A. Michalakopoulos	
23 Apr 32			K. Varvaressos
26 May 32	M. Papanastasiou	M. Papanastasiou	
5 June 32	E. Venizelos	A. Michalakopoulos	
3 Nov 32	P. Tsaldaris	J. Rallys	P. Tsaldaris
13 Jan 33	E. Venizelos	A. Michalakopoulos	M. Kaphantaris
6 Mar 33	Gen. Othonais (*ad interim*)		
10 Mar 33	P. Tsaldarus	D. Maximos	S. Loverdos
5 Mar 35		P. Tsaldaris	G. Pesmazoglou
9 Oct 35	Gen. Kondylis	J. Theotokis	Gen. Kondylis
30 Nov 35	C. Demerdjis	C. Dermerdjis	M. Mandjavinos
15 Mar 36			G. Mantzarinos
21 Jan 37	J. Metaxas	J. Metaxas	P. Rediadis
11 Feb 37			M. Apostolides
29 Jan 41	A. Korizis		
21 Apr 41	E. Tsouderos	E. Tsouderos	E. Tsouderos
30 Sep 41			K. Varvaressos
13 Apr 44	S. Venizelis	S. Venizelis	M. Manzadones
26 Apr 44	G. Papandreou	G. Papandreou	
8 June 44			P. Kanellopoulos
31 Aug 44			A. Svolos
3 Jan 45	Gen. Plastiras	J. Sophianopoulos	G. Sideris
8 Apr 45	Adm. Voulgaris		G. Mantzarinos
11 Aug 45		I. Politis	
17 Oct 45	Archp Danaskires		
1 Nov 45	P. Kanellopoulos	P. Kanellopoulos	Prof. Cassimatis
21 Nov 45	T. Sofoulis	J. Sophianopoulos	M. Mylonas
29 Jan 46		C. Rendis	
4 Apr 46	M. Poulitsas	C. Tsaldaris	S. Stephanopoulos
17 Apr 46	C. Tsaldaris		D. Helmis
27 Jan 47	D. Maximos		
29 Aug 47	C. Tsaldaris		

91

GREECE (continued)

Date of taking office	Prime Minister	Foreign Minister	Finance Minister
7 Sep 47	T. Sofoulis		
30 June 49	A. Diomedes		
6 Jan 50	J. Theotokis	P. Pipinelis	G. Mantzarinos
23 Mar 50	S. Venizelis	S. Venizelis	M. Zaimis
15 Apr 50	Gen. Plastiras	Gen. Plastiras	G. Kartalis
13 Sep 50	S. Venizelis	S. Venizelis	S. Castopoulos
2 Feb 51			G. Mavros
8 Aug 51		I. Politis	
27 Oct 51	Gen. Plastiras	S. Venizelis	C. Evelpidis
19 Nov 52	A. Papagos	S. Stephanopoulos	C. Papyannis
15 Dec 54			D. Eftaxias
6 Oct 55	C. Karamanlis	S. Theotokis	A. Apostolides
29 Feb 56			C. Thiraios
27 May 56		G. Averoff	
5 Mar 58	M. Georgakoloulos	G. Pesmajogiou	M. Mestikopoulos
17 May 58	C. Karamanlis	E. Averoff	C. Papaconstantinou
4 Nov 61			S. Theotokis
19 June 63	P. Pipinelis	P. Pipinelis	
8 Nov 63	G. Papandreou	S. Venizelos	C. Mitsotakis
30 Dec 63	J. Paraskevopoulos	C. Xanthopoulos-Palamos	
18 Feb 64	G. Papandreou	S. Kostopoulos	C. Mitsotakis
20 July 65	G. Athanasiadis-Novas	G. Melas	S. Allamanis
20 Aug 65	E. Tsirimokos	E. Tsirimokos	
17 Sep 65	S. Stephanopoulos		G. Melas
11 Apr 66		S. Stephanopoulous	
11 May 66		I. Toumbas	
22 Dec 66	I. Paraskevopoulos	P. Economou-Gouras	P. Stergiotis
3 Apr 67	P. Kanellopoulos	P. Kanellopoulos	C. Papaconstantinou
21 Apr 67	C. Kollios	P. Economou-Gouras	A. Adroutsopoulos
2 Nov 67		C. Kollios	
20 Nov 67		P. Pipinelis	
13 Dec 67	G. Papadopoulos		
1 Jan 70		G. Papadopoulos	
26 Aug 71			I. Koulis
8 Oct 73	S. Markezinis	C. Xanthopoulos-Palamos	
25 Nov 73	A. Androutsopoulos	S. Tetenes	A. Androutsopoulos

GREECE *(continued)*

Date of taking office	Prime Minister	Foreign Minister	Finance Minister
8 July 74		K. Kypreos (provisional)	
24 July 74	K. Karamanlis		
26 July 74		G. Mavros	I. Pesmazoglou

On 8 Oct 74 a caretaker government was formed, K. Karamanlis and G. Mavros retaining their posts, other ministers replaced by non-political persons. On 15 Oct 74 D. Bitsios replaced G. Mavros.

Date of taking office	Prime Minister	Foreign Minister	Finance Minister
21 Nov 74	K. Karamanlis	D. Bitsios	E. Devletoglou
28 Nov 77		P. Papaligouras	I. Boutos
10 May 78		G. Rallis	A. Kanellopoulos
9 May 80	G. Rallis	K. Mitsotakis	M. Evert
21 Oct 81	A. Papandreou	I. Charalambopoulos	E. Drettakis

HUNGARY

Date of taking office	Prime Minister	Foreign Minister	Finance Minister
14 Mar 20	A. Simonyi-Semadam	Ct. P. Teleki	Baron F. Korányi
14 Apr 21	Ct I. Bethlen	Ct D. Banffy	M. Hegedüs
1 Jan 22			T. Kállay
17 June 22		G. Daruvary	
1 June 24		T. Scitovsky	J. Bud
1 Nov 25		L. Valkó	
5 Sep 28			A. Wekerle
1 Oct 29	Ct J. Károlyi	Ct J. Károlyi	
22 Aug 31	G. Károlyi	L. Valkó	Ct J. Károlyi
1 Dec 31			Baron F. Korányi
1 Oct 32	G. Gömbös	K. Kánya	B. Imrédy
8 Jan 35			T. Fabinyi
12 Oct 36	K. Dáranyi		
9 Mar 38			L. Reményi-Schneller
13 May 38	B. Imrédy		
28 Nov 38		B. Imrédy	
10 Dec 38		Ct S. Csáky	

93

HUNGARY (continued)

Date of taking office	Prime Minister	Foreign Minister	Finance Minister
16 Feb 39	Ct P. Teleki		
15 Feb 41		L. Bárdossy	
5 Apr 41	L. Bárdossy		
10 Mar 42	I. Kállay		
23 Mar 44	D. Sztójay	D. Sztójay	
29 Aug 44	Gen. Lakatos	Fd.-Marshal Henvey	
16 Oct 44	F. Szálasi	Baron Keményi	
21 Dec 44	Gen. B. Miklos	J. Gyöngyösy	I. Vásáry
10 July 45			M. Ottványi
15 Nov 45	Z. Tildy		F. Gordon
5 Feb 46	F. Nagy		L. Dinnyés
13 Mar 47			M. Nyárády
31 May 47	L. Dinnyés	M. Mihalyti	
23 Sep 47		E. Molnár	
5 Aug 48		L. Rajk	
9 Dec 48	I. Dobi		E. Gerö
10 June 49		G. Kállai	I. Kossa
24 Feb 50			K. Olt
13 May 51		K. Kiss	
14 Aug 52	M. Rákosi		
16 Nov 52		E. Molnár	
4 July 53	I. Nagy	J. Boldoczky	
18 Apr 55	A. Hegedüs		
30 July 56		I. Horváth	
24 Oct 56	I. Nagy		
4 Nov 56	J. Kádár		I. Kossa
9 May 57			I. Antos
27 Jan 58	F. Münnich		
16 Feb 58		E. Sík	
16 Jan 60			R. Nyers
13 Sep 61	J. Kádár	J. Péter	
27 Nov 63			M. Timar
28 June 65	G. Kállai		
14 Apr 67	J. Fock		P. Vályi
13 May 71			L. Faluvégi
14 Dec 73		F. Puja	
15 May 75	G. Lázár		
27 June 80			I. Hetényi
8 July 83		P. Várkonyi	

ICELAND

Date of taking office	Prime Minister	Foreign Minister	Finance Minister
25 Feb 20	J. Magnusson		N. Gudmundsson
15 Mar 22	S. Egers		M. Jonsson
22 Mar 24	J. Magnusson		J. Thorlaksson
28 Feb 27	T. Thorhallsson		N. J. Kristjansson
20 Oct 31			E. Arnarson
3 June 32	A. Asgeirsson		A. Asgeirsson
29 July 34	H. Jonasson		E. Jonsson
17 Apr 39			J. Moller
18 Nov 41		O. Thors	
		S. Stefansson	
16 May 42	O. Thors		
16 Dec 42	B. Thordarson	V. Thor	B. Olafsson
1 Oct 44	O. Thors	O. Thors	P. Magnusson
4 Feb 47	S. J. Stefansson	B. Benediktsson	J. T. Josefsson
14 Mar 50	S. Steinthorsson		E. Jonsson
13 Sep 53	O. Thors	K. Gudmundsson	
24 July 56	H. Jonasson	G. I. Gudmundsson	
20 Dec 58	E. Jonsson		G. I. Gudmundsson
20 Nov 59	O. Thors		G. Thorodssen
14 Nov 63	B. Benediktsson		
1 Sep 65		E. Jonsson	
10 July 70	J. Hafstein		
10 Oct 70			M. Jonsson
14 July 71	O. Johannesson	E. Ágústsson	H. Sigurdsson
29 Aug 74	G. Hallgrímsson	E. Ágústsson	M. A. Mathiesen
31 Aug 78	Ó. Jóhannesson	B. Groendal	T. Arnasson
15 Oct 79	B. Groendal		S. Björgvinsson
8 Feb 80	G. Thoroddsen	Ó. Jóhannesson	R. Arnalds
26 May 83	S. Hermannsson	G. Hallgrímsson	A. Gudmundsson

IRELAND

Date of taking office	Prime Minister	Foreign Minister	Finance Minister
16 Jan 22	Provisional government: Finance and General Minister Michael Collins, Foreign Affairs Minister Gavan Duffy.		
6 Dec 22	W. Cosgrave	D. Fitzgerald	W. Cosgrave
		P. MacGilligan	E. Blythe

IRELAND (continued)

Date of taking office	Prime Minister	Foreign Minister	Finance Minister
9 Mar 32	E. de Valera	E. de Valera	S. MacEntee
27 Sep 39			S. T. O'Kelly
9 June 44			F. Aiken
18 Dec 48	J. A. Costello	S. MacBride	P. MacGilligan
30 May 51	E. de Valera	P. Aiken	A. MacEntee
2 June 54	J. A. Costello	L. Cosgrave	G. Sweetman
20 Mar 57	E. de Valera	F. Aiken	J. Ryan
23 June 59	S. Lemass		
21 Apr 65			J. Lynch
9 Nov 66	J. Lynch		
10 Nov 66			C. Haughey
2 July 69		P. Hillery	
8 May 70			G. Colley
14 Mar 73	L. Cosgrave	G. FitzGerald	R. Ryan
5 July 77	J. Lynch	M. O'Kennedy	G. Colley
11 Dec 79	C. Haughey	B. Lenihan	M. O'Kennedy
16 Dec 80			E. FitzGerald
30 June 81	G. FitzGerald	J. Dooge	J. Bruton
9 Mar 82	C. Haughey	G. Collins	R. MacSharry
14 Dec 82	G. FitzGerald	P. Barry	A. Dukes

ITALY

Date of taking office	Prime Minister	Foreign Minister	Finance Minister
21 June 19	F. Nitti	V. Scialoja	G. de Nava
15 June 20	G. Gioletti	Ct Sforza	F. Tedesco
25 Feb 22	L. Faeta	Dr C. Schauzer	G. Bertone
30 Oct 22	B. Mussolini	B. Mussolini	A. de Stefani
30 Aug 25			Ct G. Volpi
1 Jan 29			A. Mosconi
12 Sep 29		D. Grandi	
20 July 32		B. Mussolini	G. Jung
24 Jan 35			Ct P. Thaon de Reval
9 June 36		Ct G. C. de Cortellezzo	
6 Feb 43		B. Mussolini	Baron G. Acerbo

ITALY (*continued*)

Date of taking office	Prime Minister	Foreign Minister	Finance Minister
25 July 43	Marshal Badoglio	Baron Guariglea	D. Bartolini
9 June 44	I. Bonomi		M. Siglienti
10 Dec 45		A. de Gasperi	M. Presenti
19 June 45	F. Parri		M. Scoccimaro
4 Dec 45	A. de Gasperi		
17 Oct 46		P. Nenni	
30 May 47		Ct Sforza	G. Pella
23 May 48			E. Vanoni
16 July 53		A. de Gasperi	
17 Aug 53	G. Pella	G. Pella	
18 Jan 54	A. Fanfani	A. Piccione	A. Zoli
10 Feb 54	M. Scelba		R. Tremelloni
18 Sep 54		G. Martino	
6 July 55	A. Segni		G. Andreotti
20 May 57	A. Zoli	G. Pella	
19 June 58	A. Fanfani	A. Fanfani	L. Preti
16 Feb 59	A. Segni		P. E. Taviani
25 Mar 60	F. Tambroni	A. Segni	G. Trabucchi
26 July 60	A. Fanfani		
29 May 62		A. Piccione	
21 June 63	G. Leone		M. Martinelli
4 Dec 63	A. Moro	G. Saragat	R. Tremelloni
6 Mar 65		A. Fanfani	
23 Feb 66			L. Preti
24 June 68	G. Leone	G. Medici	M. F. Aggradi
12 Dec 68	M. Rumor	P. Nenni	O. Reale
5 Aug 69		A. Moro	G. Bosco
27 Mar 70			L. Preti
6 Aug 70	E. Colombo		
15 Feb 72	G. Andreotti		G. Pella
26 June 72		G. Medici	A. Valsecchi
8 July 73	M. Rumor	A. Moro	E. Colombo
15 Mar 74			M. Tanassi
23 Nov 74	A. Moro	M. Rumor	B. Visentini
12 Feb 76			G. Stammati
30 July 76	G. Andreotti	A. Forlani	F. M. Pandolfi
13 Mar 78			F. M. Malfatti
5 Aug 79	F. Cossiga	F. M. Malfatti	M. Reviglio
14 Jan 80		A. Ruffini	

ITALY *(continued)*

Date of taking office	*Prime Minister*	*Foreign Minister*	*Finance Minister*
4 Apr 80		E. Colombo	
19 Oct 80	A. Forlani		F. Reviglio
28 June 81	G. Spadolini		S. Formica
11 Dec 82	A. Fanfani		F. Forte
4 Aug 83	B. Craxi	G. Andreotti	B. Visentini

LUXEMBOURG

Date of taking office	*Prime Minister*	*Foreign Minister*	*Finance Minister*
1 Apr 21	E. Reuter		A. Neyens
1 Mar 25	P. Pruom		A. Schmit
1 July 26	J. Bech		M. Clemang
1 Aug 26			P. Dupong
5 Nov 37	P. Dupong	J. Bech	

Note: On 15 Aug 40 the government was declared void by the German forces of occupation. A government in exile continued in London.

29 Dec 53	J. Bech		P. Werner
1 Jan 58	P. Frieden		
25 Feb 59	P. Werner	E. Schauss	
15 July 64		P. Werner	
23 Dec 67		P. Gregoire	
29 Jan 69		G. Thorn	
18 June 74	G. Thorn	G. Thorn	R. Vouel
19 July 76			J. Poos
16 July 79	P. Werner		
18 July 79			P. Werner
21 Nov 80		C. Flesch	

MALTA

Date of taking office	*Prime Minister*	*Foreign Minister*	*Finance Minister*
4 Nov 47	Dr P. Boffa		
1 Jan 50			A. Colombo
26 Sep 50	E. Mizzi		F. Azzopardi
20 Dec 50	B. Olivier		
11 Mar 55	D. Mintoff		D. Mintoff

MALTA *(continued)*

Date of taking office	Prime Minister	Foreign Minister	Finance Minister

Note: Mr Mintoff resigned in Apr 58 and the constitution was suspended.

Date of taking office	Prime Minister	Foreign Minister	Finance Minister
5 Mar 62	B. Olivier		G. Felice
21 June 71	D. Mintoff	D. Mintoff	J. Abela
9 July 81			J. Cassar
20 Dec 81		A. S. Trigona	L. Spiteri

THE NETHERLANDS

Date of taking office	Prime Minister	Foreign Minister	Finance Minister
9 Sep 18	C. J. M. R. de Beerenbroeck	H. A. van Karnebeek	S. de Vries
28 July 21			D. J. de Geer
11 Aug 23			H. Colijn
31 July 25	H. Colijn		
8 Mar 26	D. J. de Geer		D. J. de Geer
30 Mar 27		F. B. van Blokland	
10 Aug 29	C. J. M. R. de Beerenbroeck		
24 May 33	H. Colijn	A. C. D. de Graeff	P. J. Oud
23 June 37		H. Colijn	J. A. de Wilde
14 Sep 37		J. A. N. Patijn	
21 May 39			H. Colijn
10 Aug 39	D. J. de Geer	E. N. van Kleffens	D. J. de Geer
4 Sep 40	P. S. Gerbrandy		J. I. M. Welter
23 Nov 41			J. W. Albarda
15 Sep 42			J. van den Broek
24 Feb 45			G. W. M. Huysmans
23 June 45	W. Schermerhorn		P. Lieftinck
26 Feb 46		J. H. van Royen	
13 July 46	L. J. M. Beel	C. G. W. H. Baron van Boetzelaer van Ooterhuit	
7 Aug 48	W. Drees	D. U. Stikker	
1 Sep 52		J. W. Beyen J. M. Λ. H. Luns *Joint Ministry*	J. A. van der Kieft

THE NETHERLANDS *(continued)*

Date of taking office	Prime Minister	Foreign Minister	Finance Minister
12 Oct 56			H. J. Hofstra
22 Dec 58	L. Beel	J. M. A. H. Luns	J. Zijlstra
19 May 59	J. E. de Quay		
24 July 63	V. G. M. Marijunen		J. H. Witteveen
12 Apr 65	J. Cals		A. Vondeling
22 Nov 66	J. Zijlstra		J. Zijlstra
3 Apr 67	P. J. S. de Jong		H. J. Witteveen
6 Jul 71	B. W. Biesheuvel	W. K. N. Schmelzer	R. J. Nelissen
11 May 73	J. den Uyl	M. van der Stoel	W. F. Duisenberg
19 Dec 77	A. van Agt	C. van der Klaauw	F. Andriessen
4 Mar 80			A. van der Stee
11 Sep 81		M. van der Stoel	
29 May 82		A. van Agt	
4 Nov 82	R. Lubbers	H. van den Broek	H. Ruding

NORWAY

Date of taking office	Prime Minister	Foreign Minister	Finance Minister
20 Feb 19	G. Knudsen	N. C. Ihlen	A. Omholt
21 June 20	O. B. Halvorsen	C. F. Michelet	E. H. Bull
22 June 21	O. A. Blehr	A. C. Raested	O. A. Blehr
5 Mar 23	O. Halvorsen	C. F. Michelet	A. Berge
1 May 23	A. Berge		
7 July 24	J. L. Mowinckel	J. L. Mowinckel	A. Holmboe
4 Mar 26	I. Lykke	I. Lykke	F. L. Konow
13 Feb 28	J. L. Mowinckel	J. L. Mowinckel	P. Lund
12 May 31	N. Kolstad	B. Bradland	F. Sundby
15 Mar 32	J. Hundseid		
27 Feb 33	J. L. Mowinckel	J. L. Mowinckel	P. Lund
14 Nov 34	.		G. Jan
19 Mar 35	J. Nygaardsvold	H. Kont	A. Indreboe
			K. Bergsvik
30 June 39			O. F. Torp
21 Feb 41		T. H. Lie	

Note: The government in exile continued in London.

NORWAY (continued)

Date of taking office	Prime Minister	Foreign Minister	Finance Minister
1 Mar 42			P. Hartmann
24 June 45	E. Gerhardsen		G. Jahn
1 Nov 45			E. Brofoss
1 Nov 47			O. Meisdalshagen
16 Nov 51	O. F. Torp		T. Bratteli
21 Jan 55	E. Gerhardsen		M. Lid
1 Mar 57			T. Bratteli
23 Apr 60			P. J. Bjerve
23 Jan 63			A. Cappelen
27 Aug 63	J. Lyng	E. Wikborg	D. Vårvik
24 Sep 63	E. Gerhardsen	H. Lange	A. Cappelen
12 Oct 65	P. Borten	J. Lyng	O. Myrvoll
22 May 70		S. Stray	
13 Mar 71	T. Bratteli	A. Cappelen	R. Christiansen
7 Oct 72	L. Korvald		
18 Oct 72		D. Vårvik	J. Norbom
16 Oct 73	T. Bratteli	K. Frydenlund	P. Kleppe
9 Jan 76	O. Nordli		
5 Oct 79			U. Sand
4 Feb 81	G. H. Brundtland		
14 Oct 81	K. Willoch	S. Stray	R. Presthus

POLAND

Date of taking office	Prime Minister	Foreign Minister	Finance Minister
19 Jan 19	I. Paderewski, provisional government.		
14 Dec 19	L. Skulski	S. Patek	W. Grabski
24 June 20	W. Grabski		
24 July 20	W. Witos	Prince Sapieha	J. K. Steczkowski
23 Sep 21	A. Ponikowski	K. Skirmunt	J. Michalski
28 June 22	M. Sliwinski		
31 July 22	M. Nowacki		
16 Dec 22	W. Sikorski	Ct A. Skrzyński	W. Grabski
28 May 23	W. Witos		
19 Dec 23	W. Grabski	Ct M. Zamoyski Ct A. Skrzyński	
29 Nov 25	Ct A. Skrzyński		J. Zdziechowski
9 June 26	K. Bartel		

POLAND *(continued)*

Date of taking office	Prime Minister	Foreign Minister	Finance Minister
2 Oct 26	J. Pitsudski	A. Zaleski	G. Czechowicz
18 Oct 28	K. Bartel		M. Grodyński
14 Apr 29	K. Świtalski		
29 Dec 29	K. Bartel		
1 Apr 30	W. Sławek		I. Matuszewski
25 Aug 30	J. Piłsudski		
4 Dec 30	W. Sławek		
29 Dec 30	K. Bartel		
27 May 31	A. Prystor		J. Piłsudski
7 Sep 32			Z. Zawadzki
2 Nov 32		J. Beck	
10 May 33	J. Jedrzejewicz		
13 May 34	L. Kozłowski		
28 Mar 35	W. Sławek		
12 Oct 35	M. Kosciałkowski-Zyndram		E. Kwiatkowski
16 May 36	F. S. Składkowski		
20 Sep 39	W. Sikorski	A. Zaleski	A. Koc

Note: The government in exile continued in Paris and later in London.

1 Jan 41			H. Strasburger
28 Aug 41		Ct E. Raczynski	
14 July 43	S. Mikołajczyk	T. Romer	L. Grosfeld
30 Nov 44	T. Arciszewski	A. Tarnowski	J. Kwapiński
28 June 45	E. Osobka-Morawski	W. Rzymowski	K. Dabrowski
6 Feb 47	J. Cyrankiewicz	Z. Modzelewski	
17 Mar 51		S. Skrzeszewski	
20 Nov 52	B. Bierut		
19 Mar 54	J. Cyrankiewicz		
27 Apr 56		A. Rapacki	
27 Jan 57			T. Dietrich
16 Nov 60			J. Albrecht
15 Jul 68			S. Majewski
22 Dec 68		S. Jędrychowski	
28 June 69			J. Trendota
23 Dec 70	P. Jaroszewicz		
22 Dec 71		S. Olszowski	S. Jedrychowski
21 Nov 74			H. Kisiel
2 Dec 76		E. Wojtaszek	
18 Feb 80	E. Babiuch		
24 Aug 80	J. Pińkowski	J. Czyrek	M. Krzak

POLAND *(continued)*

Date of taking office	Prime Minister	Foreign Minister	Finance Minister
11 Feb 81	Gen. W. Jaruzelski		
21 July 82		S. Olszowski	
8 Oct 82			S. Niekarz

PORTUGAL

Date of taking office	Prime Minister	Foreign Minister	Finance Minister
12 Mar 20	A. N. Bapista	X. da Silva	P. Lopes
2 Mar 21	B. Machado	D. Pereira	A. M. da Silva
9 Feb 22	A. M. da Silva	M. Barbosa-Magalhaes	M. Puero
1 Jan 23		D. Pereira	V. Guimarães
18 Dec 23	A. de Castro		A. de Castro
15 Feb 25	V. Guimarães	P. Martins	V. Guimarães
18 Dec 25	A. M. da Silva	V. Borges	A. M. Guedes
9 July 26	A. O. de F. Carmona	A. M. de B. Rodrigues	J. J. S. de Cordes
10 Nov 28	J. V. de Freitas	M. C. Q. Meireles	A. de O. Salazar
20 Jan 30	D. de Oliveira	F. A. Branco	
5 July 32	A. de O. Salazar	C. de S. Mendes	
11 Apr 33		J. C. da Mata	
23 Oct 34		A. de M. Guimarães	
18 Jan 36		A. R. Monteiro	
		A. de O. Salazar	
28 Aug 40			J. P. da C. L. Lumbrales
4 Feb 47		J. C. da Mata	
1 Aug 50		P. A. V. Cunha	A. A. de Oliveira
8 July 55			A. M. P. Barbosa
13 Aug 58		M. G. N. D. Matias	
3 May 61		A. M. G. F. Nogueira	
13 June 65			U. C. de A. Cortes
17 Aug 68			J. A. D. Rosas
26 Sep 68	M. J. das N. A. Caetano		
1 Apr 69		M. J. das N. A. Caetano	
14 Jan 70		R. M. de M. d'E. Patricio	
11 Aug 72			M. A. C. A. Dias

The Caetano government was overthrown by the armed forces on 25 Apr 74.

PORTUGAL (*continued*)

Date of taking office	Prime Minister	Foreign Minister	Finance Minister
16 May 74	A. da P. Carlos	M. Soares	J. da S. Lopes
17 July 74	V. dos S. Gonçalves		
25 Mar 75		E. A. de M. Antunes	J. J. Fragoso
8 Aug 75		M. Ruivo	
29 Aug 75	J. B. P. de Azevedo		
19 Sep 75		E. A. de M. Antunes	F. S. Zenha
16 July 76	M. Soares		
23 July 76		J. M. Ferreira	H. M. Carreira
10 Oct 77		M. Soares	
28 Aug 78	A. J. N. da Costa	C. G. Gago	J. da S. Lopes
25 Oct 78	C. A. M. Pinto		
22 Nov 78		J. de F. Cruz	M. J. Nunes
19 July 79	M. de L. Pintassilgo		
1 Aug 79			A. S. Franco
29 Dec 79	F. L. Sá Carneiro		
3 Jan 80		D. F. do Amaral	A. A. Cavaco e Silva
4 Dec 80	D. F. do Amaral (interim)		
22 Dec 80	F. J. P. Pinto Balsemão		
9 Jan 81		A. G. Pereira	J. A. M. Leitão
4 Sep 81			J. F. Salgueiro
4 June 82		V. G. Pereira	

F. J. P. Pinto Balsemão resigned on 19 Dec 82. Dr Pereira Crespo was appointed Prime Minister on 27 Dec 82, but his nominated ministry was not accepted. Pinto Balsemão was recalled on 23 Jan 83 to lead a caretaker government, with the Foreign and Finance Ministers who were in office at his resignation, pending elections.

Date of taking office	Prime Minister	Foreign Minister	Finance Minister
9 June 83	Dr M. Soares	J. Gama	E. Lopes

ROMANIA

Date of taking office	Prime Minister	Foreign Minister	Finance Minister
16 Mar 20	Gen. A. Averescu	D. Zamsirescu	C. Argetoianu
21 June 20		T. Ionescu	M. Titulesco
19 Jan 22	I. Brătianu	I. Duca	V. Brătianu

ROMANIA (*continued*)

Date of taking office	Prime Minister	Foreign Minister	Finance Minister
30 Mar 26	Gen. A. Averescu	M. Mitilineu	I. Lapedatu
27 Mar 27			Gen. A. Averescu
24 Nov 27	V. Brătianu	N. Titulescu	V. Brătianu
11 Nov 28	J. Maniu	G. Mironescu	M. Popovici
June 30			M. Manoilescu
19 Apr 31	N. Iorga	C. Argetoianu	C. Argetoianu
		Prince D. Ghica	Prince D. Ghica
6 June 32	A. Vaida-Voevod	G. Mironescu	
11 Aug 32		A. Vaida-Voevod	G. Mironescu
8 Oct 32		N. Titulescu	
19 Oct 32	J. Maniu		V. Madgearu
14 Jan 33	A. Vaida Voevod		
14 Nov 33	I. Duca		D. Brătianu
29 Dec 33	C. Angelescu		
3 Jan 34	G. Tatarescu		
5 Jan 35			V. Slăvescu
4 Feb 35			V. Antonescu
30 Aug 36		V. Antonescu	M. Cancicov
28 Dec 37	O. Goga	I. Micescu	E. Savu
11 Feb 38	M. Cristea	G. Tatarescu	M. Cancicov
30 Mar 38		N. Petrescu-Comnen	
21 Dec 38		G. Gafencu	
1 Feb 39			M. Constantinescu
6 Mar 39	M. Calinescu		
21 Sep 39	Gen. Argeseanu		
28 Sep 39	C. Argetoianu		
24 Nov 39	G. Tatarescu		
2 June 40		I. Gigurtu	
4 July 40	I. Gigurtu	M. Manoilescu	E. Savu
3 Sep 40	I. Antonescu		
15 Sep 40		M. Sturdza	G. Cretzianu
1 Dec 40		I. Antonescu	
27 Jan 41			N. Stoenescu
16 Oct 42			A. Neagu
24 Aug 44	C. Sănătescu	G. Niculescu-Buzeşti	G. Potopeaunu
2 Dec 44	N. Radescu	C. Vişoianu	M. Romniceanu
6 Mar 45	P. Groza	G. Tatarescu	D. Alimănişteanu
29 Nov 46			A. Alexandrini

105

ROMANIA *(continued)*

Date of taking office	Prime Minister	Foreign Minister	Finance Minister
7 Nov 47		A. Pauker	V. Luca
9 Mar 52			D. Petrescu
2 June 52	G. Gheorghiu-Dej		
5 July 52		S. Bughici	
2 Oct 55	C. Stoica	G. Preoteasa	M. Manescu
14 July 57		I. G. Maurer	
11 Jan 58		A Bunaciu	
21 Mar 61	I. G. Maurer	C. Manescu	A. Vijoli
13 July 68			V. Pirvu
19 Aug 69			F. Dŭmitrescu
18 Oct 72		G. Macovescu	
29 Mar 74	M. Manescu		
7 Mar 78			P. Niculescu
23 Mar 78		S. Andrei	
30 Mar 79	I. Verdeţ		
26 Mar 81			P. Gigea
21 May 82	G. Dăscălescu		

SPAIN

Date of taking office	Prime Minister	Foreign Minister	Finance Minister
5 May 20	M. Dato	Marquis de Lema	D. Pascual
13 Mar 21	M. Allendesalazar		M. Arguelles
8 Mar 22	S. Guerra	F. Prida	M. Bergamin
7 Dec 22	Marquis de Alhucemas	S. Alba	J. M. Pedregal

A military rebellion under General Francisco Franco forced the civil war of 1936–9. With the surrender of Madrid in Mar 39 the Loyalist government fled to France and a corporate state was set up under Franco's dictatorship.

3 Dec 25	Primo de Rivera	M. Yanguas	M. Calvo-Sotelo
27 Feb 27		P. de Rivera	
1 Jan 30	Gen. Berenguer	Duke of Alba	M. Arguelles
1 Apr 31	A. Zamora	A. Lervoux	I. Prieto
16 Dec 31	M. Azaña y Diaz	L. Z. Escolano	J. C. Romeu
1 Mar 33	A. L. Garcia	L. P. Romero	M. M. Ramon
4 Oct 34		J. J. R. Garcia	
19 Feb 36	M. Azaña y Diaz	A. Barcia y Trelles	G. F. Lopez
4 Sep 36	F. L. Caballero	J. A. del Vaijo	J. Negrín
17 May 37	J. Negrín	J. Giralt	
1 Feb 38	F. Franco	Count de Jornada	M. Amado
10 Aug 39		J. B. Atienza	J. L. Lopez

SPAIN (*continued*)

Date of taking office	Prime Minister	Foreign Minister	Finance Minister
17 Oct 40		R. S. Súñer	
20 May 41			J. B. Burin
3 Sep 42		F. Gomez-Jordana	
11 Aug 44		J. F. de Lequerica	
21 July 45		A. M. Artajo	
1 Mar 52		F. Gomez y de Llano	
1 Feb 57		F. M. Castialla y Maiz	M. Navarro Rubio
7 July 65			J. J. Espinoza
29 Oct 69		G. L. Bravo de Costro	A. M. Luque
9 Jun 73	Adm. L. Carrero Blanco		
11 Jun 73		L. López Rodó	A. Barrera de Irimo
2 Jan 74	C. Arias Navarro		
4 Jan 74		P. Cortina Mauri	
31 Oct 74			R. Cabello de Alba y Gracia
13 Dec 75		J. M. de Areilza y Martínes Rodas	J. M. Villar Mir
5 July 76	A. Suárez González		
8 July 76		M. Oreja Aguirre	E. Carriles Galarraga
5 July 77			F. F. Ordóñez
6 Apr 79			J. G. Añoveros
8 Sep 80		J. P. Pérez-Llorca	
26 Feb 81	L. Calvo Sotelo y Bustelo		
2 Dec 82	F. González		
3 Dec 82		F. Morán	M. Boyer

SWEDEN

Date of taking office	Prime Minister	Foreign Minister	Finance Minister
10 Mar 20	H. Branting	Baron Palmstierna	F. W. Thorsson
23 Feb 21	O. F. von Sydow	Count H. Wrangel	K. J. Beskow
13 Oct 21	H. Branting	H. Branting	F. W. Thorsson
9 Apr 23	E. Trygger	Baron Marcks von Wurtemburg	K. J. Beskow
24 Jan 25	R. Sandler	O. Unden	F. W. Thorsson
8 May 25			E. Wigforss

SWEDEN *(continued)*

Date of taking office	Prime Minister	Foreign Minister	Finance Minister
7 June 26	C. G. Ekman	E. Lofgren	E. Lyberg
2 Oct 28	Adm. Lindman	E. Trygger	N. Wohlin
			A. Dahl
7 June 30	C. G. Ekman	S. G. F. Ramel	F. T. Hamrin
7 Aug 32	F. T. Hamrin		
24 Sep 32	P. A. Hansson	R. J. Sandler	E. Wigforss
19 June 36	M. Pehrsson	M. Westman	V. S. Ljungdahl
27 Sep 36	P. A. Hansson	R. J. Sandler	E. Wigforss
12 Dec 39		C. Gunther	
31 July 45		O. Unden	
10 Oct 46	T. Erlander		
30 June 49			D. Hall
20 Oct 49			P. E. Sköld
25 Sep 55			G. Strang
19 Sep 62		T. Nilsson	
14 Oct 69	O. Palme		
29 June 71		K. Wickmann	
31 Oct 73		S. Andersson	
7 Oct 76	T. Fälldin		
8 Oct 76		K. Söder	I. Mundebo
13 Oct 78	O. Ullsten		
18 Oct 78		H. Blix	
11 Oct 79	T. Fälldin		
12 Oct 79		O. Ullsten	G. Bohman (Economic Affairs)
			I. Mundebo (Budget)
31 July 80			I. Mundebo (Economic Affairs)
			R. Wirtén (Budget)
22 May 81			R. Wirtén (Economic Affairs and Budget)
8 Oct 82	O. Palme	L. Bodström	K.-O. Feldt

SWITZERLAND

The Federal Council has an active Vice-President elected for one year, and seven members each responsible for a department, elected for four years.

	Vice-President	Foreign Affairs	Finance
1935	A. Meyer	G. Motta	A. Meyer
1936	G. Motta		

SWITZERLAND *(continued)*

	Vice-President	Foreign Affairs	Finance
1937	J. Baumann		
1938	P. Etter		
1939	M. Pilet-Golaz		E. Wetter
1940	H. Obrecht	M. Pilet-Golaz	
1941	P. Etter		
1942	E. Celio		
1943	W. Stampfli		
1944	M. Pilet-Golaz		E. Nobs
1945	K. Koblet	M. Petitpierre	
1946	P. Etter		
1947	E. Celio		
1948	E. Nobs		
1949	M. Petitpierre		
1950	E. von Steiger		
1951	K. Koblet		
1952	P. Etter		M. Webber
1953	R. Rubattel		
1954	J. Escher		H. Streuli
1955	M. Feldmann		
1956	H. Streuli		
1957	T. Holenstein		
1958	P. Chaudet		
1959	G. Lepovi		
1960	F. Traugott Wahlen		J. Bourgknecht
1961	P. Chaudet		
1962	J. Bourgknecht	F. Traugott Wahlen	
1963	L. van Moos		R. Bonvin
1964	H. P. Schudi		
1965	H. Schaffner		
1966	R. Bonvin	W. Spuhler	
1967	W. Spuhler		
1968	L. van Moos		N. Celio
1969	H. P. Schudi		
1970	R. Gnägi	P. Graber	
1971	N. Celio		
1972	R. Bonvin		
1973	E. Brugger		G.-A. Chevellaz
1974	P. Graber		
1975	R. Gnägi		
1976	K. Furgler		
1977	W. Ritschard		

SWITZERLAND (*continued*)

	Vice-President	Foreign Affairs	Finance
1978	H. Hürlimann	P. Aubert	
1979	G.-A. Chevallez		
1980	K. Furgler		W. Ritschard
1981	F. Honegger		
1982	P. Aubert		
1983	W. Ritschard (d. 16 Oct 83)		
16 Oct 83	G.-A. Chevallez (interim)		G.-A. Chevallez (interim)
1984	K. Furgler		O. Stich

TURKEY

Date of taking office	Prime Minister	Foreign Minister	Finance Minister
5 Apr 20	(*Grand Vizier*) Damad Ferid Pasha	Damad Ferid Pasha	Reshai Bey
21 Oct 20	(*Grand Vizier*) Tewfik Pasha	Sefa Bey	Abdullah Bey
		Izzet Pasha	Nuzhet Bey
20 Jan 21	New constitution established a Council of Commissioners instead of a cabinet.		
1 Feb 23	(*President*)Reouf Bey	Ismet Pasha	Abdul Halik Bey
30 Oct 23	Ismet Pasha		
4 Mar 25		Tevfik Rustu Bey	
			Hassan Bey
			Abdul Halik Bey
2 Nov 27			S. Saracoglu
28 Sep 30			Abdul Halik Bey
1 May 31			Fuad Agrali
1 Mar 35	Ismet Inönü		
13 Oct 37	J. Bayar		
12 Nov 38		S. Saracoglu	
27 Jan 39	R. Saydam		
11 Mar 43	S. Saracoglu	N. Menemencioglu	
15 June 44		S. Saracoglu	
14 Sep 44		H. Saka	N. E. Sumer
7 Aug 46	R. Peker		H. Nazmikismir
9 Sep 47	H. Saka	N. Sadak	
11 June 48			S. Adalan
16 Jan 49	S. Gunaltay		I. Aksal

TURKEY (continued)

Date of taking office	Prime Minister	Foreign Minister	Finance Minister
22 May 50	A. Menderes	F. Koprulu	H. Ayan
10 Mar 51			H. Polatkan
15 Apr 55		A. Menderes	
9 Dec 55		F. Koprulu	N. Okmen
20 June 56		E. Menderes	
30 Nov 56			H. Polatkan
25 Nov 57		F. R. Zorlu	
28 May 60	C. Gursel	S. Sarpa	E. Alican
24 Dec 60			K. Kurdas
20 Nov 61	I. Inönü		S. Inan
25 June 62		F. C. Erkin	F. Melen
21 Feb 65	S. H. Urguplu	H. Isik	I. Gursan
27 Oct 65	S. Demirel	I. S. Çağlayangil	
12 Nov 66			C. Bilgehan
3 Nov 69			M. Erez
1 Mar 71	N. Erim	O. Olcay	S. N. Ergin
22 May 72	F. Melen	U. H. Bayülken	S. Özbek
15 Apr 73	N. Talû	U. H. Bayülken	S. T. Müftüoglu
25 Jan 74	B. Ecevit	T. Gunes	D. Baykal
17 Nov 74	S. Irmak	M. Esenbel	B. Gürsoy
31 Mar 75	S. Demirel	I. S. Çağlayangil	Y. Ergenekon
21 June 77	B. Ecevit	G. Okçün	B. Üstünel
21 July 77	S. Demirel	I. S. Çağlayangil	C. Bilgehan
5 Jan 78	B. Ecevit	G. Okçün	Z. Müezzinoğlu
12 Nov 79	S. Demirel	H. Erkmen	I. Sezgin

The government was overthrown on 12 Sep 80 and its powers taken over by a National Security Council of the armed forces.

Date of taking office	Prime Minister	Foreign Minister	Finance Minister
21 Sep 80	B. Ülüsü	I. Turkmen	K. Erdem
14 July 82			A. B. Kafaoğlu
13 Dec 83	T. Ozal	V. Halefoğlu	V. Arikan

USSR

Date of taking office	Prime Minister	Foreign Minister	Finance Minister
8 Nov 17	V. I. Lenin	G. V. Chicherin	N. N. Krestinskii
1 Dec 22			G. Y. Sokolnikov
1 Jan 24	A. I. Rykov		
1 Mar 26			N. P. Bryukhanov

USSR (*continued*)

Date of taking office	Prime Minister	Foreign Minister	Finance Minister
1 Jan 31	V. M. Molotov	M. M. Litvinov	G. F. Grinko
1 Aug 37			V. Y. Chubar

Ministers were called People's Commissars until 1946.

Date of taking office	Prime Minister	Foreign Minister	Finance Minister
19 Jan 38			A. G. Zverev
3 May 39		V. M. Molotov	
7 May 41	J. V. Stalin		
17 Feb 48			A. N. Kosygin
28 Dec 48			A. G. Zverev
4 Mar 49		A. Y. Vyshinski	
6 Mar 53	G. M. Malenkov	V. M. Molotov	
9 Dec 55	N. A. Bulganin		
1 June 56		D. T. Shepilov	
15 Feb 57		A. A. Gromyko	
31 Mar 58	N. S. Khrushchev		
16 May 60			V. F. Garbuzov
15 Oct 64	A. N. Kosygin		
23 Oct 80	N. A. Tikhonov		

UNITED KINGDOM

Date of taking office	Prime Minister	Foreign Minister	Finance Minister
6 Dec 16	D. Lloyd-George		
10 Dec 16		A. Balfour	A. Bonar Law
10 Jan 19			A. Chamberlain
23 Oct 19		Lord Curzon	
1 Apr 21			Sir R. Horne
23 Oct 22	A. Bonar Law		
24 Oct 22			S. Baldwin
22 May 23	S. Baldwin		
27 Aug 23			N. Chamberlain
22 Jan 24	J. R. MacDonald	J. R. MacDonald	P. Snowden
4 Nov 24	S. Baldwin		
6 Nov 24		Sir A. Chamberlain	W. Churchill
5 June 29	J. R. MacDonald		
7 June 29		A. Henderson	P. Snowden
25 Aug 31		Marquis of Reading	

UNITED KINGDOM (*continued*)

Date of taking office	Prime Minister	Foreign Minister	Finance Minister
5 Nov 31		Sir J. Simon	N. Chamberlain
7 June 35	S. Baldwin	Sir S. Hoare	
22 Dec 35		A. Eden	
28 May 37	N. Chamberlain		Sir J. Simon
21 Feb 38		Viscount Halifax	
10 May 40	W. Churchill		
12 May 40			Sir K. Wood
22 Dec 40		A. Eden	
24 Sep 43			Sir J. Anderson
26 July 45	C. Attlee		
27 July 45		E. Bevin	H. Dalton
13 Nov 47			Sir S. Cripps
19 Oct 50			H. Gaitskell
9 Mar 51		H. Morrison	
26 Oct 51	Sir W. Churchill	Sir A. Eden	R. Butler
6 Apr 55	Sir A. Eden		
7 Apr 55		H. Macmillan	
20 Dec 55		S. Lloyd	H. Macmillan
10 Jan 57	H. Macmillan		
13 Jan 57			P. Thorneycroft
6 Jan 58			D. Heathcoat Amory
27 July 60		Lord Home	S. Lloyd
13 July 62			R. Maudling
18 Oct 63	Sir A. Douglas-Home		
20 Oct 63		R. Butler	
16 Oct 64	H. Wilson	P. Gordon Walker	J. Callaghan
22 Jan 65		M. Stewart	
11 Aug 66		G. Brown	
30 Nov 67			R. Jenkins
16 Mar 68		M. Stewart	
19 June 70	E. Heath		
20 June 70		Sir A. Douglas-Home	I. Macleod
25 July 70			A. Barber
4 Mar 74	H. Wilson	J. Callaghan	D. Healey
5 Apr 76	J. Callaghan		
8 Apr 76		A. Crosland	
21 Feb 77		D. Owen	

UNITED KINGDOM (*continued*)

Date of taking office	Prime Minister	Foreign Minister	Finance Minister
4 May 79	M. Thatcher		
5 May 79		Lord Carrington	Sir G. Howe
5 Apr 82		F. Pym	
12 June 83		Sir G. Howe	N. Lawson

YUGOSLAVIA

Date of taking office	Prime Minister	Foreign Minister	Finance Minister
19 Feb 21	S. Protić	M. Trumbitch	V. Janković
24 Dec 21	N. Pashić	M. Nintchić	K. Kumanudi
3 Dec 22			M. Stojadinović
8 Apr 26	N. Uzunović		N. Uzunović
1 Feb 27		N. Peritch	B. Narković
23 Feb 28	V. Vukitčević	V. Marinković	
6 Jan 29	Gen. P. Zivković		S. Svrljuga
4 Apr 32	V. Marinković		M. Georgević
11 July 32	M. Serškie	B. Jevtić	
27 Jan 34	N. Uzonivić		
Dec 34	B. Jević		
24 June 35	M. Stojadinović	M. Stojadinović	D. Letica
5 Feb 39	D. Cvetković	A. C. Marković	V. Juričić
26 Aug 39			J. Šutej
27 Mar 41	Gen. D. Simović	M. Nintchić	

In 1941 the Axis powers occupied Yugoslavia. A government-in-exile was established in London in June 1941 and eventually moved to Cairo.

11 Jan 42	S. Jovanović		
Jun 43	M. Trifimović		
10 Aug 43	B. Purić		I. Cicin-Sain
7 Mar 45	Marshal J. B. Tito	I. Subasić	S. Zejević
2 Feb 46		S. Simić	
6 May 48			D. Radosavljević
31 Aug 48		E. Kardelj	
1 Nov 51			M. Popović
14 Jan 53		K. Popović	R. Nedelković
1 Jan 54			N. Bozinović
1 Jan 57			A. Humo

YUGOSLAVIA (*continued*)

Date of taking office	Prime Minister	Foreign Minister	Finance Minister
1 Jan 59			N. Minćov
1 Jan 63			K. Gligorov
29 June 63	P. Stambolić		
23 Apr 65		M. Nikezić	
18 May 67	M. Spiljak		J. Smole
28 Apr 69		M. Tepavac	
17 May 69	M. Ribičić		
30 July 71	D. Bijedić		
1 Nov 72		J. Petrić	
5 Dec 72		M. Minich	
17 May 74			M. Cemovich
14 Feb 77	V. Djuranović		
16 May 78		J. Vrhovec	P. Kostić
16 May 82	M. Planinć	L. Mojsov	J. Florijanič

5 ELECTIONS

ALBANIA

In Mar 1920 the Lushnjë congress elected a National Assembly and a Senate. Political parties began to emerge: a group known as 'liberals' and one known as 'conservatives'.

Elections were held on 4 Feb 21 to a National Assembly of 77 deputies and a Senate of 18 (6 of whom were appointed). Alternative governments were formed by the conservative feudalistic Progressive Party and the People's Party which itself split into a right-wing faction headed by A. Zogu and a liberal faction (becoming a Democratic party) headed by Bishop Fan Noli.

At the elections of Dec 23, 40 Progressive and 35 People's Party candidates were returned, together with 20 independents. Fan Noli left the People's Party to form an opposition and seized power on 17 June 24. His government itself split into Radical and National Democrats, and Zogu seized power again in Dec 24.

By a new constitution of Feb 25 a bicameral National Assembly was set up with deputies elected every three years and a partly-elected Senate. The President was to be elected by the National Assembly for a seven-year period. In the 1925 elections opposition groups were not permitted to stand and complete victory went to the Zogists. Zogu became President.

By a new constitution of 1 Sep 28 the Senate was abolished and a National Assembly of 56 set up. Political parties were forbidden and elections were indirect and on a limited suffrage. Government-nominated candidates were presented to the electors for approval. Albania became a monarchy and Zogu its king under the name Zog I. The elections of 1932 and 1937 were held under these conditions.

On 2 Dec 45 elections were held for a new People's Assembly. 82 candidates stood on the single Democratic Front list for 82 seats. 89.9% of the electorate voted, and 93.16% of votes cast were for the Democratic Front.

At the elections of 28 May 50 the electorate was 641 241, the turn-out 99.43% of whom 98.18% voted for the 121 deputies (1 per 10 000). Turn-out in subsequent elections up to 1970 (30 May 54; 1 June 58; 3 June 62; 11 July 66; 20 Sep 70) was never less than 99% and reached (it was claimed) 100% in 1970. One deputy represents 8 000 electors. Elections are held every four years. In recent elections, in October 1974, November 1978 and November 1982, there has been 100% turnout for the 250 candidates of the Democratic Front.

Note: Some parties are referred to by initials. *See* Chapter 6, 'Political Parties', for full names.

AUSTRIA

Voting procedures. Direct secret proportional elections in multi-member constituencies. Tyrol and Vorarlberg provinces had compulsory voting by law from 1919, Styria from 1949. Universal adult suffrage for all over 20 (over 21 in 1930 and 1945).

	Electorate	Valid votes	Votes per party		Seats	% of electorate	% of votes
1919	3 554 242	2 973 454	SDP	1 211 814	69	34.1	40.7
			CSP	1 068 382	63	30.0	36.0
			Grossdeutsche Partei	545 938	24	15.4	18.4
1920	3 752 212	2 980 328	CSP	1 245 531	85	33.2	41.8
			SDP	1 072 709	69	28.6	36.0
			GdVP	514 127	28	13.7	17.2
1923	3 849 484	3 312 606	CSP	1 490 876	82	38.7	45.0
			SDP	1 311 870	68	34.1	39.6
			GdVP	422 600	15	11.0	12.8
1927	4 119 626	3 641 526	CSP } GdVP }	1 756 761[1]	73 12	42.6	41.4 6.8
			SDP	1 539 635	71	37.4	42.3
1930	4 121 282	3 687 082	SDP	1 516 913	72	36.8	41.1
			CSP	1 314 468	66	31.9	35.6
			NWbLb	427 962	19	10.4	11.6
1945	3 449 605	3 217 354	OVP	1 602 227	85	46.4	49.8
			SPO	1 434 898	76	41.6	44.6
			KPO	174 257	4	5.0	5.4
1949	4 391 815	4 193 733	OVP	1 846 581	77	42.0	44.0
			SPO	1 623 524	67	37.0	38.7
			FPO } WdU }	489 213[1]	16	11.1	11.7
1953	4 586 870	4 318 688	SPO	1 818 517	73	39.6	42.1
			OVP	1 781 777	74	38.8	41.2
			FPO } WdU }	472 866[1]	14	10.3	10.9
1956	4 614 464	4 351 908	OVP	1 999 989	82	43.3	46.1
			SPO	1 873 292	74	40.6	43.0
			FPO } WdU }	283 749[1]	6	6.1	6.5
1959	4 696 633	4 362 856	SPO	1 953 935	78	41.6	44.8
			OVP	1 928 043	79	41.0	44.2
			FPO	336 110	8	7.1	7.7
1962	4 805 351	4 456 131	OVP	2 024 501	81	42.1	45.4
			SPO	1 960 685	76	40.8	44.0
			FPO	313 895	8	6.5	7.0

[1] Two-party front

	Electorate	Valid votes	Votes per party		Seats	% of electorate	% of votes
1966	4 886 534	4 531 864	OVP	2 191 128	85	44.8	48.4
			SPO	1 928 922	74	39.5	42.6
			FPO	242 599	6	5.0	5.3
1970	5 045 841	4 588 961	OVP	2 051 012	79	40.6	44.7
			SPO	22 221 981	81	44.0	48.4
			FPO	253 425	5	5.0	5.5
1971	4 984 448	4 556 990	OVP	1 964 713	80	39.4	43.1
			SPO	2 280 168	93	45.7	50.0
			FPO	248 473	10	5.0	5.5
1975	5 019 168	4 610 533	SPO	2 324 309	93	46.3	50.4
			OVP	1 980 474	80	39.4	42.9
			FPO	249 317	10	4.9	5.4
			KPO	54 971	–	1.1	1.2
			Others	1 462	–	0.02	–
1979	5 186 676	4 728 239	SPO	2 412 778	95	46.5	51.0
			OVP	1 981 286	77	38.1	41.9
			FPO	286 644	11	5.5	6.1
			KPO	45 270	–	0.9	1.0
			Others	2 261	–	0.04	0.05
1983	5 316 438	4 750 773	SPO	2 270 997	90	42.7	47.8
			OVP	2 052 714	81	38.7	43.2
			FPO	236 320	12	4.4	5.0
			VGO	89 694	–	1.7	1.9
			ALO	60 150	–	1.1	1.3
			KPO	31 408	–	0.6	0.7
			Others	9 490	–	0.2	0.2

BELGIUM

Voting procedures. Proportional representation in single-member constituencies. Vote for all males over 25 for the Chamber of Representatives and over 30 for the Senate, until the constitutional revision of 1920–1 set the electoral age at 21. Women received the right to vote in 1948.

	Votes per party		Seats	% of votes
1919	Catholics	645 462	71	36.62
	Socialists	645 075	70	36.60
	Liberals	310 853	34	17.64
1921	Catholics	715 041	69	37.01
	Socialists	672 445	68	34.80
	Liberals	343 929	33	17.80
1925	Socialists	820 116	78	39.43
	Catholics	751 058	75	36.11
	Liberals	304 467	23	14.64

	Votes per party		*Seats*	*% of votes*
1929	Socialists	803 347	70	36.02
	Catholics	788 914	71	35.37
	Liberals	369 114	28	16.55
1932	Catholics	899 887	79	38.55
	Socialists	866 817	73	37.11
	Liberals	333 567	24	14.28
1936	Socialists	758 485	70	32.10
	Catholics	653,717	61	27.67
	Liberals	292 972	23	12.40
	Rexistes	271 491	21	11.49
1939	Catholics	764 843	73	32.73
	Socialists	705 969	64	30.18
	Liberals	401 991	33	17.19
1946	Catholics	1 006 293	92	42.53
	Socialists	746 738	69	31.56
	Communists	300 099	23	12.68
	Liberals	211 143	17	8.92
1949	Catholics	2 190 898	105	43.56
	Socialists	1 496 539	66	29.75
	Liberals	767 180	29	15.25
1950	Catholics	2 356 608	108	47.68
	Socialists	1 705 781	77	34.51
	Liberals	556 102	20	11.25
1954	Catholics	2 123 408	95	41.14
	Socialists	1 927 015	86	37.34
	Liberals	626 983	25	12.15
1958	Catholics	2 465 549	104	46.50
	Socialists	1 897 646	84	35.79
	Liberals	585 999	21	11.05
1961	Catholics	2 182 642	96	41.46
	Socialists	1 933 424	84	36.73
	Liberals	649 376	20	12.33
1965	Catholics	1 785 211	77	34.45
	Socialists	1 465 503	64	28.28
	Liberals	1 119 991	48	21.61
1968	Catholics	1 643 785	69	31.8
	Socialists	1 449 172	59	28.0
	Liberals	1 080 894	47	20.9
1971	Catholics	1 587 195	67	30.1
	Socialists	1 438 626	61	27.2
	Liberals	865 657	34	16.4
1974	Catholics	1 699 233	72	32.3
	Socialists	1 401 288	59	26.7
	Liberals	798 896	30	15.2
	FDF/Rassemblement	575 616	25	11.0
	Volksunie	536 195	22	10.2

	Votes per party		Seats	% of votes
	Communists	169 668	4	3.2
	Others	75 758	–	1.4
1977	Catholics	1 459 997	56	26.2
	Socialists/PSC	543 608	24	9.7
	PSB ⎫	1 473 329	35	13.4
	BSP ⎭		27	13.0
	PVV	475 912	17	8.5
	PRLW ⎫	328 571	14 ⎫	7.0
	PL ⎭	63 041	2 ⎭	
	Volksunie	559 634	20	10.0
	FDF	237 280	10	4.7
	RW	158 559	5	2.4
	Communists	151 421	2	2.7
	Vlaams Blok ⎫		– ⎫	
	RAD-UDRT ⎬	122 878	– ⎬	2.2
	Others ⎭		– ⎭	
1978	Catholics (CVP)	1 446 056	57	26.1
	Socialists (PSC)	560 565	25	10.1
	PSB	719 926	32	13.0
	BSP	684 465	26	12.4
	PVV	571 520	22	10.3
	PRLW ⎫	287 942 ⎫	14	6.0
	PL ⎭	42 156 ⎭	1	
	Volksunie	388 368	14	7.0
	FDF	235 152	11	4.2
	RW	158 563	4	2.9
	Communists	180 088	4	3.2
	Vlaams Blok		1	
	RAD-UDRT ⎬	258 405	1 ⎬	4.7
	Others ⎭		0	
1981	CVP	1 165 155	43	19.3
	PSC	430 712	18	7.1
	PS	765 055	35	12.7
	SP	744 586	26	12.4
	PRL	516 291	24	8.6
	PVV	776 882	28	12.9
	VU	588 430	20	9.8
	FDF ⎫			
	RW ⎭	253 703	8	4.2
	Communists	138 992	2	2.3
	UDRT	163 725	3	2.7
	Ecology	289 901	4	4.8
	Vlaams Blok	66 424	1	1.1
	Others	123 250	–	2.1

BULGARIA

By 1918 Bulgaria was a constitutional monarchy with an electoral system established by the 1879 *Turnovo* constitution. The legislature was the unicameral National Assembly, *Narodno Sŭbranie*, of deputies each representing 10 000 electors, elected by universal suffrage at 21 years for three- (later four-) year terms. To pass any constitutional amendment a Grand National Assembly, *Veliko Narodno Sŭbranie*, was elected of twice the usual number of deputies. Elections were on the proportional representation system.

		Votes per party	*Seats*
1923 (23 Apr)	Agrarians	569 000	212
	Communists	204 000	16
	Social Democrats	28 000	2
	Middle class and		
	traditional parties	275 000	15
1923 (18 Nov)	Democratic *entente*		
	in a bloc with		202⎫
	Social Democrats	638 675	29⎭
	Left-wing Agrarians		
	in a bloc with		31⎫
	Communists	217 607	8⎭
	Right-wing Agrarians	42 737	19
	National Liberals	36 507	7

By an electoral law of 1927 proportional representation (abolished in 1923) was restored in a system favourable ti the government party, Democratic *entente*, enabling it to win 168 of the 273 seats with 39% of the votes in the election of 29 May 27:

Votes per party	*Seats*
Democratic *entente*	504 703	168
'Iron bloc' of Agrarians,		42
Social Democrats and		10
Artisans	285 758	4
Workers (*i.e.* Communists)	29 210	4
National Liberals		14
Democrats		12
Macedonians		11
Radicals		2

A new proportional representation system was introduced for the elections of 21 June 31, the results of which were:

Votes per party	*Seats*
Agrarians		69
'Popular bloc' of Democrats		43
Kyorchev Liberals and		32
Radicals	590 000	8
Democratic *entente*		
in a bloc with		63
Smilov Liberals	417 000	15
Workers (*i.e.* Communists)	166 000	33
Macedonians		8
Social Democrats		5

121

The government was taken over on 19 May 34 in a *coup d'état* by a group of army officers in alliance with a group of intellectuals associated with the journal *Zveno*. Tsar Boris overthrew this government in turn on 22 Jan 35 and set up a royal dictatorship.

By an electoral law of 1937 the number of deputies was reduced to 160, political parties were banned and unmarried women disfranchised.

At the election of Mar 38 Agrarians and Social Democrats stood in opposition to the government in the Bulgarian version of the Popular Front called the 'Constitutional bloc', and won 63 seats. At the elections of 30 Jan 40 opposition candidates (including 9 Communists) won 20 seats.

On 9 Sep 44 at the beginning of the Soviet occupation a 'Fatherland Front' government of Communists and anti-fascists was set up.

18 Nov 45 (Opposition boycotted election)	Fatherland Front, 88.2% (85.6% of electorate voted)

A referendum was held on 8 Sep 46 at which 92.7% of the electorate voted, 3 801 160 for a Republic, and 197 176 to retain the monarchy. 119 168 votes were invalid. A People's Republic was proclaimed on 15 Sep 46.

The elections of 27 Oct 46 were for a 'Grand' National Assembly as was necessary to carry a constitutional change. The Communists and their allies stood in a Fatherland Front bloc; the opposition parties campaigned as the 'United opposition'.

		Votes per party	*Seats*
1946	Fatherland Front	2 980 000	366
	Communists	2 260 000	277
	Obbov Agrarians		67
	Neikov Social Democrats		9
	Zveno group		8
	Radicals		4
	United opposition	1 300 000	99
	Agrarians		89
	Social Democrats		9
	Independent		1

On 4 Dec 47 the 'Dimitrov' constitution was promulgated. The National Assembly was elected for four-year terms by all citizens of 18 and over. Each deputy represented 20 000 electors. The President was to be elected by the National Assembly.

Before the elections of 1949 the Social Democrats merged with the Communists and the *Zveno* group dissolved. 97.66% of votes cast were for the single Fatherland Front list of Communist or Agrarian candidates.

	Electorate	*Votes per party*	*% of votes*
1953	5 017 667 (99 48% voted)	Fatherland Front (465 deputies elected)	99.8

	Electorate	Votes per party	% of votes
1957	5 218 602	Fatherland Front 5 204 027	99.95
	(99.77% voted)	(number of deputies reduced to 253)	
	(Votes = 5 206 428)		
1962	5 485 607	Fatherland Front (321 deputies elected)	99.9
	(99.71% voted)		
	(Votes = 5 466 517)		
1966	5 774 251	Fatherland Front 5 744 072	99.85
	(99.63% voted	(number of candidates = 416)	
	(Votes = 5 752 817)		
1971	(99.85% voted)	Fatherland Front	99.9

A new constitution was promulgated on 18 May 71 by which the number of deputies was fixed at 400 and their term of service altered to five years.

In elections in May 1976, of an electorate of 6 378 348, some 6 375 092 voted (99.99%). Of these, 6 369 762 (99.92%) voted for the Fatherland Front, returning 272 members for the Bulgarian Communist Party, 100 for the Bulgarian Agrarian Party and 28 non-party members.

In elections in June 1981, of the total electorate some 6 524 086 (99.96%) cast their votes. Of these 6 519 674 (99.93%) were for the Fatherland Front. The members returned comprised 271 Bulgarian Communist Party, 99 Agrarian Union and 30 non-party.

CZECHOSLOVAKIA

A National Assembly was set up on 14 Nov 18 of 260 delegates of the following party composition:

Agrarians	54
Social Democrats	50
Slovaks	50
National Democrats	44
National Socialists	28
Catholics	28
Progressive Liberals	6

Representatives of the German minority refused to take part.

A constitution was promulgated on 29 Feb 20 providing for a bicameral National Assembly, *Národni Shromážděni*, to be elected by direct universal suffrage on the proportional representation method. The Chamber of Deputies of 300 members was to be elected for six years by citizens over 21; the Senate for eight years by voters over 26, and to have 150 senators.

The head of state was to be a President elected by both chambers for seven years.

Elections to the Chamber of Deputies were held on 18 Apr 20 and to the

Senate on 25 Apr 20. The electorate was 6 917 956 (for the Chamber of Deputies; the Senate electorate was a proportion of this which remained more or less constant throughout later elections. At this election it was 5 804 134). Turn-out was 89.9%. Valid votes cast for the Chamber of Deputies: 6 130 318.

Pre-war Czechoslovak politics were dominated by the problem of national minorities, and the official classification of the voting figures in this election reflects this preoccupation: Czechoslovak parties polled 4 255 623 votes (68.64% of votes cast) and gained 199 seats in the Chamber of Deputies, and gained 102 seats in the Senate with 70.07% of votes cast. German parties: 72; 1 586 060 (25.58%) and 37; 26.09%. Hungarian-German parties: 9; 247 901 (4%) and 2; 1.93%. Hungarian parties: 1; 30 734 (0.50%) and 1; 0.77%.

Seats gained and proportion of votes polled by individual, successful parties were:

Chamber of Deputies:		*Seats*	*%*
	Social Democrats	74	25.65
	Populist Catholics	33	11.29
	Agrarians	28	9.74
Czechoslovak	National Socialists	24	8.08
parties	National Democrats	19	6.25
	Slovak National Agrarians	12	3.9
	Professional Middle Class	6	1.98
	Working People (Progressive Socialists)	3	0.95
	German Social Democrats	31	11.12
	German Electoral Union	15	5.3
German parties	Union of German Peasants	11	3.9
	German Christian Social Party	10	3.44
	German Democratic Liberals	5	1.78
Hungarian-German	Hungarian-German Christian Socialists	5	2.25
parties	Hungarian-German Social Democrats	4	1.75
Hungarian parties	Hungarian Agrarians	1	0.43

Senate		*Seats*	*%*
	Social Democrats	41	28.07
	Populist Catholics	18	11.91
	Agrarians	14	10.15
Czechoslovak	National Socialists	10	7.15
parties	National Democrats	10	6.78
	Slovak National Agrarians	6	3.47
	Professional Middle Class	3	2.06
	German Social Democrats	16	11.35
	German Electoral Union	8	5.75
German parties	Union of German Peasants	6	4.03
	German Christian Social Party	4	2.7
	German Democratic Liberals	3	2.26
Hungarian-German	Hungarian-German Christian Socialists	2	1.93
Hungarian	Hungarian Agrarians	1	0.77

At the elections of 15 Nov 25 all 300 seats in the Chamber of Deputies and all 150 in the Senate were filled by election. The electorate was 7 855 822, the turn-out was 91.4% and 7 105 276 votes were cast.

(Czechoslovak parties):	Chamber of Deputies			Senate		
	Votes	% of votes	Seats	Votes	% of votes	Seats
Agrarians	970 489	13.66	45	841 647	13.81	23
Populist Catholics	691 238	9.73	31	618 033	10.14	16
Social Democrats	630 894	8.88	29	537 470	8.82	14
National Socialists	609 195	8.57	28	516 250	8.47	14
Professional Middle Class	285 928	4.02	13	257 171	4.22	6
National Democrats	284 628	4.01	13	256 360	4.2	7
German Social Democrats	411 040	5.79	17	363 310	6.84	12
German Christian Social Party	314 440	4.43	13	289 055	4.74	7
German Nationalists	240 879	3.39	10	214 589	3.52	5
Nazis	168 278	2.37	7	139 945	2.3	3
Union of German Peasants	571 198	–8.04	24	505 597	8.29	12
Hlinka's Populist Slovak Catholics	489,027	6.88	23	417 206	6.84	12
Sub-Carpathian Russian Agrarians	35 674	0.5	1			
Polish People's and Workers' Union	29 884	0.42	1			
Hungarian Christian Social Party	98 383	1.39	4	85 777	1.41	2
Communists	933 711	13.14	41	774 454	12.7	20

At the elections of 27 Oct 29 the electorate was 8 183 462, the turn-out 91.6% and 7 385 084 votes cast.

(Czechoslovak parties):	Chamber of Deputies			Senate		
	Votes	% of votes	Seats	Votes	% of votes	Seats
Agrarians	1 105 429	14.97	46	978 291	15.17	24
Social Democrats	963 312	13.05	39	841 331	13.04	20
National Socialists	767 571	10.39	32	666 607	10.33	16
Populist Catholics	623,522	8.44	25	559 700	8.68	13
National Democrats	359 533	4.87	15	325 023	5.04	8
Professional Middle Class	291 238	3.94	12	274 085	4.25	6
Anti-Electoral Scrutiny	70 857	0.96	3	51 617	0.8	1
German Social Democrats	506 750	5.76	19	446 940	6.93	11
German Electoral Coalition	396 383	5.37	16	359 002	5.57	9
German Christian Social Party	348 097	4.71	14	313 544	4.86	8
Nazis	204 096	2.77	8	171 181	2.65	4
German Nationalist and Sudeten German Union	189 071	2.56	7			
Hlinka's Populist Slovak Catholics	425 052	5.76	19	377 498	5.85	9
Hungarian Christian Socialists	257 231	3.48	9	233 772	3.62	6
Polish and Jewish Union	104 539	1.42	4			
Communists	753 444	10.2	30	644 896	10.00	15

At the elections of 19 May 35 the electorate was 8 957 572, turn-out was 92.8% and 8 231 412 votes were cast.

(Czechoslovak parties):	Chamber of Deputies			Senate		
	Votes	% of votes	Seats	Votes	% of votes	Seats
Agrarians	1 176 593	13.29	45	1 042 924	14.33	23
Social Democrats	1 034 774	12.57	38	910 252	12.51	20
National Socialists	755 880	9.18	18	672 126	9.24	14

	Chamber of Deputies			Senate		
	Votes	% of votes	Seats	Votes	% of votes	Seats
Populist Catholics	615 877	7.48	22	557 684	7.66	11
Artisans and Tradesmen	448 047	5.44	17	393 732	5.41	8
Fascists	167 433	2.04	6			
National Union	456 353	5.55	17	410 095	5.64	9
Sudeten Germans	1 249 531	15.18	44	1 092 255	15.01	23
German Social Democrats	299 942	3.64	11	271 097	3.73	6
German Christian Social Party	162 781	1.98	6	155 234	2.13	3
Union of German Peasants	142 399	1.73	5			
Autonomous bloc (Hlinka's Slovaks, Poles and Hungarians)	564 273	6.86	22	495 166	6.8	11
Hungarian-German Christian Social bloc	291 831	3.55	9	259 832	3.57	6
Communists	849 509	10.32	30	740 696	10.18	16

With the dismemberment and annexation of Czechoslovakia by Germany in 1938 all political parties were proscribed and two puppet organizations set up: The Party of National Unity and the Party of Labour.

On 3 Apr 45 Beneš established a provisional government at Košice with a cabinet of seven Communists, three Slovak Democrats, three Populist Catholics, three National Socialists and two Social Democrats. This organized an indirect election in Sep and Oct 45 of a provisional National Assembly which met on 28 Oct 45. Four parties were recognized in the Czech lands (Communists, Agrarians, National Socialists, Social Democrats) and allotted 40 deputies each, 2 in Slovakia (Populist Catholics and Slovak Democrats) 50 each, 32 seats went to the Trade Union organization and 8 to outstanding individuals in the cultural sphere, making 300 in all.

At the elections of 26 May 46 to a Constituent Assembly eight official parties were allowed to stand: no independents, no fascist parties and (at Soviet insistence) no Agrarians. The electorate was 7 583 784 (all citizens over 18 of whom 7 138 694 voted.

Party	Votes	Seats
Communists	2 695 915	114
National Socialists	1 298 917	55
Populist Catholics	1 110 920	47
Slovak Democrats	988 275	43
Social Democrats	905 654	36
Slovak Freedom	67 575	3
Slovak Labour	49 983	2

Elections were held on 30 May 48 in which the electorate of 7 998 035 were invited to vote for a single list of National Front candidates. 7 419 253 votes were cast, 6 424 734 for the National Front.

President Beneš resigned and was succeeded by K. Gottwald.

A new constitution of 9 June 48 provided for a single-chamber National Assembly, *Národni Shromáždĕni*, of 368 deputies elected by universal suffrage of citizens over 18 for a six-year period. The President was to be elected by the National Assembly for seven years.

An electoral law of May 54 permitted only one candidate to stand per constituency; all candidates had to be nominated by the National Front.

At the elections of 28 Nov 54 the electorate was 8 783 816, votes cast numbered 8 711 718 (99.18%), of which 8 494 102 (97.89%) were for the National Front. At the elections of 12 June 60, 9 085 432 votes were cast (99.68% of the electorate), of which 9 059 838 (99.86% of votes cast) went to the National Front.

On 11 July 60 a new constitution made Czechoslovakia a 'Socialist' instead of a 'People's' Republic, and fixed the number of National Assembly deputies at 300. The President was henceforth to be elected for a five-year term, the National Assembly for four.

At the elections of 14 June 64, 9 418 349 votes were cast (99.98% of the electorate), 9 412 309 for the National Front (99.99% of votes cast).

Czechoslovakia became a Federal Republic of the Czech lands and Slovakia as of 1 Jan 69. Each federative republic elects a National Council. The Federal Assembly consists of two chambers: the Chamber of the People of 200 deputies, and the Chamber of the Nations composed of 75 Czech and 75 Slovak deputies. Elections are held every five years, to coincide with Communist Party congresses.

The elections due in 1968 were postponed until 26–27 Nov 71. In 1968 a new electoral law had permitted more than one candidate to stand for each seat, but this was annulled in the 1971 elections in which the number of candidates was once again equivalent to the number of seats. The electorate was 10 253 796 of whom 99.45% voted. Votes for candidates: Federal Assembly Chamber of the People, 99.81%; Federal Assembly Chamber of the Nations, 99.77%; Czech National Council, 99.78%; Slovak National Council, 99.94%.

In elections in October 1976, of the 10 649 261 voters, 99.7% cast their votes. Of these, 10 605 672 (99.97%) voted for National Front candidates.

In elections in June 1981, of the 10 789 574 voters, 99.51% cast their votes. Of these, 10 725 609 (99.9%) voted for the National Front.

DENMARK

In 1918, the capital had direct proportional elections, the provinces had direct elections in single-member constituencies with some additional seats allotted in proportion to the vote. From 1920, direct proportional elections in multi-member seats. Suffrage of men and women over 29, except those working as servants and farm helpers without their own household. Age reduced to 25 at the third election of 1920, to 23 in 1953 and to 21 in 1961. From 1918–53 there was a second chamber, the Landsting. For this there was indirect election, electors being selected by city or parish, voters having one vote per elector allocated. Voters were all men and women over 35. Electors in turn elected 53 (first two elections of the period) of the 66 Landsting members, and 55 of them in the last ten elections.

	Votes per party		Seats	% of votes
1918	Liberals	269 005	44	29.4
	Soc. Dem.	262 796	39	29.4
	Rad. Lib.	192 478	33	21.0
	Con.	167 865	22	18.3
1920(1)	Liberals	350 563	48	34.2
	Soc. Dem.	300 345	42	29.3
	Con.	201 499	28	19.7
	Rad. Lib.	122 160	17	11.9
1920(2)	Liberals	343 351	51	36.1
	Soc. Dem.	285 166	42	29.9
	Con.	180 293	26	18.9
	Rad. Lib.	110 931	16	11.6
1920(3)	Liberals	411 661	51	34.0
	Soc. Dem.	389 653	48	32.2
	Con.	216 733	27	17.9
	Rad. Lib.	147 120	18	12.1
1924	Soc. Dem.	469 949	55	36.6
	Liberals	362 682	44	28.3
	Con.	242 955	28	18.9
	Rad. Lib.	166 476	20	13.0
1926	Soc. Dem.	497 106	53	37.2
	Liberals	378 137	46	28.3
	Con.	275 793	30	20.6
	Rad. Lib.	150 931	16	11.3
1929	Soc. Dem.	593 191	61	41.8
	Liberals	402 121	43	28.3
	Con.	233 935	24	16.5
	Rad. Lib.	151 746	16	10.7
1932	Soc. Dem.	660 839	62	42.7
	Liberals	381 862	38	24.7
	Con.	289 531	27	18.7
	Rad. Lib.	145 221	14	9.4
1935	Soc. Dem.	759 102	68	46.1
	Liberals	292 247	28	17.8
	Con.	293 393	26	17.8
	Rad. Lib.	151 507	14	9.2
1939	Soc. Dem.	729 619	64	42.9
	Liberals	309 355	30	18.2
	Con.	301 625	26	17.8
	Rad. Lib.	161 834	14	9.5

	Votes per party		Seats	% of votes
1943	Soc. Dem.	894 632	66	44.5
	Con.	421 523	31	21.0
	Liberals	376 850	28	18.7
1945	Soc. Dem.	671 755	48	32.8
	Liberals	479 158	38	23.4
	Con.	373 688	26	18.2
1947	Soc. Dem.	834 089	57	40.0
	Liberals	574 895	49	27.6
	Con.	259 324	17	12.4
1950	Soc. Dem.	813 224	59	39.6
	Liberals	438 188	32	21.3
	Con.	365 236	27	17.8
1953(1)	Soc. Dem.	836 507	61	40.4
	Liberals	456 896	33	22.1
	Con.	358 509	26	17.3
1953(2)	Soc. Dem.	894 913	74	41.3
	Liberals	499 656	42	23.1
	Con.	364 960	30	16.8
1957	Soc. Dem.	910 170	70	39.4
	Liberals	578 932	45	25.1
	Con.	383 843	30	16.6
1960	Soc. Dem.	1 023 794	76	42.1
	Liberals	512 041	38	21.1
	Con.	435 764	32	17.9
1964	Soc. Dem.	1 103 667	76	41.9
	Liberals	547 770	38	20.8
	Con.	527 798	36	20.1
1966	Soc. Dem.	1 068 911	69	38.2
	Liberals	539 028	35	19.3
	Con.	522 027	34	18.7
1968	Soc. Dem.	974 833	62	34.1
	Liberals	530 167	34	18.6
	Cons.	581 051	37	20.4
1971	Soc. Dem.	1 074 777	70	37.3
	Liberals	450 904	30	15.6
	Cons.	481 335	31	16.7
1973	Soc. Dem.	783 145	46	25.6
	Soc. People's Party	183 522	11	6.0
	Com.	110 715	6	3.6
	Left Soc.	44 843	0	1.5
	Lib. Dem.	374 283	22	12.3
	Rad. Lib.	343 117	20	11.2
	Chr. People's Party	123 573	7	4.0
	Con.	279 391	16	9.2
	Centre Dem.	236 784	14	7.8
	Pro. Party	414 212	24	13.6
	STP	54 067	–	1.8

	Votes per party		Seats	% of votes
1975	Soc. Dem.	913 155	53	30.0
	Soc. People's Party	150 963	9	4.9
	Com.	127 837	7	4.2
	Left Soc.	63 579	4	2.1
	Lib. Dem.	711 298	42	23.3
	Rad. Lib.	216 553	13	7.1
	Chr. People's Party	162 734	9	5.3
	Con.	168 164	10	5.5
	Centre Dem.	66 316	4	2.2
	Pro. Party	414 212	24	13.6
	STP	54 067	–	1.8
1977	Soc. Dem.	1 150 355	65	37.0
	Soc. People's Party	120 357	7	3.9
	Com.	114 022	7	3.7
	Left Soc.	83 667	5	2.7
	Lib. Dem.	371 728	21	12.0
	Rad. Lib.	113 330	6	3.6
	Chr. People's Party	106 082	6	3.4
	Con.	263 262	15	8.5
	Centre Dem.	200 347	11	6.4
	Pro. Party	453 782	26	14.6
	STP	102 149	6	3.3
	Pensioners Party	26 889	0	0.9
1979	Soc. Dem.	1 213 456	68	38.3
	Lib. Dem	396 484	22	12.5
	Con.	395 653	22	12.5
	Pro. Party	349 243	20	11.0
	Soc. People's Party	187 284	11	5.9
	Rad. Lib.	172 365	10	5.4
	Left Soc.	116 047	6	3.7
	Centre Dem.	102 132	6	3.2
	Chr. People's Party	82 133	5	2.6
	STP	83 238	5	2.6
	Com.	58 901	0	1.9
	Com. Workers Party	13 070	0	0.4
1981	Soc. Dem.	1 027 376	59	32.9
	Con. People's Party	450 970	26	14.4
	Soc. People's Party	353 167	21	11.3
	Lib.	353 435	20	11.3
	Pro. Party	278 454	16	8.9
	Centre Dem.	258 720	15	8.3
	Rad. Lib.	159 933	9	5.1
	Left Soc.	82 106	5	2.6
	Chr. People's Party	72 020	4	2.3
	Others	85 744	–	2.7

ESTONIA

Elections for a Constituent Assembly were held 7 and 8 Apr 19, and a coalition government formed headed by the Social Democratic Party. A constitution was adopted on 15 June 20 which provided for a single-chamber parliament (*Riigikogu*) of 100 deputies elected every 3 years by proportional representation. Elections were held in 1920, 1923, 1926, 1929 and 1932. The system favoured the proliferation of political parties. There were also national minority parties: Swedish, German and Russian. The Communist Party was outlawed in Feb 25 after an abortive *coup*. The fascist ex-servicemen's organization Vaps began to gain influence at a time of increasing dissatisfaction with government instability (between 1919 and 1933 there were 20 coalition governments) and instigated a referendum to amend the constitution in Oct 1933. The amendment was approved by 416 879 votes (56.3% of the electorate), but the President (K. Päts) on 12 Mar 34 assumed direct control under emergency powers and presented a third constitution to the people in Feb 36. This was approved by a majority of 76.1% and came into force on 1 Jan 38. It provided for a new two-chamber parliament: a 40-strong National Council of appointed specialists, and an 80-strong Chamber of Deputies elected every five years on the single-member constituency system. The President was to be directly elected every six years.

At the elections of 24 Apr 38 the poll was a record 90%. Päts was elected President. 55 members of the pro-Päts Patriotic League were elected. Social Democrats and extreme left-wing groups were in opposition.

EUROPEAN COMMUNITIES

EUROPEAN PARLIAMENT

DIRECT ELECTIONS 1979

	Votes per party	Seats	% of votes
Belgium			
CVP	1 607 925	7	29.5
PSC	445 940	3	8.2
BSP	698 892	3	12.8
PSB	575 886	4	10.6
PVV	512 355	2	9.4
PRL	372 857	2	6.9
FDF/RW	414 412	2	7.6
Volksunie	324 569	1	6.0
Others	490 031	–	9.0
Turnout 91.4%			
Denmark*			
Peoples Movement against EEC	365 760	4	20.5
Social Democrats	382 487	3	21.5

* In Greenland, with 1 seat, the successful candidate was from the ruling SIUMUT (Socialist) Party. The turnout was 33.5%.

131

	Votes per party	Seats	% of votes
Liberal Democrats	252 767	3	14.2
Conservatives	245 309	2	13.8
Centre Democrats	107 790	1	6.1
Progress Party	100 702	1	5.7
Socialist People's Party	81 991	1	4.6
Left Socialists	60 964	0	3.4
Single Tax Party	59 379	0	3.3
Radical Liberals	56 944	0	3.2
Christian People's Party	30 985	0	1.7
Others	36 426	0	2.0
Turnout 47.8%			

Federal Republic of Germany

SPD	11 377 818	35	40.8
CDU	10 890 355	34	39.1
CSU	2 816 758	8	10.1
FDP	1 663 506	4	6.0
Greens	893 510	–	3.2
Others	109 026	–	0.8
Turnout 65.9%			

France

UFE	5 588 026	26	27.6
PS/MRG	4 764 341	21	23.5
Communists	4 154 512	19	20.5
DIFE	3 302 131	15	16.3
Europe-Ecologie	887 863	–	4.4
Others	1 545 543	–	7.6
Turnout 60%			

Ireland

Fianna Fail	464 451	5	34.7
Fine Gael	443 652	4	33.1
Labour Party	193 129	4	14.5
Independents	193 898	2	14.4
Others	43 942	–	3.3
Turnout 63.6%			

Italy

DC (+ SVP)	12 971 528	30	36.5
PCI (+ PDUP)	10 768 000	25	30.7
PSI	3 866 946	9	11.0
MSI/DN	1 909 055	4	5.4
PSDI	1 514 272	4	4.3
PR	1 285 065	3	3.7
PLI ⎫	1 271 159	3	3.6
PRI ⎭	896 139	2	2.6
DP	252 342	1	0.7
Others	505 303	0	1.3
Turnout 85.5%			

	Votes per party	Seats	% of votes
Luxembourg			
PCS	352 296	3	36.2
PD	274 307	2	28.1
LSAP	211 106	1	21.7
PC	48 813	–	4.9
Others	14 570	–	9.2
Turnout 88.9%			
Netherlands			
CDA	2 017 692	10	35.6
PvdA	1 721 949	9	30.4
VVD	914 661	4	16.4
D-66	511 590	2	9.0
SGP	126 397	–	2.2
Others	373 933	–	6.5
Turnout 57.8%			
United Kingdom*			
Conservative	6 508 512	60	50.7
Labour	4 253 117	17	33.1
Liberal	1 690 598	–	13.2
Scottish Nationalist	219 142	1	1.7
Plaid Cymru	83 399	–	0.6
Others	88 486	–	0.7
Turnout 32%			

* In Ulster, where the single-transferable vote system was used, the results were one representative each for the Democratic Unionists, Official Unionists and the SDLP.

DIRECT ELECTIONS 1984

	Votes per party	Seats	% of votes
Belgium			
PS	762 377	5	13.3
SP	980 668	4	17.1
CVP	1 134 012	4	19.8
PSC	436 126	2	7.6
PRL	540 597	3	9.4
PVV	494 585	2	8.6
Volksunie	484 925	2	8.5
Agalev	246 879	1	4.3
Ecologistes	220 704	1	3.9
FDF	142 871	–	2.5
RW	51 899	–	0.9
Others	230 194	–	4.0
Turnout 92.0%			
Denmark*			
Conservatives	414 175	4	20.8
Peoples Movement (against EEC)	413 807	4	20.8

* Greenland also elected one EEC MP, not included in above figures.

	Votes per party	Seats	% of votes
Social Democrats	387 098	3	19.4
Liberal Democrats	248 497	2	12.5
Socialist People's Party	183 589	1	9.2
Centre Democrats	131 984	1	6.6
Progress Party	68 747	–	3.5
Radical Liberals	62 558	–	3.1
Christian People's Party	54 624	–	2.7
Left Socialists	25 305	–	1.3
Turnout 52.3%			

Federal Republic of Germany

CDU	9 306 775	34	37.5
SPD	9 294 916	33	37.4
CSU	2 104 590	7	8.5
Die Grünen	2 024 801	7	8.2
FDP	1 192 138	–	4.8
Others	918 082	–	3.6
Turnout 56.8%			

France

UDF/RPR	8 683 596	41	43.0
PSF	4 188 875	20	20.8
PCF	2 261 312	10	11.2
National Front	2 210 334	10	11.0
Others	2 836 817	–	14.0
Turnout 56.7%			

Greece

PASOK	2 451 409	10	41.6
ND	2 246 896	9	38.1
KKE (ext)	685 387	3	11.6
KKE (int)	200 531	1	3.4
Others	311 997	1	5.3
Turnout 77.2%			

Ireland

Fianna Fail	438 946	8	39.2
Fine Gael	361 034	6	32.2
Independents	113 067	1	10.1
Labour Party	93 656	–	8.4
Sinn Fein	54 672	–	4.9
Others	59 141	–	5.3
Turnout 47.6%			

Italy

PCI/PDUP	11 624 183	27	33.3
DC	11 532 342	26	33.0
PSI	3 909 027	9	11.2
MSI–DN	2 265 619	5	6.5
PLI/PRI	2 131 457	5	6.1
PSDI	1 208 071	3	3.5

	Votes per party	Seats	% of votes
PR	1 193 141	3	3.4
Others	1 043 395	3	3.0

Luxembourg

PCS	345 363	3	35.3
POSL	295 993	2	30.3
PD	206 763	1	21.2
Others	129 266	–	13.2

Turnout 87.0%

Netherlands

PvdA	1 785 399	9	33.7
CDA	1 590 601	8	30.0
VVD	1 002 825	5	18.9
GPA	296 516	2	5.6
CC	275 824	1	5.2
Dem 66	120 848	–	2.3
Others	225 608	–	4.3

Turnout 50.5%

United Kingdom

Conservative	5 426 796	45	40.8
Labour	4 865 220	32	36.5
Liberal/SDP Alliance	2 591 657	–	19.5
Scottish Nationalists	230 590	1	1.7
Plaid Cymru	103 031	–	0.8
Ecology Party	74 176	–	0.6
Others	21 348	–	0.2

Turnout 32.0%

FEDERAL REPUBLIC OF GERMANY

From 1949, direct elections for 60% of the seats in the Bundestag, the others filled by election from lists. From 1953, each voter votes (1) for a candidate in his constituency and (2) for a party list. Seats are distributed proportionally to the second vote. Suffrage since 1949 is for men and women over 21.

		Votes per party	Seats	% of votes
1949	CDU/CSU	7 359 100	139	31.0
	SPD	6 935 000	131	29.2
	FDP	2 829 900	52	11.9
1953	CDU/CSU	12 444 000	244	45.2
	SPD	7 994 900	151	28.8
	FDP	2 629 200	48	9.5
1957	CDU/CSU	15 008 400	270	50.2
	SPD	9 495 600	169	31.8
	FDP	2 307 100	41	7.7

		Votes per party	Seats	% of votes
1961	CDU/CSU	14 298 400	242	45.4
	SPD	11 427 400	190	36.2
	FDP	4 028 800	67	12.8
1965	CDU/CSU	15 524 100	245	47.6
	SPD	12 813 200	202	39.3
	FDP	3 096 800	49	9.5
1969	CDU/CSU	15 195 187	242	46.1
	SPD	14 065 716	224	42.7
	FDP	1 903 422	30	5.8
1972	CDU/CSU	16 806 020	225	44.9
	SPD	17 175 169	230	45.8
	FDP	3 129 982	41	7.6
1976	SPD	16 099 019	214	42.6
	CDU	14 367 302	190	38.0
	CSU	4 027 403	53	10.6
	FDP	2 995 085	39	7.9
	NPD	122 428	–	0.3
	DKP	118 488	–	0.3
	Others	92 571	–	0.4
1980	CDU	12 992 334	174	34.2
	CSU	3 908 036	52	10.3
	SPD	16 262 096	218	42.9
	FDP	4 030 608	53	10.6
	Die Grünen	568 265	–	1.5
	Others	181 713	–	0.4
1983	SPD	14 866 210	193	38.2
	CDU	14 856 835	191	38.2
	CSU	4 140 351	53	10.6
	FDP	2 705 795	34	6.9
	Die Grünen	2 164 988	27	5.6
	Others	203 391	–	0.4

FINLAND

Voting procedures. Direct proportional elections from multi-member constituencies. Suffrage for all adults over 24 until 1945, and then over 21. In 1919, part of the population disenfranchised by the civil war.

		Votes per party	Seats	% of votes
1919	SSP	365 046	80	38.0
	MI	189 297	42	19.7
	KK	151 018	28	15.7
	KE	123 090	26	12.8
	RK	116 582	22	12.1

		Votes per party	*Seats*	*% of votes*
1922	SSP	216 861	53	25.1
	MI	175 401	45	20.3
	KK	157 116	35	18.1
	RK	107 414	25	12.4
	KE	79 676	15	9.2
1924	SSP	255 068	60	29.0
	MI	177 982	44	20.3
	KK	166 880	38	19.0
	RK	105 733	23	12.0
	KE	79 937	17	9.0
1927	SSP	257 572	60	28.3
	MI	205 313	52	22.5
	KK	161 450	34	17.7
	RK	111 005	24	12.2
	KE	61 613	10	6.8
1929	SSP	260 254	59	27.4
	MI	248 762	60	26.1
	KK	138 008	28	14.5
	RK	108 886	23	11.4
	KE	53 301	7	5.6
1930	SSP	386 026	66	34.2
	MI	308 280	59	27.3
	KK	203 958	42	18.1
	RK	113 318	20	10.0
	KE	65 830	11	5.8
1933	SSP	413 551	78	37.3
	MI	249 758	53	22.6
	RK	131 440	21	11.2
	KK	121 619	20	10.4
	IK	97 891	14	8.3
1939	SSP	515 980	85	39.8
	MI	296 529	56	22.9
	KK	176 215	25	13.6
	RK	124 720	18	9.6
1945	SSP	425 948	50	25.1
	SKDI	398 618	49	23.5
	MI	362 662	49	21.3
	KK	255 394	28	15.0
1948	MI	455 635	56	24.2
	SSP	494 719	54	26.3
	SKDI	375 820	38	20.0
	KK	320 366	33	17.1
1951	SSP	480 754	53	26.5
	MI	421 613	51	23.2
	SKDI	391 362	43	21.6
	KK	264 044	28	14.6

	Votes per party		Seats	% of votes
1954	SSP	527 094	54	26.2
	MI	483 958	53	24.1
	SKDI	433 528	43	21.6
	KK	257 025	24	12.8
1958	SKDI	450 506	50	23.2
	SSP	450 212	48	23.2
	MI	448 364	48	23.1
	KK	297 094	29	15.3
1962	MI	528 409	53	23.0
	SKDI	507 124	47	22.0
	SSP	448 930	38	19.5
	KK	346 638	32	15.0
1966	MI	503 047	49	21.2
	SKDI	502 635	41	21.2
	SSP	645 339	55	27.2
	KK	326 928	26	13.8
1970	MI	434 150	37	17.1
	SKDI	420 556	36	16.6
	SSP	594 185	51	23.4
	KK	457 582	37	18.0
1972	MI	423 039	35	16.4
	SKDI	438 757	37	17.0
	SSP	664 724	55	25.8
	KK	453 434	34	17.6
1975	SSDP	695 394	54	24.9
	SKDL	528 026	40	18.9
	KP	488 930	39	17.5
	KK	512 213	35	18.4
	SFP	141 381	10	5.0
	LKP	121 722	9	4.4
	SKL	92 108	9	3.3
	Others	214 364	4	7.6
1979	SSDP	691 256	52	23.9
	KK	626 108	47	21.7
	KP	501 012	36	21.0
	SKDL	516 276	35	17.9
	SFP	122 450	10	4.6
	LKP	106 609	4	4.2
	SKL	137 850	9	4.8
	Others	180 744	7	1.7
1983	SSDP	795 813	57	26.7
	KK	658 975	44	22.1
	KP	525 091	38	17.6
	SKDL	400 483	26	13.5

Votes per party		Seats	% of votes
SMP	288 435	17	9.7
SFP	137 189	10	4.6
SKL	90 374	3	3.0
Others	79 506	5	2.7

FRANCE

Voting procedures. From 1919–27, mixed proportional and majority representation. From 1927–45 the system was as in 1852. In 1945 proportional representation was restored as the sole system; this lasted until 1951 when mixed representation returned. Universal male suffrage until 1945, when women received the vote.

	Votes per party		Seats	% of votes
1919	Rep. U.	1 820 000	201	22.3
	Rad. Soc.	1 420 000	106	17.4
	Rep. (left)	889 000	79	10.9
	Soc.	1 615 000	67	20.1
1924	Rep. U.	3 191 000	204	35.5
	Rad. Soc.	1 613 000	162	17.9
	Soc.	1 814 000	104	20.2
1928	Rep. U.	2 082 000	182	22.0
	Rad. Ind.⎫ Rep. (left)⎭	2 196 000	126	23.2
	Soc.	1 709 000	99	18.0
1932	Rad. Soc.	1 837 000	157	19.2
	Soc.	1 964 000	129	20.5
	Rep. U.	1 233 000	76	12.9
	Rep. (left)	1 300 000	72	13.6
	Rad. Ind.	956 000	62	10.0
1936	Centre party	2 536 000⎫	222	25.8
	Right-wing	1 666 000⎭		16.9
	Soc.	1 955 000	149	19.9
	Rad. Soc.	1 423 000	109	14.5
	Communist	1 502 000	72	15.3
1945	Communist⎫ Progressive⎭	5 005 000	148	26.1
	Soc.	4 561 000	134	23.8
	Chr. Dem.	4 780 000	141	24.9

		Votes per party	*Seats*	*% of votes*
1946(1)	Chr. Dem.	5 589 000	160	28.1
	Communist ⎫ Progressive ⎭	5 119 000	146	25.7
	Soc.	4 188 000	115	21.1
1946(2)	Communist ⎫ Progressive ⎭	5 489 000	166	28.6
	Chr. Dem.	5 058 000	158	26.3
	Soc.	3 432 000	90	17.9
	Moderates	2 566 000	70	13.4
1951	Gaulliste	4 125 000	107	21.6
	Com. and Prog.	5 057 000	97	26.4
	Soc.	2 745 000	94	14.3
	Moderates	2 657 000	87	13.9
	Chr. Dem.	2 370 000	82	12.4
1956	Com. and Prog.	5 514 000	147	25.8
	Moderates	3 258 000	95	15.2
	Soc.	3 247 000	88	15.2
	Rep. Front ⎫ Radicals	1 996 000		9.3
	Right ⎬		73	
	Centre ⎭ Radicals	838 000		3.9
	Chr. Dem.	2 366 000	71	11.1
1958	Gaulliste	4 165 000	198	20.4
	Moderates	4 502 000	133	22.1
	Chr. Dem.	2 273 000	57	11.1
	Soc.	3 194 000	44	15.7
	Com. and Prog.	3 908 000	10	19.2
1962	Gaulliste	5 847 000	234	31.9
	Soc.	2 320 000	64	12.6
	Com. and Prog.	3 992 000	41	21.7
	Moderates	1 743 000	37	9.6
	Chr. Dem.	1 635 000	37	8.9
1967	Gaulliste	8 454 000	232	37.7
	Dem. Soc. Fed.	4 207 000	116	18.8
	Com. and Prog.	5 030 000	72	22.4
1968	Gaulliste	10 201 024	349	46.1
	Communist	4 435 357	33	20.0
	F.G.D.S.	3 654 003	57	16.5
	Moderates	2 700 864	31	12.2
1973	Communists	4 438 834	73	20.6
	PSU, extreme left	85 678		0.3
	Socialists	4 722 886		21.9
	Other Left	823 084	102	3.8

	Votes per party		Seats	% of votes
	Reformers	1 325 058	34	6.1
	URP UDR	6 730 147	183	31.3
	Ind Rep.	1 658 060	55	7.7
	CDP	841 576	30	3.9
	Various	706 942		3.2
	Others	139 236	13*	0.6
1977	RPR	6 651 756	154	26.1
	UDF	5 907 603	124	23.2
	Communists	4 744 868	86	18.6
	Socialists	7 212 916 ⎫	103	28.3
	Left Radicals	595 478 ⎭		2.3
	Other Parties (inc	357 418 ⎫	14	0.2
	Presidential Majority)	305 763 ⎭		1.2
1981	Socialists + Left Radicals	9 198 332	285	
	RPR	4 191 482	85	
	UDF	3 481 849	65	
	Communists	1 303 587	44	
	Other Right-wing	408 861	8	
	Other Left-wing	112 481	4	
	Extreme Left	3 517	–	

* unaffiliated (non-inscrits)

GERMANY

From 1918–33, direct proportional elections by list system with a uniform quota of 60 000 votes for one representative. Suffrage for all men and women over 20. From 1933 to 1945 there were three elections, but these are not recognized as free elections and no figures are given.

	Votes per party		Seats	% of votes
1919	SPD	11 509 100	163	37.9
	BVP	5 980 200	91	19.7
	DDP	5 641 800	75	18.6
	DNVP	3 121 500	44	10.3
1920	SPD	6 104 400	102	21.6
	BVP	5 083 600	85	17.8
	USPD	5 046 800	84	18.0
	DVP	3 929 400	65	14.0
1924	SPD	6 008 900	100	20.5
	DNVP	5 696 500	95	19.5
	BVP	4 861 100	81	16.6
	KPD	3 693 300	62	12.6

		Votes per party	Seats	% of votes
1924	SPD	7 881 000	131	26.0
	DNVP	6 205 800	103	20.5
	BVP	5 252 900	88	17.3
	DVP	3 049 100	51	10.7
1928	SPD	9 153 000	153	29.8
	BVP	4 657 800	78	15.2
	DNVP	4 381 600	73	14.2
	KPD	3 264 800	54	10.6
1930	SPD	8 577 700	143	24.5
	NSDAP	6 409 600	107	18.3
	BVP	5 187 000	87	14.8
	KPD	4 592 100	77	13.1
1932	NSDAP	13 745 800	230	37.4
	SPD	7 959 700	133	21.6
	BVP	5 782 000	97	15.7
	KPD	5 282 600	89	14.6
1932	NSDAP	11 737 000	196	33.1
	SPD	7 248 000	121	20.4
	KPD	5 980 200	100	16.9
	BVP	5 325 200	90	15.0
	DNVP	2 959 000	52	8.8
1933	NSDAP	17 277 200	288	43.9
	SPD	7 181 600	120	18.3
	BVP	5 498 500	92	13.9
	KPD	4 848 100	81	12.3
	DNVP	3 136 800	52	8.0

GERMAN DEMOCRATIC REPUBLIC

Electors vote at 18 and may be candidates at 21. Elections to the People's Chamber (*Volkskammer*) are 'universal, equal, direct and secret' and are held every four years. East Berlin has its own Assembly (*Ostberliner Abgeordenetenhaus*) of 200 and does not elect to the *Volkskammer*. However, it nominates 66 representatives thereto without voting rights.

There are 434 seats in the *Volkskammer* (500 in all when the East Berlin nominees are added). The parties are represented in pre-arranged proportions. Since 1967 more candidates have been allowed to stand than there are seats. All candidates who receive more than 50% of the votes are considered elected; those in excess of the number of seats are placed on a reserve list in order of votes gained. As well as to parties, seats are allotted to social and cultural organizations, *e.g.* to trade unions.

The *Volkskammer* evolved through a series of People's Congresses dominated by the USSR and East German Communists which claimed to speak for all Germany. At the *Länder* elections of Oct 46 the SED failed to gain 50% of the vote and elections thereafter were conducted on the Soviet single-list model.

	Electorate	Valid votes	Seats	
1949	13 533 071	12 887 234	SED	90
			CDU	45
			LDPD	45
			NDPD	15
			DBP	15
			others	130

These elections resulted in the 3rd People's Congress of 1525 delegates, which elected from among its members a German People's Council of 330 on 3 May 49.

On 7 Oct 49 the formation of a go-it-alone German Democratic Republic was announced and the People's Council became the Provisional *Volkskammer* of 400 representatives.

West Germany declared the GDR illegal in that it was not founded upon free elections. (West Germany and the Western Allies still do not recognize East Germany *de jure*.)

An upper chamber of representatives of provinces (*Länderkammer*) was formed in 1949 but abolished in 1958. The term 'Provisional' was dropped from the title of the *Volkskammer* after that Chamber had been confirmed by the 1950 elections.

	Electorate	Valid votes	Seats	
1950	12 331 905	12 139 932	SED	100
			CDU	60
			LDPD	60
			NDPD	30
			others	150
1954	12 085 380	11 892 849	SED	102
			CDU	47
			LDPD	46
			NDPD	45
			DBD	45
			others	115
1958	11 839 217	11 707 715	SED	102
			CDU	47
			LDPD	46
			NDPD	45
			DBD	45
			others	115

At the 1963 elections the electorate was 11 621 158 (valid votes, 11 533 859); 1967, 11 341 729 (11 208 816); 1971, 11 401 090 (11 227 535). The distribution

143

of seats in all 3 elections was the same: SED, 128; CDU, 52; LDPD, 52; NDPD, 52; DBP, 52; others 164.

In elections held on 17 October 1976, of the total electorate of 11 425 194 some 11 262 948 (98.58%) cast their vote. Of the valid votes, 99.85% were cast for the National Front list.

In elections held on 14 June 1981, of the total electorate of 12 356 263 some 12 255 006 (99.21%) cast their vote. Of the valid votes, 99.86% were cast for the National Front list.

GREECE

Voting procedures. Party list system in electoral departments. Direct election, majority vote. Universal male suffrage. From 1926, proportional representation until 1928, and then again for the election of Sep 32 and the elections of Jan 36, Mar 46, Mar 50, Sep 51 and May 58 onwards. Vote extended to women in 1955.

	Votes per party		Seats	% of votes
1926	Liberals	303 140	102	31.6
	Populists	194 243	60	20.3
	Freedom Party	151 044	51	15.8
1928	Liberals	477 502	178	46.9
	Pro-Liberals	74 976	25	2.5
	Workers and Agrarian	68 278	20	6.7
	Populists	243 543	19	23.9
1932	Liberals	391 521	98	33.4
	Populists	395 974	95	33.8
	Progressive	97 836	15	8.4
1933	Populists	434 550	118	38.1
	Liberals	379 968	80	33.3
1935	Populists ⎱ Nat. Radical ⎰	669 434	287	65.0
	Royalists	152 285	7	14.8
1936	Liberals	474 651	126	37.3
	Populists	281 597	72	22.1
	Populists and Rad. Union	253 384	60	19.9
1946	Nationalist (union of Populists, Nat. Lib., Reformist and others)	610 995	206	55.1
	Nat. Pol. Union (Venizelos Liberals, Soc. Dem., Nat. United Party and others)	213 721	68	19.3
	Liberals	159 525	48	14.4

	Votes per party		*Seats*	*% of votes*
1950	Populists	317 512	62	18.8
	Liberals	291 083	56	17.2
	Nat. Prog. Union	277 739	45	16.4
	Papandreou Party (ex-Soc. Dem.)	180 185	35	10.7
1951	Hellene Party	624 316	114	36.5
	Nat. Prog. Union	401 379	74	23.5
	Liberals	325 390	57	19.0
1952	Hellenes	783 541	247	49.2
	Nat. Prog. Union } Liberals	544 834	51	34.2
1956	Nat. Rad. Union	1 594 112	165	47.4
	Dem. Union (Populists, Liberals, Nat. Prog. Union, Agrarians and Centre)	1 620 007	132	48.2
1958	Nat. Rad. Union	1 583 885	171	41.2
	United Democratic Left	939 902	79	24.4
	Liberals	795 445	36	20.7
1961	Nat. Rad. Union	2 347 824	176	50.8
	Centre Union } Progressives	1 555 442	100	33.7
	Un. Dem. Left (under title Pandemocratic Agrarian Front)	675 867	24	14.6
1963	Centre Union	1 962 079	138	42.0
	Nat. Rad. Union	1 837 377	132	39.4
	Un. Dem. Left	669 267	28	14.3
1964	Centre Union	2 424 477	171	52.7
	Nat. Rad. Union } Progressives	1 621 546	108	35.3
	Un. Dem. Left	542 865	21	11.8

Note: On 21 April 67 dictatorial power was seized by right wing army colonels, aiming to forestall the expected electoral victory of the Centre Union under George Papandreou. Democracy was restored in 1974 when Constantine Karamanlis returned from exile in Paris to head a government of National Unity.

	Votes per party		*Seats*	*% of votes*
1974	New Democracy	2 670 804	220	54.4
	Panhellenic Socialist Union	666 806	12	13.6
	Centre Union	1 002 908	60	20.4
	Communists/United Left	464 331	8	9.4
	National Democratic Union	54 162	–	1.1
	Others	53 345	–	1.1
1977	New Democracy	2 146 687	172	41.8
	Panhellenic Socialist Movement	1 299 196	93	25.3

Votes per party		Seats	% of votes
Democratic Centre Union	613 113	15	11.9
Communist Party (KKE)	480 188	11	9.4
Left-Wing and Progressive Alliance	139 762	2	2.7
Others	405 411	7	7.9
1981 Panhellenic Socialist Movement	2 725 395	172	48.1
New Democracy	2 033 774	115	35.9
Communists (KKE exterior)	619 296	13	10.9
Progressive Party	95 697	–	1.7
KKE (interior)	77 465	–	1.4
Others	119 314	–	2.0

HUNGARY

Before its extensive territorial reduction in 1918 the kingdom of Hungary formed part of the Austro-Hungarian empire. It had no codified written constitution. There was a bicameral parliament (*Országház*), but only 6% of the population possessed the vote.

Towards the close of the war M. Károlyi's Party of Independence emerged on the political scene, standing for independence from Austria and unilateral withdrawal from hostilities. At a time of popular unrest Károlyi was appointed prime minister on 31 Oct 18, leading a coalition government of Party of Independence, Radicals and Social Democrats. On 13 Nov 18 King Charles IV renounced participation in affairs of state, and on 16 Nov 18 Hungary was proclaimed a Republic with Károlyi as provisional President (he became President on 11 Jan 19). Parliament was dissolved and replaced by a provisional unicameral National Assembly.

This government resigned on 22 Mar 19 in protest at Allied territorial demands, and was succeeded by a Soviet republic of Communists and Social Democrats led by Béla Kun. Elections to the Soviets were held on 17 Apr 19. The Communist régime was short-lived and harassed by hostilities with foreign invaders and native anti-Communist forces. Kun resigned on 1 Aug 19, and Romania occupied Budapest until M. Horthy entered on 16 Nov 19 at the head of an anti-Communist army.

At Allied insistence an election with universal secret suffrage was held on 25 Jan 20. The Christian Nationalists (government party) gained 77 seats, the Smallholders 49. The Social Democrats refused to take part in the election.

This government annulled all Károlyi's and Kun's legislation and re-established the former constitution. The link with Austria was dissolved. On 23 Mar 20 Hungary was proclaimed a kingdom again; Horthy had been chosen as regent on 1 Mar 20.

This government decreed a new electoral system. The upper house (House of Magnates) was re-established. Secret ballot was abolished except in towns (20% of constituencies were urban). Some 1.5m. lost the vote. Educational, property and residence qualifications were introduced. Men voted at 24, women at 30. Candidates had to be nominated by 10 000 electors. The National Assembly was to consist of 245 deputies.

On 7 Mar and 29 Oct 21 Charles IV made unsuccessful attempts to regain the throne.

At the elections of 28 May and 2 June 22 Smallholders and Christian Nationalists combined to form the Party of National Unity, which gained 143 seats. The opposition parties gained 78 (including 25 Social Democrats).

An electoral law of 11 Nov 26 gave definitive form to the House of Magnates, which was to consist of nominated members of the nobility and upper middle class, and other dignitaries. A small proportion of members were elected for ten-year terms.

1926   Party of National Unity, 171; Christian Social Union, 35; Social Democrats, 14; others, 25.

1931   Party of National Unity, 155; Christian Social Union, 32; Social Democrats, 14; Independent Smallholders, 11; independents, 21; others, 12.

1935   Party of National Unity, 170; Independent Smallholders, 23; Christian Social Union, 14; Social Democrats, 11.

By an electoral law of Dec 38 residential and educational qualifications were made stricter, and male voting age raised from 24 to 26. In order to vote women over 30 had to be self-supporting or the wives of electors. The number of deputies was raised to 260. 135 single-member constituencies were formed, election requirement being a simple majority over 40%. Multi-member constituencies elected the remainder on a proportional representation scheme.

Secret ballot was introduced in May 39, and many Jews were disenfranchised.

1939   Party of Hungarian Life (formerly Party of National Unity) in alliance, 186; Christian Union, 3; Arrow Cross (fascists), 29; Independent Smallholders, 14; National Social Front Union, 5; Citizens' Freedom Party, 5; Social Democrats, 5; Racialists, 4; National Front, 3; Christian National Social Front, 3; People's Will, 1; Independents, 2.

During the war an Independence Front began to take shape of Social Democrats, crypto-Communists, Smallholders, National Peasants and Legitimists.

With the Soviet invasion a provisional government was set up at Debrecen on 21 Dec 44, which ultimately consisted of 127 Communists, 123 Smallholders, 94 Social Democrats, 63 Trade Unionists, 39 National Peasants, 22 Democrats and 30 independents.

By an electoral law of 19 Sep 45 universal secret suffrage at 20 was introduced.

		Votes	Seats
1945	Smallholders	2 688 161	245
	Social Democrats	821 566	69
	Communists	800 257	70
	National Peasants	322 988	23
	Democrats	78 522	2
			409

1947 Electorate: 5 407 893. Voted: 4 996 100 (93%). Seats 411.

Government bloc	Votes	Seats
Communists	1 082 497	100
Smallholders	757 821	68
Social Democrats	732 178	67
National Peasants	435 170	36
	3 007 027	271

Opposition	Votes	Seats
Popular Democrats	805 450	60
Hungarian Independence Party	718 193	49
Independent Democrats	256 396	18
Radicals	93 270	6
Christian Women's Union	67 792	4
Citizen Democrats	48 055	3
	1 989 156	140

During the next two years the opposition parties were eliminated or amalgamated into the People's Front. The Social Democrats merged into the Communists in June 48. At the election of 15 May 49 candidates were presented on a single list, the People's Front. Electorate: 6 053 972. Voted: 5 730 519 (94.6%). For the People's Front. 5 478 515 (95.6%).

A new constitution of Soviet type was promulgated on 18 Aug 49. Hungary was proclaimed a 'People's Republic'. Voting age was lowered to 18. The National Assembly was to be elected every four years by universal secret suffrage.

At the election of 17 May 53 there was a single list of People's Front.

Electorate: 6 501 869. Voted: 6 370 519 (98%). Votes for People's Front: 6 256 653 (98.2%).

On 27 Oct 56 there was a major reorganization of the government in response to armed insurrection: independent Smallholders and National Peasants were co-opted in. Revolutionary councils sprang up demanding a free general election. On 30 Oct 56 I. Nagy proclaimed the restoration of multi-party government. On 3 Nov 56 the government was reorganized as a coalition of Communists, Smallholders, National Peasants and Social Democrats.

This government was overthrown by armed Soviet intervention and a 'Revolutionary Worker-Peasant government' set up under J. Kádár.

At the election of 16 Nov 58, 6 493 680 voted (98.4% of electorate). For People's Patriotic Front: 6 431 832 (99.6%). There were 338 candidates for 338 seats.

At the election of 24 Feb 63 the electorate was 7 114 855. Voted: 6 915 644 (97.2%). Voted for the single list of People's Patriotic Front 6 813 058 (98.9%). 340 deputies elected.

On 11 Nov 66 an electoral law brought an end to the strict rigidity of the one seat – one candidate system by replacing the 20 multi-seat mega-constituencies by 349 single-member constituencies. All candidates remained nominees of the People's Patriotic Front, but it became possible for more than one candidate to contest a single seat.

In the election of 19 Mar 67 this happened in nine constituencies. None of the nine challengers was elected. 7 131 151 votes were cast (99.7% of the electorate) and 98.8% of these were for the People's Patriotic Front candidates.

In Oct 70 another electoral law liberalized the position further by introducing the participation of the ordinary citizenry in the nomination of candidates. In the election of 25 Apr 70, 49 seats were contested by more than one candidate. Electorate: 7 432 420. Voted: 7 334 918 (98.7%). Voted for the People's Patriotic Front: 7 258 121 (98.9%). 352 deputies were elected.

In elections held on 15 June 1975, 7 527 169 votes were cast (97.6% of a total electorate of 7 760 464). Of these, 99.6% of votes were cast for official candidates.

In elections held on June 1980, only 15 of the 352 seats were contested by more than one candidate. Of the 7.7 million who voted, 99.3% of votes cast were for the official People's Patriotic Front.

ICELAND

Voting procedures. From 1915–20, the Althing had 40 members directly elected, 6 proportionally and 34 by majority. Majority elections were in 25 constituencies, 9 of them two-member, the rest single. Suffrage for the election of 34 members, all men and women property-holders over 25; for the 6, all those over 35. From 1920 onwards the Althing had additional members, including some elected by direct proportional election in Reykjavic. From 1934, suffrage extended to all men and women over 21 'in charge of their own finances and properties'.

	Votes per party		Seats	% of votes
1923	Citizens Party	16 272	21	53.6
	Progressives	8 062	13	26.6
	Soc. Dems.	4 912	1	16.2
1927	Progressives	9 532	17	29.8
	Liberals	15 474	13	5.8
	Conservatives			42.0
	Soc. Dem.	6 097	4	19.1
1931	Progressives	13 844	12	35.9
	Independence	16 891	21	43.8
1933	Independence	17 131	17	48.0
	Progressives	8 530	14	23.9
1934	Independence	21 974	20	42.3
	Progressives	11 377	15	21.9
	Soc. Dem.	11 269	10	21.7
1937	Progressives	14 556	19	24.9
	Independence	24 132	17	41.3
	Soc. Dem.	11 084	8	19.0
1942(1)	Progressives	16 033	20	27.6
	Independence	22 975	17	39.5
	United Soc.	11 059	10	18.5
1942(2)	Independence	23 001	20	38.5
	Progressives	15 869	15	26.6
	United Soc.	11 059	10	18.5
1946	Independence	26 428	20	39.4
	Progressives	15 429	13	23.1
	United Soc.	13 049	10	19.5
	Soc. Dem.	11 914	9	17.8
1949	Independence	28 546	19	39.5
	Progressives	17 659	17	24.5
	United Soc.	14 077	9	19.5
1953	Independence	28 738	21	37.1
	Progressives	16 959	16	21.9
	United Soc.	12 422	7	16.1
1956	Independence	35 027	19	42.4
	Progressives	12 925	17	15.6
	People's Un.	15 859	8	19.2
	Soc. Dem.	15 153	8	18.3

	Votes per party		*Seats*	*% of votes*
1959(1)	Independence	36 029	20	42.5
	Progressives	23 061	19	27.2
	People's Un.	12 929	7	15.3
1959(2)	Independence	33 800	24	39.7
	Progressives	21 882	17	25.7
	People's Un.	13 621	10	16.0
	Soc. Dem.	12 909	9	15.2
1963	Independence	37 021	24	41.4
	Progressives	25 217	19	28.2
	People's Un.	14 274	9	16.0
1967	Independence	36 036	23	37.5
	Progressives	27 029	18	28.1
	People's Un.	13 403	9	13.9
	Soc. Dem.	15 059	9	15.7
1971	Independence	38 170	22	36.2
	Progressives	26 645	17	25.3
	People's Un.	18 055	10	17.1
	Soc. Dem.	11 020	6	10.5
1974	Independence	48 758	25	42.8
	People's Alliance	20 922	11	18.3
	Soc. Dem.	10 321	5	9.1
	Progressives	28 388	17	24.9
	Liberal and Leftist Union	5 244	2	4.6
1978	Independence	39 973	20	32.7
	People's Alliance	27 962	14	22.9
	Soc. Dem.	26 912	14	22.0
	Progressives	20 561	12	16.9
	Liberal and Leftist Union	na	0	3.5
1979	Independence	42 957	21	33.6
	People's Alliance	24 390	11	19.1
	Soc. Dem.	27 078	10	21.2
	Progressives	30 871	17	24.2
	Others	2 433	1	1.9
1983	Independence	50 251	23	38.7
	Progressives	24 095	14	18.5
	People's Alliance	22 490	10	17.3
	Soc. Dem.	15 214	6	11.7
	Soc. Dem. Alliance	9 489	4	7.3
	Others	8 423	3	6.5

IRELAND

Voting procedures. From 1918–21, single-member constituencies, spot voting and plurality counting. From 1921, multi-member constituencies with preferential voting and quota counting. Suffrage for men of 21 and over, and women of 30 and over, until 1923 when the age limit for both was 21. From 1918–23, University graduates and owners of businesses had extra votes.

	Electorate	Valid votes	Votes per party		Seats	% of electorate	% of votes
1918	1 936 673	1 046 541	Sinn Fein	496 961	73	–	47.5
			Unionists	298 726	26	–	28.5
			Nationalists	233 690	6		22.3
1921	–	–	Sinn Fein	–	124	–	–
			Unionists	–	4		

(Note: This was not a normal election; no poll took place; all borough and county seats were taken by Sinn Fein and the Unionists were returned for Dublin University.)

	Electorate	Valid votes	Votes per party		Seats	% of electorate	% of votes
1922	1 026 289	627 623	Pro-Treaty	245 336	58	–	39.1
		(first preference)	Anti-Treaty	134 801	36	–	21.5
			Labour	132 511	17		21.1

(Note: Pro- and Anti-Treaty parties were the result of the division of Sinn Fein.)

	Electorate	Valid votes	Votes per party		Seats	% of electorate	% of votes
1923	1 785 436	1 052 495	Fine Gael	409 184	63	22.9	38.9
			Fianna Fail	291 191	44	16.3	27.7
			Labour	130 659	16	7.3	12.4
1927(1)	1 730 426	1 146 460	Fine Gael	314 711	46	18.2	27.5
			Fianna Fail	299 476	44	17.3	26.1
			Labour	159 046	23	9.2	13.9
1927(2)	1 728 340	1 170 856	Fine Gael	453 013	61	26.2	38.7
			Fianna Fail	411 833	57	23.8	35.2
			Labour	111 287	13	6.4	9.5
1932	1 601 933	1 274 026	Fianna Fail	566 498	72	33.5	44.5
			Fine Gael	449 506	56	26.6	35.3
			Independents	106 466	12	6.3	8.4
			Labour	114 163	9	6.7	9.0
1933	1 724 420	1 386 558	Fianna Fail	689 054	76	40.0	49.7
			Fine Gael	422 495	48	24.5	30.5
			Labour	88 347	9	5.1	6.4
1937	1 775 055	1 324 449	Fianna Fail	599 040	68	33.7	45.2
			Fine Gael	461 171	48	26.0	34.8
			Labour	147 728	15	8.3	11.2
1938	1 697 323	1 286 259	Fianna Fail	667 996	76	39.4	51.9
			Fine Gael	428 633	45	25.3	33.3
			Labour	140 099	9	8.3	10.9
1943	1 816 142	1 331 709	Fianna Fail	557 525	66	30.7	41.9
			Fine Gael	307 499	32	16.9	23.1
			Labour	214 743	17	11.8	16.1
1944	1 776 850	1 217 349	Fianna Fail	595 259	75	33.5	48.9
			Fine Gael	249 329	30	14.0	20.5
			Labour	140 245	12	7.9	11.5

	Electorate	Valid votes	Votes per party		Seats	% of electorate	% of votes
1948	1 800 210	1 323 443	Fianna Fail	553 914	67	30.8	41.9
			Fine Gael	262 393	31	14.6	19.8
			Labour	150 229	19	8.3	11.4
1951	1 785 144	1 331 573	Fianna Fail	161 212	68	34.5	46.3
			Fine Gael	342 922	40	19.2	25.8
			Labour	151 828	16	8.5	11.4
1954	1 763 209	1 335 202	Fianna Fail	578 960	65	32.8	43.4
			Fine Gael	427 031	50	24.2	32.0
			Labour	163 982	18	9.3	12.3
1957	1 738 278	1 227 019	Fianna Fail	592 994	78	34.1	48.3
			Fine Gael	326 699	40	18.8	26.6
			Labour	111 747	11	6.4	9.1
1961	1 670 860	1 168 404	Fianna Fail	512 073	70	30.6	43.8
			Fine Gael	374 099	47	22.4	32.0
			Labour	139 822	16	8.4	12.0
1965	1 683 019	1 253 122	Fianna Fail	597 414	72	35.4	47.7
			Fine Gael	427 081	47	25.4	34.1
			Labour	192 740	22	11.5	15.4
1969	1 735 388	1 318 953	Fianna Fail	602 234	75	34.7	45.7
			Fine Gael	449 749	50	25.9	34.1
			Labour	224 498	18	12.9	17.0
1973			Fianna Fail	624 530	69		
			Fine Gael	473 779	54		
			Labour	185 117	19		
			Others	67 111	2		

In the four elections of 1977–1982, the seats won were as follows:

	1977	1981	1982 (Feb)	1982(Nov)
Fianna Fail	34	78	81	75
Fine Gael	43	65	66	70
Labour	17	15	15	16
Independents	4	8	7	5

ITALY

The elections of 1919 and 1921 were fought on adult male suffrage and the
d'Hondt system of proportional representation. The election of 1924 was not a
free election because of Fascist intimidation. After 1945, the new Constitution
provided for a bicameral Parliament, with a minimum voting age of 21.
Deputies are chosen by proportional representation using the *Imperiali*
system.

	Votes per party		*Seats*	*% of votes*
1919	Socialist	1 834 792	156	32.3
	Popular	1 167 354	100	20.5
	Centre coalition	904 195	96	15.9
	Democrats	622 310	60	10.9
1921	Socialist	1 631 435	123	24.7
	Popular	1 377 008	108	20.4
	Nat. Bloc.	1 260 007	105	19.1
	Lib. Dem.	684 855	68	10.4
1924	Fascist	4 671 550	375	65.3
	Popular	645 789	39	9.0
1946	Chris. Dem.	8 101 004	207	35.2
	Socialist	4 758 129	115	20.7
	Communist	4 356 686	104	18.9
1948	Chris. Dem.	12 741 299	305	48.5
	Communist[1] Socialist }	8 137 047	183	31.0
1953	Chris. Dem.	10 864 282	263	40.1
	Communist	6 121 922	143	22.6
	Socialist	3 441 305	75	12.7
	Monarchist	1 855 843	30	6.9
1958	Chris. Dem.	12 520 556	273	42.4
	Communist	6 704 763	140	22.7
	Socialist	4 206 777	84	14.2
1963	Chris. Dem.	11 763 418	260	38.3
	Communist	7 763 854	166	25.3
	Socialist	4 251 966	87	13.8
1968	Chris. Dem.	12 441 553	266	39.1
	Communist	8 557 404	177	26.9
	Socialist	4 605 832	91	14.5
1972	Chris. Dem.	12 943 675	267	38.8
	Communist	9 085 927	179	27.2
	Socialist	4 925 700	89	14.7
1976	Chris. Dem.	14 211 005	262	38.7
	Communists	12 620 509	228	34.4
	Socialists	3 541 383	57	9.6
	Social Democrats	1 237 483	15	3.4
	Republicans	1 134 648	14	3.1
	Liberals	478 157	5	1.3
	Italian Social Movement	2 243 849	35	6.1
	Others	1 248 543	14	3.4
1979	Chris. Dem.	14 007 594	262	38.3
	Communists	11 107 883	201	30.4
	Socialists	3 586 256	62	9.8
	Italian Social Movement	1 924 251	30	5.3
	Social Democrats	1 403 873	20	3.8

[1] Under the name Democratic Popular Front

Votes per party		Seats	% of votes
Republicans	1 106 766	16	3.0
Liberals and Radicals	1 967 384	27	5.3
Others	1 462 578	12	4.1
1983	Chris. Dem.	12 145 800	225	32.9
	Communists	11 028 158	198	29.9
	Socialists	4 222 487	73	11.4
	Italian Social Movement	2 511 722	42	6.8
	Republicans	1 872 536	29	5.1
	Social Democrats	1 507 431	23	4.1
	Liberals and Radicals	1 875 505	27	5.1
	Others	1 726 642	13	4.7

LATVIA

A Constituent Assembly in May 1920 established a parliament (*Saeima*) of 100 deputies to be elected every three years. Elections were held in 1922, 1925, 1928 and 1931. The system favoured a proliferation of parties: 22 in 1922; 27 in 1925; 25 in 1928 and 24 in 1931. The more numerous parties were, from right to left: Farmers' Union; Catholics; Democratic Centre; New Settlers; Right-wing Socialists; Social Democrats. The Communist Party was illegal, but ran as the Workers' Bloc in 1931, gaining seven seats. The Social Democrats had 30 deputies in each government, except that of 1931, when they had 22. There were Jewish, Polish, Russian and German national minority parties, and a fascist party, Thunder Cross (*Perkonkrusts*).

On 15 May 32 Ulmanis assumed dictatorial powers by dismissing the Saeima and prohibiting all party political activity.

The country was occupied by Soviet troops on 16 June 40 and an election was held on 14 and 15 July 40. The resultant People's *Saeima* voted unanimously for incorporation into the USSR.

LITHUANIA

On 22 Sep 17 a congress of 214 Lithuanian delegates elected a 20-strong council (*Taryba*) which proclaimed independence and organized elections for a Constituent Assembly. These were held by universal suffrage on the proportional representation system on 15 May 20. One representative stood for 15 000 inhabitants. There were 112 seats in the Constituent Assembly, distributed as follows: Christian Democrats, 59; Social Populist Democrats, 29; Social Democrats, 13; Jews, 6; Poles, 3; Independents, 2.

This enacted that a parliament (*Semias*) of 80 was to be elected every three years by universal suffrage on the proportional representation system, one deputy representing 25 000 electors.

At the elections of 10 Oct 22 the results were: Christian Democrats (including the Farmers' Union and the Workers' Federation), 38; Social Populist Democrats, 19; Social Democrats, 11; Workers' Party, 5; Jews, 3; Poles, 2. A Stulginskis was elected President.

A further election was held on 5 June 23: Christian Democrats, 40; Social Populist Democrats, 16; Social Democrats, 8; Jews, 5; Poles, 5; Germans, 2; Russians, 2.

Elections 8 and 10 May 26: Christian Democrats, 30; Socialist Populist Democrats, 22; Social Democrats, 15; Poles, 4; Jews, 3; Germans, 1; and from Memel (Klaipeda) Agrarians, 3; People's Party, 2.

By a *coup d'état* of 17 Dec 26, A. Smetona assumed dictatorial powers as President, and parliamentary government lapsed.

MALTA

In the first elections held after independence (held in 1966), the Nationalists under Dr Borg Olivier won 28 seats, the Labour Party won 22. Thereafter the results were as follows:

	Votes per party		*Seats*	% of votes
1971	Malta Labour	85 448	28	50.8
	Nationalist Party	80 753	27	48.1
	Others	1756	–	–
1976	Malta Labour Party	105 854	34	51.5
	Nationalist Party	99 551	31	48.5
	Independent	35	–	–
1981	Malta Labour Party	109 990	34	49.1
	Nationalist Party	114 132	31	50.9

THE NETHERLANDS

Voting procedures. Direct proportional elections on the party list system. Elections to 100 seats, the rest allocated according to the greatest remainder vote. Suffrage for men over 25, until 1922 when it was extended to women the same age. In 1946, extended to all citizens 23 and over and in 1967 all citizens over 21.

	Votes per party		*Seats*	% of votes
1918	RKS	402 908	30	30.0
	S-DA-P	296 145	22	22.0
	PvV	202 972	15	15.1
	ARP	179 523	13	13.4

	Votes per party		Seats	% of votes
1922	RKS	874 745	32	29.9
	S-DA-P	567 769	20	19.4
	ARP	402 277	16	13.7
1925	RKS	883 333	30	28.6
	S-DA-P	706 689	24	22.9
	ARP	377 426	13	12.2
1929	RKS	1 001 589	30	29.6
	S-DA-P	804 714	24	23.9
	ARP	391 832	12	11.6
	CHU	354 548	11	10.5
1933	RKS	1 037 364	28	27.9
	S-DA-P	798 632	22	21.5
	ARP	499 892	14	13.4
1937	RKS	1 170 431	31	28.8
	S-DA-P	890 661	23	22.0
	ARP	665 501	17	16.4
1946	KV	1 466 582	32	30.8
	PvA	1 347 940	29	28.3
	ARP	614 201	13	12.9
1948	KV	1 531 154	32	31.0
	PvA	1 263 058	27	25.6
	ARP	651 612	13	13.2
1952	KV	1 529 508	30	28.7
	PvA	1 545 867	30	29.0
	ARP	603 329	12	11.3
1956	PvA	1 872 209	50	32.7
	KV	1 529 508	49	31.7
	ARP	567 535	15	9.9
1959	KV	1 895 914	49	31.6
	PvA	1 821 825	48	30.3
	VVD	732 658	19	12.2
	ARP	563 091	14	9.4
1963	KV	1 993 352	50	31.9
	PvA	1 753 084	43	28.0
	VVD	643 839	16	10.3
	ARP	545 836	13	8.7
	CHU	536 801	13	8.6
1967	KV	1 822 904	42	26.5
	PvA	1 620 112	37	23.5
	VVD	738 202	17	10.7
	ARP	681 060	15	9.9
1971	KV	1 379 672	35	21.8
	PvA	1 554 280	39	24.6
	VVD	653 370	16	10.3
	ARP	542 742	13	8.6

		Votes per party	Seats	% of votes
1972	KV	1 305 401	27	17.7
	PvA	2 021 454	43	27.3
	VVD	1 068 375	22	14.4
	ARP	653 609	14	8.8
1977	CDA	2 652 278	49	31.9
	PvdA	2 813 793	53	33.8
	VVD	1 492 689	28	17.9
	D-66	452 423	8	5.4
	PSP	77 972	1	0.9
	CPN	143 481	2	1.7
	Others	684 976	9	8.2
1981	CDA	2 676 525	48	30.8
	PvdA	2 455 424	44	28.3
	VVD	1 504 293	26	17.3
	D-66	959 661	17	11.0
	PSP	184 039	3	2.1
	CPN	178 147	3	2.0
	Others	728 298	9	8.5
1982	PvdA	2 499 562	47	30.4
	CDA	2 141 176	45	29.3
	VVD	1 897 986	36	23.0
	D-66	355 830	6	4.3
	PSP	187 150	3	2.3
	SGP	156 782	3	1.9
	CPN	147 510	3	1.8
	PPR	136 095	2	1.6
	RPF	124 018	2	1.5
	Others	313 711	3	3.8

NORWAY

Voting procedures. Direct proportional elections in multi-member constituencies. Suffrage for men and women over 23 until 1949, when it was extended to men and women over 21.

		Votes per party	Seats	% of votes
1918	Left	187 657	51	28.3
	Right	101 325	50	30.4
	Labour	209 560	18	31.6
1921	Right	301 372	57	33.3
	Left	181 989	37	20.1
	Labour	192 616	29	21.3
	Agrarian	18 657	17	13.1
1924	Right	316 846	54	32.5
	Left	180 979	34	18.6
	Labour	179 567	24	18.4
	Agrarian	131 706	22	13.5

	Votes per party		Seats	% of votes
1927	Labour	388 106	59	36.8
	Conservative	240 091	30	24.0
	Liberal	172 568	30	17.3
	Agrarian	149 026	26	14.9
1930	Labour	374 854	47	31.4
	Conservative	327 731	41	21.1
	Liberal	241 355	33	20.2
	Agrarian	190 220	25	15.9
1933	Labour	500 526	69	40.1
	Conservative	252 506	30	20.2
	Liberal	213 153	24	17.1
	Agrarian	173 634	23	13.9
1936	Labour	618 616	70	42.5
	Conservative	310 324	36	21.3
	Liberal	232 784	23	16.0
	Agrarian	168 038	18	11.6
1945	Labour	609 348	76	41.0
	Conservative	252 608	25	27.0
	Liberal	204 852	20	13.8
1949	Labour	803 471	85	45.7
	Conservative	311 819	23	17.7
	Liberal	235 876	21	13.4
1953	Labour	830 448	77	46.7
	Conservative	344 067	27	18.8
	Liberal	177 662	15	10.0
	Chr. People's	186 627	14	10.5
	Agrarian	160 583	14	9.0
1957	Labour	865 675	78	48.3
	Conservative	338 651	29	18.9
	Liberal	173 525	15	9.7
	Agrarian	166 757	15	9.3
1961	Labour	860 526	74	46.8
	Conservative	368 340	29	20.0
	Agrarian	170 645	16	9.3
	Chr. People's	176 896	15	9.6
1965	Labour	883 320	68	43.1
	Conservative	432 025	31	21.1
	Liberal	211 853	18	10.4
	Agrarian	202 396	18	9.9
1969	Labour	1 000 348	74	46.5
	Conservative	406 209	13	18.8
	Liberal	202 553	13	9.4
	Agrarian	194 128	20	9.0
1973	Labour	759 482	62	35.3
	Conservative	375 782	29	17.5
	Centre (Agrarian)	237 073	21	11.0
	Christian Democrats	261 869	20	12.2

	Votes per party		Seats	% of votes
	Left Socialists	241 816	16	11.2
	Liberals	76 155	2	3.5
	Others	200 966	5	9.3
1977	Labour	962 728	76	42.4
	Conservative	560 025	41	24.7
	Centre (Agrarian)	196 005	12	8.6
	Christian Democrats	274 516	22	12.1
	Left Socialists	102 371	2	4.5
	Liberals	73 371	2	3.2
	Others	80 929	–	3.6
1981	Labour	896 796	66	37.6
	Conservative	746 614	53	31.3
	Centre	220 827	10	9.3
	Christian Democrats	160 224	16	6.7
	Left Socialists	116 637	4	4.9
	Progress Party	107 971	4	4.5
	Liberals	92 266	2	3.9
	Others	40 860	–	1.7

POLAND

J. Piłsudski proclaimed independence on 10 Nov 18 and appointed governments on 18 Nov 18 and 16 Jan 19.

Elections to the Sejm (parliament) were held in non-occupied Poland on 26 Jan 19 and supplemented by by-elections in Nov. There were 394 deputies from 14 parties including:

National Democrats and allies (dubbed 'Endecja' from the initials)	140 (of these 116 were National Democrats, *i.e.* 37% of all deputies)
Polish Peasant Party 'Liberation' (*i.e.* left-wing)	71
Polish Peasant Party 'Piast' (*i.e.* right-wing)	46
Polish Socialist Party	35
National Workers' Party	32
National minority parties	13

A constitution was promulgated on 17 Mar 21 by which a bicameral parliament was set up, to be elected by universal suffrage every five years by proportional representation, consisting of a Senate of 111 senators and the Sejm of 444 deputies.

At the elections of 5 and 12 Nov 22 the electorate was 13 109 793 of whom 8 760 195 (67%) voted. Representatives of 15 parties were elected to the Sejm, including:

	Votes	%	Seats
Christian League of National Union	2 551 000	29.1	169
Polish Peasant Party 'Piast'	1 150 000	13.1	70
Polish Peasant Party 'Liberation'	963 000	11	49
Polish Socialist Party	906 000	10.3	41
National Workers' Party	474 000	5.4	18
Polish Centre	260 000	3	6
Communist Party	121 000	1.4	2
National minority parties	1 963 000	22.4	86

On 14 May 26 Piłsudski staged a *coup d'état* and issued a constitution in June which restricted the powers of the Sejm.

At the elections of 4 Mar 28 the electorate was 15m. and 11 408 218 voted.

	Votes	Seats
Non-party pro-Piłsudski Bloc (BBWR)	2 399 032	130
Polish Peasant Party 'Liberation'		66
Polish Socialist Party	1 148 279	63
People's Party (SN; formerly National Democrats)	925 744	37
Polish Peasant Party 'Piast'		21
Christian Democratic Party		19
National Workers' Party		14
Communist Party (illegal, but running under the name 'Union of Town and Country Proletariat')	940 000	8
National minority parties		86

This Sejm was dissolved on 30 Aug 30.

During the campaign before the elections of 16 and 23 Nov 30 opposition politicians were imprisoned.

The electorate was 15 520 342, of whom 13 078 682 voted. 372 deputies were elected to the Sejm, and the number was made up to 444 by allotments according to proportional representation:

	Votes	Seats
Non-party pro-Piłsudski Bloc (BBWR)	5 292 725	247
People's Party (SN)	1 455 399	62
6-Party Centre-Left coalition	1 907 380	
Polish Peasant Party 'Liberation'		33
Polish Socialist Party		24
Christian Democrats		15
Polish Peasant Party 'Piast'		15
National Workers' Party		10
Communist Party		5
National minority parties		33

A new constitution was promulgated on 23 Apr 35. The Sejm was reduced to 208 deputies, elected by universal suffrage at 24 years. The Senate was reduced to 96, of whom one-third were appointed by the President and the remainder elected by a college of 300 000. Methods of election were not changed but district electoral assemblies acquired a decisive role in the designation of candidates.

All political parties boycotted the elections of 8 and 15 Sep 35. The electorate was 16 332 100, of whom according to the government's own figures only 45.9% voted (7 512 102). 153 BBWR members were returned to the Sejm and 22 members of national minority groups.

President Móscicki dissolved Sejm and Senate on 22 Sep 35.

All political parties abstained from the elections of 6 and 13 Nov 38. The turn-out was 67.4%. 161 members of the non-party Camp of National Unity (OZN) were returned to the Sejm.

The liberation of part of Poland from German occupation by Soviet forces enabled the Polish Committee of National Liberation (PKWN) to be set up on 21 July 44, proclaiming itself the sole legal Polish executive power. It was composed of Communists, left-wing socialists, left-wing peasants and Democratic Party representatives. It became the provisional government on 31 Dec 44. At the Yalta conference (Feb 45), it was agreed that a Provisional Government of National Unity should be formed based on this government, and this was done on 28 June 45. It contained Communists (PPR, *i.e.* Polish Workers' Party) and representatives of the Polish Socialist Party (PPS), and the Polish Peasant (PSL), Democratic (SD) and Christian Democratic Labour (SP) parties.

A referendum was held on 30 June 46, at which the electorate were asked to approve (1) the abolition of the Senate, (2) basic nationalization and land reform, (3) the fixing of Poland's borders on the Baltic and the Oder-Neisse line. The turn-out was 80.8% (11 530 551), and affirmative answers were recorded as follows: (1) 68%, (2) 77.2%, (3) 91.4%.

An electoral law of Sep 46 disfranchised collaborators: approximately 1m. people lost their vote in this way.

During the elections of 19 Jan 47 some 12.7m. votes were cast, of which 11 244 873 were valid (89.19% of electorate voted). The Communists together with the Polish Socialist, Peasant and Democratic parties stood as the Democratic Bloc, polling 9m. votes (80.1% of the vote) and gaining 392 seats in the Sejm. Other parties:

	Votes %	Seats
Polish Peasant Party	10.3	27
Christian Labour Party (SP)	4.7	15
Peasant Party 'Liberation'		7
Catholic independents		3

162

On 19 Feb 47 the Sejm passed an interim constitution, which became known as the 'Little Constitution'. A permanent constitution was passed on 22 July 52. This gives the ground plan of the electoral provisions now extant, although these have been liberalized by later amendments. The Sejm is elected every four years by all citizens over 18. Citizens may stand as candidates at 21. There is one deputy per 60 000 inhabitants. Only political and social organizations (trade unions, youth and cultural organizations) may nominate candidates, who must be on the single list of the National Unity Front (FJN), which groups three parties: Communist (PZPR), United Peasant (ZSL) and Democratic (SD).

The office of President was abolished. The Chairman of the Council of State would henceforth be head of state.

At the elections of 26 Oct 52 the number of candidates was the same as the number of seats. The electorate was 16 305 891: votes cast, 15 495 815. The single list of National Front candidates gained 99.8% of valid votes and took up seats in the Sejm:

	Seats
Communist Party (PZPR)	273
United Peasant Party (ZSL)	90
Democratic Party (SD)	25
Independents	37
	425

By an electoral law of 24 Oct 56 the single list of candidates was allowed to include up to two-thirds more candidates than seats. All electors were to make their vote behind curtains. Negative votes were to be recorded by crossing out the candidates' names.

At the elections of 20 Jan 57 there were 717 candidates (51% of whom were Communists) for 459 seats. Turn-out was 94.14% (16 892 213 votes were cast from an electorate of 17 944 081). 280 002 votes (1.6% of votes) were made against National Front candidates. Seats:

	Seats
Communists (PZPR)	239
United Peasant Party (ZSL)	118
Democratic Party (SD)	39
Independents (including 12 Catholics, 9 of whom from the Znak group)	63
	459

An electoral law of 22 Dec 60 reduced the ratio of candidates to seats.

At the elections of 16 Apr 61 there were 616 candidates for 460 seats. The turn-out was 94.83%. There were 292 009 votes against the National Front list (1.57% of votes).

163

	Seats
Communists (PZPR)	256
United Peasant Party (ZSL)	117
Democratic Party (SD)	39
Independents (including 5 Catholics of the Znak group)	48
	460

After the elections of 30 May 65, 1 June 69 and 19 Mar 72 the parties' positions were the same.

	Seats
Communists (PZPR)	255
United Peasant Party (ZSL)	117
Democratic Party (SD)	39
Independents (including 14 Catholics)	49
	460

	1965	*1969*	*1972*
Electorate	19 645 893	21 148 879	21 854 481
Turn-out	96.62%	97.61%	97.94%
Votes against	226 324	161 569	–
National Front List	(1.15% of votes)	(0.78% of votes)	–

In elections held on 21 Mar 76, 631 candidates contested the 460 seats. Of the 24 069 579 registered voters, 23 652 256 (98.27%) cast their votes. Some 99.43% voted for the official candidates of the National Unity Front.

In elections held on 23 Mar 80, 646 candidates contested the 460 seats. Official figures stated that 98.87% of the 25 098 816 total electorate voted. Of these 99.52% voted for the list of National Unity Front candidates.

DANZIG

Danzig was created a Free City by the Versailles Treaty of 28 June 19, under a League of Nations High Commissioner and in customs union with Poland. It was incorporated into Germany during World War II, and into Poland (as Gdańsk) after it.

The constitution provided for a Senate of 20 plus a President and Vice-President elected by the People's Assembly for four years. The President was head of state: 1918, H. Sahm; 1931, E. Ziehm; 1933, H. Rauschning; 1934, A. Greiser. The Assembly (*Volkstag*) of 120 (reduced to 72 in 1930) was elected by universal secret suffrage at 20 for four-year terms on a proportional representation system.

Election 16 May 20. Social Democrats, 37 seats; German Nationalists, 34; Centre (Catholics), 17; German Democrats, 10; Poles, 7; Populists, 6; National Liberals, 3; German Liberals, 3; Communists, 3.

Election 9 Nov 23. Social Democrats, 30; German Nationalists, 26; Centre (Catholics), 15; Communists, 11; German Social Party, 7 (10 301 votes; the first appearance of a racialist party); Populists, 6; German Democrats, 5; German Liberals, 5; Poles, 5; National Liberals, 4; Middle-class Federation, 2; Independents, 4.

Election 13 Nov 27. Social Democrats, 42; German Nationalists, 25; Centre (Catholics), 18; Communists, 8; Populists, 5; National Liberals, 5; German Liberals, 4; Middle-class Federation, 3; Poles, 3; German Social Party, 1 (2130 votes); Nazis, 1 (1483 votes).

Elections

	16 Nov 30		28 May 33		7 Apr 35	
	Votes	*Seats*	*Votes*	*Seats*	*Votes*	*Seats*
Social Democrats	49 965	19	38 703	13	37 804	14
Nazis	32 457	12	107 335	38	128 619	40
Centre (Catholics)	30 232	11	31 339	10	31 576	11
German Nationalists	25 938	10	13 595	4	9 822	3
Communists	20 194	7	44 766	5	7 935	2
Poles	6 377	2	6 738	2	8 311	2
People's Union		3				
Populists		2				
National Liberals		2				
Middle-class Federation		2				
German Liberals		1				
Independent		1				

The 1935 election was fought for a two-thirds majority to enable the Nazis to ask the League of Nations to revise the constitution. The Polish government and the opposition parties alleged terror and unlawful practices by the Nazis. The Danzig Court found for some illegality, and reduced the Nazi vote and number of seats as first officially proclaimed. The final figures are given above.

By dissolutions and amalgamations the Nazis became supreme in the Assembly by 1939, except for the two Polish deputies. On 22 Mar 39 it was declared that the elections then due were 'unnecessary' and would not be held.

PORTUGAL

On 19 Mar 33, the *Estado Novo* constitution (providing for an authoritarian Republic on a corporative basis) was voted upon and adopted. This constitution provides for a President, to be elected for seven years by direct suffrage by male Portuguese citizens, of age or emancipated, able to read or write, and those unable to read or write, being taxpayers to the state or administrative corporations for direct taxes, and Portuguese citizens, females, of age or emancipated, with a special, secondary school, or university diploma; and for a National Assembly (one chamber) of 90 deputies elected for four years by direct suffrage. In the two elections for the National Assembly (1934 and 1938) the only lists presented were those organized by the National Union, an association legally recognized, but without the character of a party, whose aim was to defend the principles contained in the constitution. The electoral law permitted, however, the presentation of more than one list of the deputies to be elected.

At the elections of 8 Nov 53 the União Nacional (National Union) obtained all 120 seats; the 28 opposition candidates were defeated. At subsequent elections only government candidates stood for re-election.

On 25 Apr 74, an almost bloodless *coup* took place in Portugal. The new military government promised a return of normal political life. After a troubled period, the first elections to a Constituent Assembly were held in Apr 75.

The outcome was

	Votes	Seats	% of votes
Portuguese Socialist Party (PSP)	2 145 392	115	37.9
Portuguese Democratic Party (PDP)	1 494 575	80	26.4
Portuguese Communist Party (PCP)	709 639	30	12.5
Social Democratic Centre (CDS)	433 153	16	7.6
Portuguese Democratic Movement (MDP)	233 362	5	4.1
Portuguese Socialist Front (FSP)	66 161	–	1.2
Movement of the Socialist Left (MES)	57 682	–	1.0
Others	132 579	1	2.3

Elections for a legislative assembly were subsequently held in Apr 76, the Socialists again emerging as the largest party.

Portuguese Socialist Party (PSP)	1 887 180	107	35.0
Popular Democratic Party (PPD)	1 296 432	73	24.0
Social Democratic Centre (CDS)	858 783	42	15.9
Portuguese Communist Party (PCP)	785 620	40	14.6
Popular Democratic Union (UDP)	91 383	1	1.7
Popular Socialist Front (FSP)	41 954	0	0.8

After a succession of political crises, Parliament was dissolved prematurely and elections took place on 2 Dec 79.

Democratic Alliance	2 497 019	118	42.2
Socialists	1 621 950	73	27.4
Communists	1 121 224	47	19.0
Others	503 933	8	8.6

Under the new constitution, elections had still to be held in Oct 80.

Democratic Alliance			47.1%
PSD	82		
CDS	46	= 134	
PPM	6		
Republican and Socialist Front			28.0
PSP	66		
UEDS	4	= 74	
ASDI	4		
United Peoples Alliance			16.9
PCP	39		
MDP	2	= 41	
Popular Democratic Union	1		1.4

Elections were next held in 1983. The results were:

		% of vote
PSP	101	36.3
PSD	75	27.0
PCP	44	18.2
CDS	30	12.4
PPM	–	0.5
Pop. Dem. Un.	–	0.5
Others	–	5.1

ROMANIA

1919	Chamber of Deputies: 568 of which:	
	National Party of Transylvania	199
	Peasants	130
	National Liberals	120
	Nationalists and Democrats	27
	Conservative Democrats	16

In 1920 the number of deputies was reduced to 369 and conducted under proportional representation.

1920	People's Party	224
	Peasants	40
	National Party of Transylvania	30
	Socialists	19
	National Liberals	17
	Germans	8

		% of votes
1922	National Liberals	227
	Peasants and National Party of Transylvania	62
	People's Party	11
	Conservative Democrats	8
	Germans	8
	Social Democrats	1
	Jews	1

Opposition parties challenged validity of this election and withdrew.

A new constitution of 23 Mar 23 reorganized the Senate to consist of 249 seats elected on a more restricted suffrage (over 40-year-olds and members of the ruling élite). The Chamber of Deputies was to be elected by universal secret suffrage at 21 years of age on a constituency basis.

By an electoral law of 1926 that party which obtained 40% of the vote was awarded 50% of the seats plus a proportionate share of the seats remaining.

Party	Number of votes	% of votes	Seats gained
1926 Electorate: 3 496 814, of which 75% voted.			
National Liberals	192 309	7	16
National Peasants	727 202	28	69
People's Party	1 306 100	52	292
Christian League of National Defence	124 778	5	10

1927   The electorate was 3 586 806, of which 77% voted.

	Number of votes	% of votes	Seats gained
National Liberals ⎫ Peasants ⎭	1 704 435	62	⎧ 298 ⎩ 22
National Peasants	610 149	22	54
Hungarians	173 517	6	15

1928   The electorate was 3 671 352, of which 77.4% voted.

	Number of votes	% of votes	Seats gained
National Peasants	2 228 922	78	348
National Liberals	185 939	7	13
People's Party	70 490	2	5
Peasants	70 506	2	5
Hungarians	172 699	6	16

1931   The electorate was 4 038 464, of which 72.5% voted.

	Number of votes	% of votes	Seats gained
National Union	1 389 901	48	289
National Peasants	438 747	15	30
National Liberals (G. Brătianu)	173 586	6	12

Party	Number of votes	% of votes	Seats gained
People's Party	141 141	5	10
Hungarians	139 003	5	10
Christian League of National Defence	113 863	4	8
Peasant Party	100 682	3	7
Social Democrats	94 957	3	6
Peasant Democrats Union in alliance with League against Usury	80 570	3	6
Labour and Peasant Group	73 716	3	5
Jews	64 193	2	4

1932 The electorate was 4 220 731, of which 70.8% voted.

National Peasants	1 203 700	41	274
National Liberals (Duca)	407 023	14	28
National Liberals (Brătianu)	195 048	7	14
Peasants	170 860	6	12
Christian League of National Defence	159 071	5	11
Hungarians	141 894	5	14
National Agrarians	108 857	4	8
Social Democrats	101 068	3	7
Iron Guard	70 674	2	5
National Union	68 116	2	5
Jews	67 582	2	5
People's Party	64 525	2	4

1933 The electorate was 4 380 354, of which 68% voted.

National Liberals	1 518 864	51	300
National Peasants	414 685	14	29
Peasants	152 167	5	11
National Liberals (Brătianu)	147 665	5	10
Christian League of National Defence	133 205	5	9
National Agrarians	121 748	4	9
Hungarians	119 562	4	8
Radical Peasants	82 930	3	6
Agrarian Union	73 208	2	5

1937 66% of the electorate voted.

Government Party (National Liberals, etc.)	1 103 323	36	152
National Peasants	626 642	20	86
'All-for-Country' (i.e. Iron Guard)	478 378	16	66
Christian League of National Defence	281 167	9	39

Party	Number of votes	% of votes	Seats gained
Hungarians	136 139	4	19
National Liberals (Brătianu)	119 361	4	16
Radical Peasants	69 208	2	9

The government failed to get its necessary 40% of the votes. King Carol II picked on the Christian League of National Defence to form a government. He dismissed this government on 10 Feb 38 and instituted a royal dictatorship, called the Government of National Concentration.

A new constitution of 20 Feb 38 reduced the electorate to some 2m. (voting was universal and secret at age 30) and established a Senate. Political parties were banned except for the royalist monolithic National Renaissance Front. A plebiscite of 24 Feb 38, conducted by open voting, confirmed the new constitution by 4 283 395 to 5413 votes. Turn-out (compulsory): 92%. A corporatist parliament was returned at the election of 2 June 39: 86 representatives of agrarian and labour interests, 86 of commerce and industry, 86 intelligentsia and 88 senators. Turn-out was 85%. There were twice as many candidates as seats.

An electoral law of 14 July 46 abolished the Senate, enfranchised all at 21 and provided for a unicameral Assembly elected for four-year terms.

At the election of 19 Nov 46 the government bloc (National Democratic Front) obtained 71% of the votes cast and 347 seats. The National Peasants gained 33, the National Liberals 3. The validity of the results has been challenged.

1947   Electorate: 7 859 212. Voted: 6 934 563 (88.9%).

National Democratic Front	(348)	(4 766 630)
National Liberals	75	
Social Democrats	75	
Communists	73	
Ploughmen's Front	70	
National People's Party	26	
Dissident National Peasants	20	
Jews	2	
Independents	7	
Opposition parties	(66)	(1 361 536)
National Peasants	32	879 927
National Liberals	3	259 306
Democratic Peasants	2	156 775
Hungarian People's Union	29	569 651

170

The opposition parties protested at the falsification and terror used in these elections.

In Dec 47 King Michael abdicated, and a People's Republic was proclaimed on the 30th. On the 28 Mar 48, an election was held for a new National Assembly to pass a new constitution.

The remnants of the Social Democrats were merged with the Communists to form the Workers' Party, which ran for election in the single-list monolithic National Democratic Front comprising also the Ploughmen's Front, the National Peasants and the Hungarian People's Union. Electorate 8 417 467. Voted: 7 663 675 (91% turn-out). Voted for National Democratic Front: 6 958 531 (90.8%). The Front gained 405 of the 414 Assembly seats, the Liberals 7, the Democratic Peasants 1 with 1 Independent.

On 13 Apr 48 a new constitution, of the Soviet type, was promulgated: vote at 18, stand at 23, universal secret suffrage.

A further constitution was instituted on 24 Sep 49, in general outline the same as that of 1948. Deputies to the Grand National Assembly (*Marea Adunare Naţională*) were to represent 40 000 electors for four-year terms.

1952 Electorate: 10.5m. Voted: 97%. For National Democratic Front: 98%.
1957 Electorate: 11.7m. Voted: 99.15%. For National Democratic Front: 99.88%.

At the elections of 5 Mar 61, 7 Mar 65 and 2 Mar 69 a single list of candidates was presented, the number of candidates equalling the number of seats. At least 99% of the voters turned out, at least 99% of these voted for the National Democratic Front (Socialist Unity Front since 19 Nov 68).

In elections held on 9 March 75 for the first time 139 of the 349 seats were contested by more than one candidate (although all belonged to the Socialist Unity Front). According to official figures, 99.96% of the 14 900 000 registered voters went to the polls.

In elections held on 9 March 80, officially some 15 629 098 voters (99.99%) of the total electorate voted. Of these, 98.52% voted for official candidates.

SPAIN

Elections held in Feb 18 were followed by a long period of political stability.

On 12 Sep 23 Primo de Rivera took over the country in a *coup d'état*. In Sep 27 the National Assembly met, members having been nominated by Primo de Rivera.

In Feb 31 elections were announced but postponed because of a government crisis and elections under a provisional government were held for the constituent *Cortes*. Franchise minimum voting age reduced from 25 to 23 years. Eligibility for *Cortes* membership extended to women and priests.

Electoral divisions revised to give one deputy for every 50 000 inhabitants to a *Cortes* which was a single chamber elected by direct popular vote.

		Seats
Feb 31	Socialists	116
	Radical Socialists	60
	Azañaś Republican Action Party	30
	Radicals (following Lerroux)	90
	Progressives (following Zamona)	22
	Catalan Esquerra	43
	Casares Quirozaś Gallegan Nationalists	16
	Parties of the right of which only 19 were members of the Monarchist Party	60

Nov 33	*Parties of the left centre*	Acción Republicana	8
		Socialists	58
		Remainder of pro-government parties	33
		Radicals (following Lerroux)	167
		Parties to the right	207

Feb 36	Parties of the left	278
	Centre parties	55
	Parties of the right	134

Traditionally designated as the *Cortes* (courts), the Spanish parliament was revived by General Franco in 1942 as a unicameral body with strictly limited powers under the official name of Spanish Legislative Assembly (*Las Cortes Españolas*). Until 1967 it had no directly elected members but was made up of appointed and *ex officio* dignitaries, representatives of syndical (trade-union) and professional and business associations, and 108 indirectly elected representatives from the 53 Spanish and African provinces and the two North African *presidios*. Under the Organic Law of 1967, its membership was expanded by the addition of 108 'family representatives' to be directly elected for a four-year term by heads of families, married women and widows. The first elections of family representatives were held 10 Oct 67.

In 1969, the membership of the *Cortes* was made up of the categories and approximate numbers listed below; however, since some members sat in more than one capacity, the total membership was somewhat less than the indicated 563. The succession law of 22 July 69 was adopted by a vote of 491 in favour, 19 opposed, 9 abstaining, and 15 absent, making a total of 534.

High Officials	23
Appointed	25
Members of the National Council of the Movement	102
Representatives of cultural bodies	18
Representatives of professional associations	22
Syndical representatives	150
Municipal and provincial representatives	115
Family representatives	108
	563

	Party	
1977	UCD	165
	PSOE	118
	PCE	20
	CD	16
	CU	11
	PNV	8
	Others	12
1979	UCD	168
	PSOE	121
	PCE	23
	CD	9
	CU	8
	PNV	7
	PSA	5
	Others	9

	Votes per party		Seats	% of votes
1982	PSOE/PSC-PSOE	10 127 392	202	48.7
	AP/AP-PDP	5 543 107	106	26.6
	UCD	1 425 093	12	6.8
	CU	772 726	12	3.7
	PNV	395 656	8	1.9
	PCE-PSUC	844 976	4	4.1
	CDS	600 842	2	2.9
	HB	210 601	2	1.0
	ERC	138 116	1	0.7
	EE	100 326	1	0.5
	Others	648 346	–	3.1

SWEDEN

Voting procedures. Election to the First Chamber indirect through electoral colleges. Direct election to the Second Chamber. Proportional representation. Suffrage – for the First Chamber, universal suffrage at age 27; for the Second, suffrage for men at 24. In 1927, the First Chamber suffrage extended to age 23, and to age 21 in 1941. In 1945 suffrage for the Second Chamber altered to universal suffrage at 21.

	Votes per party		Seats	% of votes
1917	Högern (Con.)	181 333	59	16.1
	Agrarians/Centre	62 658	12	5.6
	Liberaler (Lib.)	202 936	62	18.0
	Social Dem.	288 020	97	25.6
	Others	1037	0	0.1
1920	Högern (Con.)	183 019	70	15.3
	Agrarians/Centre	92 941	30	7.8
	Liberaler (Lib.)	144 946	48	12.2
	Social Dem.	237 177	82	19.9
	Others	100	0	0.0
1921	Högern (Con.)	449 302	62	13.9
	Agrarians/Centre	192 269	21	6.0
	Liberaler (Lib.)	332 765	41	10.3
	Social Dem.	687 096	99	21.3
	Soc. and Comm.	80 355	7	2.5
	Others	165	0	0.0
1924	Högern (Con.)	461 257	65	13.8
	Agrarians/Centre	190 396	23	5.7
	Liberaler (Lib.)	69 627	5	2.0
	Frisinnade (Lib.)	228 913	28	6.9
	Social Dem.	725 407	104	21.7
	Soc. and Comm.	89 902	5	2.7
	Others	84	0	0.0
1928	Högern (Con.)	692 434	73	19.8
	Agrarian/Centre	263 501	27	7.5
	Liberaler (Lib.)	70 820	4	2.1
	Frisinnade (Lib.)	303 995	28	8.7
	Social Dem.	873 931	90	25.0
	Soc. and Comm.	151 567	8	4.4
	Others	2563	0	0.1
1932	Högern (Con.)	585 248	58	15.8
	Agrarians/Centre	351 215	36	9.5
	Liberaler (Lib.)	48 722	4	1.3
	Frisinnade (Lib.)	244 577	20	6.6
	Social Dem.	1 040 689	104	28.0
	Socialist	132 564	6	3.6
	Communist	74 245	2	2.0
	Others	17 846	0	0.5
1936	Högern (Con.)	512 781	44	13.0
	Agrarians/Centre	418 840	36	10.7
	Folkpartiet (Lib.)	376 161	27	9.6
	Social Dem.	1 338 120	112	34.0
	Socialist	127 832	6	3.3
	Communist	96 519	5	2.5
	Others	47 500	0	1.2
1940	Högern (Con.)	518 346	42	12.6
	Agrarian/Centre	344 345	28	8.4
	Folkpartiet (Lib.)	344 113	23	8.4
	Social Dem.	1 546 804	134	37.6
	Socialist	18 430	0	0.4

	Votes per party		Seats	% of votes
	Communist	101 424	3	2.5
	Others	995	0	0.0
1944	Högern (Con.)	488 921	39	11.3
	Agrarians/Centre	421 094	35	9.8
	Folkpartiet (Lib.)	398 293	26	9.2
	Social Dem.	1 436 571	115	33.3
	Socialist	5279	0	0.1
	Communist	318 466	15	7.6
	Others	17 680	0	0.4
1948	Högern (Con.)	478 786	23	10.2
	Agrarians/Centre	480 421	30	10.2
	Folkpartiet (Lib.)	882 437	57	18.7
	Social Dem.	1 789 459	112	38.0
	Communist	244 826	8	5.2
	Others	3062	0	0.0
1952	Högern (Con.)	543 825	31	11.3
	Agrarians/Centre	406 183	26	8.5
	Folkpartiet (Lib.)	924 819	58	19.2
	Social Dem.	1 742 284	110	36.3
	Communist	164 194	5	3.4
	Others	2402	0	0.0
1956	Högern (Con.)	663 693	42	13.6
	Agrarians/Centre	366 612	19	7.5
	Folkpartiet (Lib.)	923 564	58	18.9
	Social Dem.	1 729 463	106	35.4
	Communist	194 016	6	4.0
	Others	1 982	0	0.0
1958	Högern (Con.)	750 332	45	15.0
	Agrarians/Centre	486 760	32	9.7
	Folkpartiet (Lib.)	700 019	38	14.0
	Social Dem.	1 776 667	111	35.6
	Communist	129 319	5	2.6
	Others	1 155	0	0.0
1960	Högern (Con.)	704 365	39	14.2
	Agrarians/Centre	579 007	34	11.6
	Folkpartiet (Lib.)	744 142	40	15.0
	Social Dem.	2 033 016	114	40.9
	Communist	190 560	5	3.8
	Others	3 024	0	0.0
1964	Högern (Con.)	582 609	33	11.4
	Agrarians/Centre	559 632	36	11.0
	Folkpartiet (Lib.)	720 733	43	14.1
	Social Dem.	2 006 923	113	39.4
	Communist	221 746	8	4.4
	Others	154 137	0	3.0
1968	Högern (Con.)	621 031	29	12.9
	Agrarians/Centre	757 215	37	15.7
	Folkpartiet (Lib.)	688 456	32	14.3
	Social Dem.	2 420 277	125	50.1

	Votes per party		Seats	% of votes
	Communist	145 172	3	3.0
	Others	197 228	7	4.1
1970	Högern (Con.)	573 812	41	11.5
	Agrarians/Centre	991 208	71	19.9
	Folkpartiet (Lib.)	806 667	58	16.2
	Social Dem.	2 256 369	163	45.3
	Communist	236 659	17	4.8
	Others	111 481	0	2.3
1973	Social Democrats	2 247 727	156	43.6
	Communist Left	274 929	19	5.3
	Centre Party	737 584	51	14.3
	Moderates	1 295 246	90	25.1
	Liberals	486 028	34	9.4
	Minor Parties	117 325	–	2.3
1976	Social Democrats	2 320 818	152	42.9
	Communist Left	257 967	17	4.7
	Centre Party	845 580	55	15.6
	Moderates	1 307 927	86	24.1
	Liberals	600 249	39	11.0
	Minor Parties	90 790	–	1.7
1979	Social Democrats	2 356 234	154	43.5
	Communist Left	305 420	20	5.6
	Moderates	1 108 406	73	20.5
	Centre Party	984 589	64	18.2
	Liberals	577 063	38	10.6
	Minor Parties	86 855	–	1.6
1982	Social Democrats	2 533 250	166	45.6
	Communist Left	308 899	20	5.6
	Moderates	1 313 337	86	23.6
	Centre Party	859 618	56	15.5
	Liberals	327 770	21	5.9
	Minor Parties	211 670	0	3.8

SWITZERLAND

A general election takes place by ballot every four years. Every citizen of the Republic who has entered on his 20th year is entitled to vote, and any voter, not a clergyman, may be elected as a deputy. Laws passed by both chambers may be submitted to direct popular vote, when 30 000 citizens or eight cantons demand it; the vote can be only 'Yes' or 'No'. This principle, called the *referendum*, is frequently acted on.

Women's suffrage, although advocated by the Federal Council and the Federal Assembly, was repeatedly rejected but at a *referendum* held on 7 Feb 71 women's suffrage was carried.

	Votes per party		Seats	% of votes
1919	Liberal Democratic	28 497	9	3.8
	Peasant and Middle Class	114 337	31	15.3
	Catholic Conservative	156 702	41	21.0
	Radical	215 566	58	28.8
	Socialist	175 292	41	23.5
	Others	59 360	9	7.6
1922	Liberal Democratic	19 041	10	4.0
	Peasant and Middle Class	118 382	35	16.1
	Catholic Conservative	153 836	44	20.9
	Radical	208 144	58	28.3
	Socialist	170 974	43	23.3
	Communist	13 441	2	1.8
	Others	43 605	6	5.6
1925	Liberal Democratic	30 523	7	4.1
	Peasant and Middle Class	113 512	31	15.3
	Catholic Conservative	155 467	42	20.9
	Radical	206 485	59	27.8
	Socialist	192 208	49	25.8
	Communist	14 837	3	2.0
	Others	34 106	7	4.1
1928	Liberal Democratic	23 752	6	2.9
	Peasant and Middle Class	126 961	31	15.8
	Catholic Conservative	172 516	46	21.4
	Radical	220 135	58	27.4
	Socialist	220 141	50	27.4
	Communist	14 818	2	1.8
	Others	29 149	5	3.3
1931	Liberal Democratic	24 573	6	2.8
	Peasant and Middle Class	131 809	30	15.3
	Catholic Conservative	184 602	44	21.4
	Radical	232 562	52	26.9
	Socialist	247 946	49	28.7
	Communist	12 778	2	1.5
	Others	32 305	4	3.4
1935	Independent	37 861	7	4.2
	Liberal Democratic	30 476	7	3.3
	Peasant and Middle Class	100 300	21	11.0
	Catholic Conservative	185 052	42	20.3
	Radical	216 664	48	23.7
	Socialist	255 843	50	28.0
	Communist	12 569	2	1.4
	Others	78 810	10	8.1
1939	Independent	43 735	9	7.1
	Liberal Democratic	10 241	6	1.6
	Peasant and Middle Class	91 182	22	14.7
	Catholic Conservative	105 018	43	17.0
	Radical	128 163	51	20.8
	Socialist	160 377	45	25.9
	Communist	15 962	4	2.6
	Others	69 062	7	10.3

	Votes per party		Seats	% of votes
1943	Independent	48 557	7	5.5
	Liberal Democratic	28 434	8	3.2
	Peasant and Middle Class	101 998	22	11.6
	Catholic Conservative	182 916	43	20.8
	Radical	197 746	43	22.5
	Socialist	251 576	56	28.6
	Others	76 449	11	7.8
1947	Independent	42 428	9	4.4
	Liberal Democratic	30 492	7	3.2
	Peasant and Middle Class	115 976	21	12.1
	Catholic Conservative	203 202	44	21.2
	Radical	220 486	52	23.0
	Socialist	251 625	48	26.2
	Communist	49 353	7	5.1
	Others	53 118	6	4.8
1951	Independent	49 100	10	5.1
	Liberal Democratic	24 813	5	2.6
	Peasant and Middle Class	120 819	23	12.6
	Catholic Conservative	216 616	48	22.5
	Radical	230 687	51	24.0
	Socialist	249 857	49	26.0
	Communist	25 659	5	2.7
	Others	50 438	5	4.5
1955	Independent	53 450	10	5.5
	Liberal Democratic	21 688	5	2.2
	Peasant and Middle Class	117 847	22	12.1
	Catholic Conservative	226 122	47	23.2
	Radical	227 370	50	23.3
	Socialist	263 664	53	27.0
	Communist	25 060	4	2.6
	Others	46 819	5	3.4
1959	Independent	54 049	10	5.5
	Liberal Democratic	22 934	5	2.3
	Peasant and Middle Class	113 611	23	11.6
	Catholic Conservative	229 088	47	23.3
	Radical	232 557	51	23.7
	Socialist	259 139	51	26.3
	Communist	26 346	3	2.7
	Others	51 281	6	4.1
1963	Independent	48 224	10	5.0
	Liberal Democratic	21 501	6	2.2
	Peasant and Middle Class	109 202	22	11.4
	Catholic Conservative	225 160	48	23.4
	Radical	230 200	51	24.0
	Socialist	256 063	53	26.6
	Communist	21 088	4	2.2
	Others	49 693	6	4.2
1967	Independent	89 950	16	9.1
	Liberal Democratic	23 208	6	2.3
	Peasant and Middle Class	109 621	21	11.0
	Catholic Conservative	219 184	45	22.1
	Radical	230 095	49	23.2

Votes per party		*Seats*	*% of votes*
Socialist	233 873	51	23.5
Communist	28 723	5	2.9
Others	59 194	7	3.6
1971 Independent	150 684	13	7.6
Liberal Democratic	43 338	6	2.2
Peasant and Middle Class	217 909	23	11.0
Catholic Conservative	402 528	44	20.4
Radical	431 364	49	21.8
Socialist	452 194	46	22.9
Communist	50 834	5	2.6
Republican Movement	88 327	7	4.5
Others	138 417	7	5.3
1975 Social Democrats		55	25.4
Radical Democrats		47	22.2
Christian Democrats		46	20.6
Swiss People's Party		21	10.1
Independent Party		11	6.2
Liberal Democrats		6	2.3
Republican Movement		4	3.0
Party of Labour (Communists)		4	2.2
Others		6	8.0
1979 Social Democrats		51	24.4
Radical Democrats		51	24.1
Christian Democrats		44	21.5
Swiss People's Party		23	11.6
Independents Party		8	4.1
Liberal Democrats		8	2.8
Republican Movement		1	1.9
Party of Labour (Communist)		3	1.7
Others		11	7.9
1983 Radical Democrats		54	23.4
Social Democrats		47	22.8
Christian Democrats		42	20.2
Swiss People's Party		23	11.1
Independents Party		8	4.0
Liberal Party		8	2.8
Others		18	11.5

TURKEY

The first Turkish Grand National Assembly met in Ankara on 23 Apr 20. In these circumstances, only indirect elections proved possible, every province putting forward five delegates. The Assembly consisted of 337 members, 232 of whom had been newly elected. Under the constitution of 20 Jan 21, which the Assembly adopted and which legalized the organization it had set up, the deputies' term of office was set at two years.

In the 1920 elections Kemalists held 197 seats; Opposition, 118; Non-aligned, 122. In 1923, Grand National Assembly Party; Progressive Republican Party; Republican People's Party, 304. In 1946, Democratic Party,

179

64; Republican People's Party, 64; Independents, 6.

The first Assembly was prorogued on 1 Apr 23 after deciding that new elections should be held. On 19 Oct 23, the Republic was proclaimed and the 1924 constitution extended the franchise to all men aged 18 or over. Candidates had to be at least 30 years old, and the deputies' term of office was lengthened to four years. A constitutional amendment adopted on 5 Jan 34 extended the franchise to women, but raised the minimum voting age to 22. Elections continued to be indirect: voters chose an electoral college which then elected the Assembly. This practice was continued until 1946. The membership of the Assembly increased constantly until the adoption of the 1961 constitution, since it had been laid down that there should be one deputy per 40 000 citizens.

The first effective political party in the history of the Turkish Republic, the People's Party, was formed in Oct 23; in Nov 24 its name was changed to Republican People's Party. This party remained in power until 1950. The Free Republican Party, formed in 1930, had a brief existence. Then between 1930 and 1945 Turkey had a single-party regime. On 5 June 45 the authorities allowed the formation of political parties without a preliminary permit, and as a consequence the elections held on 21 July 46 were for the first time contested by more than one party. Voting was direct and public, electors were allowed to divide their votes between party lists of candidates (producing 'mixed' lists), but votes were counted in secret. To win, candidates needed to obtain the simple majority of the votes cast. Two changes were introduced in the elections held on 14 May 50: voting became secret, and the counting of votes open. In 1957 mixed lists were banned, but electors were allowed to delete the names of individual candidates from the party lists of their choice. After 27 May 60, the National Unity Committee first assumed all the powers vested in the Grand National Assembly under the 1924 constitution. This transfer of power, legalized by the provisional constitution of 12 June 60, was followed on 13 Dec of the same year by a law setting up a Constituent Assembly, which was opened on 6 Jan 61. The constitution which this Assembly drew up governed the elections held on 15 Oct 61 which produced a new Turkish Grand National Assembly. Article 55 of the constitution required voting to be free, direct, universal and secret, and the counting of votes to be open. However, the constitution did not define the system of representation which was to be used, and this was regulated by electoral laws. Proportional representation was introduced for the first time in the elections of 15 Oct 61 and has been retained since, although the basic d'Hondt formula has been varied: first candidates had to obtain a minimum number of votes (known as the 'barrage') to qualify for consideration: then the country-wide pooling and redistribution of wasted votes ('the national residue') was introduced in time for the elections of 12 Oct 65, but dropped together with the 'barrage' requirement before the 1969 elections.

		Votes per party	*Seats*
1950	Democratic Party	4 242 831	396
	Republican People's Party	3 165 096	68
	Nation Party	240 209	1
	Independents	258 698	7
1954	Republican People's Party	3 161 696	31
	Republican Nation Party	434 085	5
	Democratic Party	5 151 550	505
	Peasant Party	57 011	–
	Independents	137 318	1
1957	Republican People's Party	3 753 136	178
	Republican Nation Party	652 064	4
	Democratic Party	4 372 621	424
	Freedom Party	350 497	4
	Independents	4 944	–
1961	Justice Party	3 527 435	158
	Republican People's Party	3 724 752	173
	Republican Peasants and Nation Party, renamed Nationalist Action Party	1 415 390	54
	New Turkey Party	1 391 934	65
	Independents	81 732	–
1965	Justice Party	4 921 235	240
	Republican People's Party	2 675 785	134
	Republican Peasants and Nation Party, renamed Nationalist Action Party	208 696	11
	Nation Party	582 704	31
	Turkish Workers' Party	276 101	14
	New Turkey Party	346 514	19
	Independents	296 528	1
1969	Justice Party	4 219 712	256
	Republican People's Party	2 487 006	143
	Republican Peasants and Nation Party, renamed Nationalist Action Party	275 091	1
	Nation Party	292 961	6
	Turkish Workers' Party	243 631	2
	New Turkey Party	197 929	6
	Independents	511 023	13
	Unity Party	254 695	8
	Reliance Party, renamed National Reliance Party in 1971	597 818	15

Senators are elected for six years, but one-third of the membership is re-elected every other year. Voting is free, equal, universal, direct and secret, and counting open. The Senate was first set up in 1961. That year and in 1964, a simple majority sufficed for the election of a senator; in 1966 and 1968 proportional representation (with 'national residue') was introduced.

		Votes per party	Seats
1961	Justice Party	3 560 675	71
	Republican People's Party	3 734 285	76
	Republican Peasants and Nation Party	1 350 892	16
	New Turkey Party	1 401 636	27
	Independents	39 558	–
1964	Justice Party	1 385 655	31
	Republican People's Party	1 125 783	19
	Republican Peasants and Nation Party	88 400	–
	New Turkey Party	96 427	–
	Independents	64 498	1
1966	Justice Party	1 688 316	35
	Republican People's Party	877 066	13
	Republican Peasants and Nation Party	57 367	1
	Nation Party	157 115	1
	Turkish Workers' Party	116 375	1
	New Turkey Party	70 043	1
	Independents	980	–
1968	Justice Party	1 656 802	38
	Republican People's Party	899 444	13
	Republican Peasants and Nation Party	66 232	–
	Reliance Party, renamed National Reliance Party	284 234	1
	Nation Party	200 737	1
	Turkish Workers' Party	157 062	–
	Independents	58 317	–

After a period of disguised military rule, Parliament reasserted its influence in 1973. In the elections of Oct 73 there was a shock rebuff for Mr Demirel with major gains by Ecevit (much more in the Social Democrat mould).

		Votes	Seats	% votes
1973	Republican Peoples Party	3 570 583	185	33.3
	Justice Party	3 179 897	149	29.8
	National Salvation Party	1 265 771	48	11.8
	National Action Party	362 208	3	3.4

		Votes	Seats	% votes
	Democratic Party	1 275 502	15	11.9
	Republican Reliance Party	564 343	13	5.3
	Turkish Unity Party	121 759	1	1.1
	Others	365 595	6	3.4
1977	Republican Peoples Party	6 117 280	213	41.4
	Justice Party	5 457 649	189	36.9
	National Salvation Party	1 271 620	24	8.6
	National Action Party	942 606	16	6.4
	Republican Reliance Party	277 059	3	1.9
	Democratic Party	273 426	1	1.8
	Turkish Unity Party	58 319	–	0.4
	Others	387 855	4	2.6

On 10 Sept 80, for the third time in 20 years, the military took control of Turkey. A general election took place on 6 Nov 83. The result was

	Votes	Seats	% votes
Motherland Party	7 823 827	212	45.7
Populist Party	5 277 698	117	30.8
Nationalist Democracy Party	4 032 046	71	23.5

USSR

In 1917 the Provisional Government had been organizing elections to establish a Constituent Assembly, and these the Bolsheviks allowed to take place on 25 Nov 17. Suffrage was universal, and the electorate numbered 41.7m. Figures are uncertain and contradictory (some reputable variant figures are given in brackets).

	Votes cast	Delegates returned
	17.1m. (17.4m.)	419 (of whom 380 of the right-wing faction)
Bolsheviks	9.6m. (9.8m.)	168 (175)
Mensheviks	1.4m.	18
Kadets	2m.	17
Monarchists	300 000	. .
Various national minority parties	1.7m.	. .

The Kadets were proscribed at the end of 1917. The Constituent Assembly met on 18 Jan 18, just over half the delegates being present. It was dissolved by the Bolsheviks the following day after rejecting by 237 votes to 136 a Bolshevik motion which would have recognized the Congress of Soviets to be the supreme government authority.

The Congress of Soviets was therefore the supreme organ of state power until it was replaced by the Supreme Soviet in 1937. There were altogether ten All-Russian Congresses until the formation of the USSR (30 Dec 22) and eight All-Union Congresses thereafter.

Elections were indirect, from amongst the deputies in the hierarchy of soviets throughout the country. The latter were elected on a franchise restricted to workers, peasants and the armed forces. Deputies to town soviets were elected on a basis of 1 per 25 000 electors; to rural soviets on a basis of 1 per 125 000.

By 1922 all public opposition to the Communist Party had been brought to an end. Party allegiance in the early Congresses of Soviets (for the first two see above):

> 3rd (Jan 18) Bolsheviks 61%
>
> 4th Extraordinary (Mar 18)   Bolsheviks 66%
>
> 5th (July 18) Bolsheviks (now called Communists) 66%
>
> 6th (Nov 18) Communists 90%
>
> 7th (Dec 19) Communists 95%
>
> 8th (Dec 20) Communists 95%

The 'Stalin' Constitution of 1936 replaced the Congresses of Soviets with the Supreme Soviet (*Verkhovnyi Sovet*). This has two chambers: the Soviet of the Union (*Sovet Soyuza*) and the Soviet of Nationalities (*Sovet Natsionalnostei*). Elections are held every four years. Suffrage universal at 18 years; candidates may stand at 23. The Soviet of the Union is elected on a basis of 1 deputy per 300 000 electors. Deputies to the Soviet of Nationalities are elected in the following proportions: 32 from each federative republic, 11 from each Autonomous Republic, 5 from each Autonomous Oblast (Province) and 1 from each National District.

Although it is constitutionally the supreme legislative body, the Supreme Soviet has no significance in the realm of policy-making: *de facto* supreme power is in the hands of the Communist Party. Candidates for election may be nominated only by recognized organizations: the Communist Party, trade unions, industrial co-operatives, agricultural collectives, youth organizations and cultural organizations. Candidates need not belong to the party, but they must support its programme. On the average, some 75% of deputies are party members.

More than one candidate may be nominated, and there is no constitutional bar to more than one standing for election, but the practice is that one only of the nominees is selected to stand by local party officials, and the elector's choice is thus limited to voting for or against him.

The ballot is secret but so arranged that only a contrary vote actually requires entry into the polling booth.

Elections were held in Dec 37, Feb 46, Mar 50, Mar 54, Mar 58, Mar 62,

June 66, June 70, June 74 and Mar 79. In 1937, 91 113 153 votes were cast out of an electorate of 93 139 478, and subsequently the turn-out has always exceeded 99%. Less than 1% of votes cast have been against candidates, and no candidate has ever failed to be elected.

INDEPENDENT TERRITORIES (1918–21)

Armenia, Azerbaijan and Georgia proclaimed independence jointly as the Transcaucasian Federative Republic on 22 Apr 18; reconquered respectively 29 Nov 20, 27 Apr 20 and 18 Mar 21.

The Transcaucasian Federative Republic was governed by a *Seim* of delegates based upon the elections to the Russian Constituent Assembly (dissolved on 18 Jan 18): Mensheviks, 33; Musavat (Moslem Nationalists), 30; Dashnaktsutiun (Armenian Nationalists), 27; Moslem Socialists, 7; Socialist revolutionaries, 5; others, 10.

The Federation collapsed upon the secession of Georgia on 26 May 18, and each republic became separately independent.

Armenia set up a National Council (*Khorhurd*) on 1 Aug 18, the party composition of which was: Dashnaktsutiun, 18; Populists, 6; Moslems, 6; Mensheviks, 5; independents, 2; Bolsheviks, 1; Yezidis, 1; Russians, 1.

Azerbaijan set up a National Council composed as follows: Musavat (Moslem Nationalists) and Neutral Democratic Group (Sunni Moslems), 30; Socialists, 11; Moslem Union, 3. In June 18 the Council was reformed under the insistence of the Turkish military commander to exclude socialists and give predominance to the conservative Moslem Union. In turn the British military commander after the surrender of the Turks objected to the Council as unrepresentative. A new Council was created in Dec 18: Musavat, 38; Neutral Democratic Group, 7; Unity Party, 13; Socialists, 11; Dashnaktsutiun (Armenian Nationalists), 7; other Armenian parties, 4; Bolsheviks, 1; others, 15.

Georgia. In Feb 19 the National Council held elections for a Constituent Assembly. Suffrage was universal and by proportional representation. 15 parties presented candidates for election. 505 477 votes were cast (some 60% of the electorate). The Assembly had 130 deputies, distributed as follows:

	Votes cast	*Deputies in the Assembly*
Mensheviks	409 766	109
National Democrats	30 154	8
Social-Federalists	33 721	8
Social-Revolutionaries	21 453	5

UNITED KINGDOM

In 1911 the maximum duration of a parliament, which since 1715 had been seven years, was reduced to five years.

By 1918 virtually all men were enfranchised together with all women over 30 years of age who were householders or the wives of householders. Voting in more than two constituencies was prohibited. General elections which had hitherto been spread over two weeks and more were concentrated on a single day. Candidates were required to provide a deposit of £150 to be forfeit if they failed to secure one-eighth of the votes cast in their constituency. Seats were redistributed, for the first time on the basis of approximately equal electorates, and the House of Commons was increased to 707 members (this fell to 615 in 1922, with the independence of Southern Ireland).

The age of women voting was lowered to 21 in 1928 and they were given the vote on exactly the same basis as men.

In 1948 university seats and all plural voting were abolished. Machinery was set up for Permanent Boundary Commissions to redraw constituencies once in the life of every normal five-year parliament, but because the first routine distribution of seats in 1954-5 (which increased the House to 630 members) had caused so much annoyance and difficulty, an Act was passed in 1958 to reduce the frequency of redistribution to between 10 and 15 years.

		Votes	% share of total vote	Members	Candi-dates	Unopposed returns
1918	Electors:	21 392 322	Turnout: 58.9%			
	Total votes cast	10 766 583	100.0	707	1625	107
	Coalition Unionist	3 504 198	32.6	335	374	42
	Coalition Liberal	1 455 640	13.5	133	158	27
	Coalition Labour	161 521	1.5	10	18	−
	(Coalition)	(5 121 259)	(47.6)	(478)	(550)	(69)
	Conservative	370 375	3.4	23	37	−
	Irish Unionist	292 722	2.7	25	38	−
	Liberal	1 298 808	12.1	28	253	−
	Labour	2 385 472	22.2	63	388	12
	Irish Nationalist	238 477	2.2	7	60	1
	Sinn Fein	486 867	4.5	73	102	25
	Other	572 503	5.3	10	197	−
1922	Electors:	21 127 663	Turnout: 71.3%			
	Total votes cast	14 393 632	100.0	615	1443	57
	Conservative	5 500 382	38.2	345	483	42
	National Liberal	1 673 240	11.6	62	162	5
	Liberal	2 516 187	17.5	54	328	5
	Labour	4 241 383	29.5	142	411	4
	Other	462 340	3.2	12	59	1
1923	Electors:	21 281 232	Turnout: 70.8%			
	Total votes cast	14 548 521	100.0	615	1446	
	Conservative	5 538 824	38.1	258	540	35
	Liberal	4 311 147	29.6	159	453	11
	Labour	4 438 508	30.5	191	422	3
	Other	260 042	1.8	7	31	1

		Votes	% share of total vote	Members	Candidates	Unopposed returns
1924	Electors:	21 731 320	Turnout: 76.6%			
	Total votes cast	16 640 279	100.0	615	1428	32
	Conservative	8 039 598	48.3	419	552	16
	Liberal	2 928 747	17.6	40	340	6
	Labour	5 489 077	33.0	151	512	9
	Communist	55 346	0.3	1	8	–
	Other	126 511	0.8	4	16	1
1929	Electors:	28 850 870	Turnout: 76.1%			
	Total votes cast	22 648 375	100.0	615	1730	7
	Conservative	8 656 473	38.2	260	590	4
	Liberal	5 308 510	23.4	59	513	–
	Labour	8 389 512	37.1	288	571	–
	Communist	50 614	0.3	–	25	–
	Other	243 266	1.0	8	31	3
1931	Electors:	29 960 071	Turnout: 76.3%			
	Total votes cast	21 656 373	100.0	615	1292	67
	Conservative	11 978 745	55.2	473	523	56
	National Liberal	341 370	1.6	13	20	–
	Liberal National	809 302	3.7	35	41	–
	Liberal	1 403 102	6.5	33	112	5
	(National government)	(14 532 519)	(67.0)	(554)	(696)	(61)
	Independent Liberal	106 106	0.5	4	7	–
	Labour	6 649 630	30.6	52	515	6
	Communist	74 824	0.3	–	26	–
	New Party	36 377	0.2	–	24	–
	Other	256 917	1.2	5	24	–
1935	Electors:	31 379 050	Turnout: 71.2%			
	Total votes cast	21 997 054	100.0	615	1348	40
	Conservative	11 810 158	53.7	432	585	26
	Liberal	1 422 116	6.4	20	161	–
	Labour	8 325 491	37.9	154	552	13
	Independent Labour Party	139 577	0.7	4	17	–
	Communist	27 117	0.1	1	2	–
	Other	272 595	1.2	4	31	1
1945	Electors	33 240 391	Turnout: 72.7%			
	Total votes cast	25 085 978	100.0	640	1682	3
	Conservative	9 988 306	39.8	213	624	2
	Liberal	2 248 226	9.0	12	306	–
	Labour	11 995 152	47.8	393	604	1
	Communist	102 780	0.4	2	21	–
	Common Wealth	110 634	0.4	1	23	–
	Other	640 880	2.0	19	104	–
1950	Electors:	33 269 770	Turnout: 84.0%			
	Total votes cast	28 772 671	100.0	625	1868	2
	Conservative	12 502 567	43.5	298	620	2
	Liberal	2 621 548	9.1	9	475	–
	Labour	13 266 592	46.1	315	617	
	Communist	91 746	0.3	–	100	–
	Other	290 218	1.0	3	56	–

		Votes	% share of total vote	Members	Candi- dates	Unopposed returns
1951	Electors	34 645 573	Turnout: 82.5%			
	Total votes cast	28 595 668	100.0	625	1376	4
	Conservative	13 717 538	48.0	321	617	4
	Liberal	730 556	2.5	6	109	–
	Labour	13 948 605	48.8	295	617	–
	Communist	21 640	0.1	–	10	–
	Other	177 329	0.6	3	23	–
1955	Electors:	34 858 263	Turnout: 76.7%			
	Total votes cast	26 760 493	100.0	630	1409	–
	Conservative	13 286 569	49.7	344	623	–
	Liberal	722 405	2.7	6	110	–
	Labour	12 404 970	46.4	277	620	–
	Communist	33 144	0.1	–	17	–
	Other	313 410	1.1	3	39	–
1959	Electors	35 397 080	Turnout: 78.8%			
	Total votes cast	27 859 241	100.0	630	1536	–
	Conservative	13 749 830	49.4	365	625	–
	Liberal	1 638 571	5.9	6	216	–
	Labour	12 215 528	43.8	258	612	–
	Communist	30 897	0.1	–	18	–
	Other	224 405	0.8	1	56	–
1964	Electors:	35 892 572	Turnout: 77.1%			
	Total votes cast	27 655 374	100.0	630	1757	–
	Conservative	12 001 396	43.4	304	630	–
	Liberal	3 092 878	11.2	9	365	–
	Labour	12 205 814	44.1	317	628	–
	Communist	45 932	0.2	–	36	–
	Other	302 982	1.1	–	98	–
1966	Electors	35 964 684	Turnout: 75.8%			
	Total votes cast	27 263 606	100.0	630	1707	–
	Conservative	11 418 433	41.9	253	629	–
	Liberal	2 327 533	8.6	12	311	–
	Labour	13 064 951	47.9	363	621	–
	Communist	62 040	0.2	–	57	–
	Other	390 649	1.4	2	89	–
1970	Electors	39 384 364	Turnout: 72%			
	Total votes cast	28 344 807	100.0	630	1837	–
	Conservative	13 144 692	46.4	330	628	–
	Liberal	2 117 638	7.5	6	332	–
	Labour	12 179 166	42.9	287	624	–
	Communist	38 431	0.1	–	58	–
	Other	864 880	3.1	7	195	–
1974 (Feb)	Electors	39 798 899	Turnout 78.7%			
	Total votes cast	31 333 226	100.0	635	2135	–
	Conservative	11 868 906	37.9	297	623	–
	Liberal	6 063 470	19.3	14	517	–
	Labour	11 639 243	37.1	301	623	–
	Communist	32 741	0.1	–	44	–
	Plaid Cymru	171 364	0.6	2	36	–
	SNP	632 032	2.0	7	70	–

		Votes	% share of total vote	Members	Candidates	Unopposed returns
	National Front	76 865	0.3	–	54	–
	Others (G.B.)	131 059	0.4	2	120	–
	Others (N.I.)	717 986	2.3	12	48	–
1974	Electors	40 072 971	100.0	Turnout 72.8%		
(Oct)	Conservative	10 464 817	35.8	277	623	–
	Liberal	5 346 754	18.3	13	619	–
	Labour	11 457 079	39.2	319	623	–
	Communist	17 426	0.1	–	29	
	Plaid Cymru	166 321	0.6	3	36	
	SNP	839 617	2.9	11	71	
	National Front	113 843	0.4	–	90	
	Others (G.B.)	81 227	0.3	–	118	–
	Others (N.I.)	702 094	2.4	12	43	–
1979	Electors	41 093 264	100.0	Turnout 76.0%		
	Conservative	13 697 690	43.9	339	622	–
	Liberal	4 313 811	13.8	11	577	–
	Labour	11 532 148	36.9	269	523	–
	Communist	15 938	0.1	–	38	–
	Plaid Cymru	132 544	0.4	2	36	–
	SNP	504 259	1.6	2	71	–
	National Front	190 747	0.6	–	303	–
	Ecology	38 116	0.1	–	53	–
	WRP	13 535	0.1	–	60	–
	Others (G.B.)	85 338	0.3	–	129	–
	Others (N.I.)	695 889	2.2	12	64	–
1983	Conservatives	13 012 602	42.4	397		
	Liberal/SDP Alliance	7 780 577	25.4	23*		
	Labour	8 457 124	27.6	209		
	Plaid Cymru	125 309	0.4	2		
	SNP	331 975	1.1	2		
	Others G.B.	289 033	1.0	–		
	Others N.I.	674 275	2.1	17		

* SDP 6, Liberals 17

YUGOSLAVIA

The 1920 elections were held on proportional principles by universal male suffrage. 65% of electorate voted.

	Party	Seats	% of votes
1920	Democrats (a combination of S. Pribičević's Hapsburg Serbs and the Independent Radicals)	92	19.9
	Radicals	91	17

Party	Seats	% of votes
Communists (became illegal 1921)	58	12.4
Croat Peasants	50	14.3
Serbian Agrarians	39	
Moslems	32	
Slovene Catholic People's Party	27	
Social Democrats	10	
Others	19	

The proportional system was modified in the 1923 election. 73% of the electorate voted.

	Party	Seats	% of votes
1923	Radicals	108	25.8
	Croat Peasants	70	21.8
	Democrats	51	
	Slovene Catholic People's Party	22	
	Moslems of Bosnia	18	
	Moslems of Macedonia	14	
	Serbian Agrarians	10	
	Germans	8	
	Social Democrats	2	
	Others	9	

At the 1925 elections 76.9% of the electorate voted.

	Party	Seats
1925	Radicals	142
	Independent Democrats	22
	Croat Peasants	67
	Slovene Catholic People's Party	20
	Moslems	15
	Serbian Agrarians	5
	Germans	5
	Montenegrans	3
	Others	34

At the 1927 elections 68% of the electorate voted.

	Party	Seats
1927	Radicals	112
	Croat Peasants	61
	Democrats	59

Party	Seats
Independent Democrats	22
Slovene Catholic People's Party	21
Moslems	18
Serbian Agrarians	9
Germans	6
Social Democrats	1
Others	6

The *Vidovdan* constitution and the *Skupština* were abolished on 6 Jan 29 by King Alexander, who set up a royal dictatorship which found permanent expression in the constitution of 3 June 31. This instituted a bicameral legislature: a National Assembly elected every four years publicly by all males over 21, each deputy representing 50 000 inhabitants; and a Senate half appointed and half elected by regional colleges of electors. The powers of the *Skupština* were reduced. In an attempt to eliminate regionalism all parties centred about ethnic or religious particularities were declared illegal. The name of the kingdom was changed to Yugoslavia in a similar gesture against separatism. Proportional representation was abolished: any party which won a majority of votes would henceforth be allotted two-thirds of the seats in the *Skupština*.

At the elections of 8 Nov 31 only the government list was presented. 65% of the electorate voted.

In 1933 this electoral law was relaxed. The winning party was to receive three-fifths of the seats; and conditions for establishing countrywide lists of candidates were made easier.

On 9 Oct 34 King Alexander was assassinated, and Prince Paul became Regent.

The elections of 25 May 35 were public. The opposition parties (Croat Peasants, Independent Democrats, Democrats, Serbian Agrarians and Moslems) formed a united bloc. 73.7% of the electorate voted.

	Votes	Seats
The Government	1 746 982	303
The Opposition	1 076 345	67

At the elections of 11 Dec 38, 74.5% of the electorate voted.

	Votes	Seats
The Government	1 643 783	306
(Yugoslav Radical Union)		
The Opposition	1 364 524	67

All opposition parties abstained from the elections to the Constituent Assembly of 11 Nov 45 leaving only a single Popular Front list. 88% of the electorate voted, 90% for the Popular Front.

In 1950 an electoral law abolished the single list system, and candidates were nominated individually. In the election of 26 Mar 50 the number of candidates was still the same as the number of seats: there was no contest. Popular Front candidates polled 93.25% of the votes cast.

At the elections of 22 Nov 53 the electorate for the Federal Council was 10 580 648. 527 candidates stood for 484 seats (Federal Council, 282; Council of Producers, 202, of whom 135 were industrial and 67 were agricultural). 89.4% of the electorate voted.

At the elections of 23–26 Mar 58, 307 candidates stood for the 301 seats of the Federal Council. The electorate was 11 331 727: 94% of the electorate voted. 216 representatives were elected to the Council of Producers: 168 industrial, 48 agricultural.

By the constitution of 7 Apr 63 Yugoslavia became a 'Socialist' instead of a 'People's' Republic. This constitution did away almost entirely with direct elections, replacing these by an electoral filtering system. The electoral emphasis moved from the formal act of voting to the nominating process in which citizens participate through their local government wards and workers through their workplace. The Council of Producers was abolished and replaced by four specialised councils (Administration; Culture; Economy; Welfare). The Federal Assembly of 670 was to be elected for four-year terms. Every second year one-half of each council was renewed.

Elections were held on 25 May and 16 June 63. The number of candidates was the same as the number of seats. 95.5% of the electorate voted. Half the seats came up for renewal on 19 Mar and 18 Apr 65, when a few constituencies had more than one candidate. 93.6% of the electorate voted.

By a constitutional amendment in 1968 the Federal Council was abolished and divided into its two political components: (1) Social and Political Council, elected by citizens in local government wards; (2) Council of Nations, representing the republican legislatures.

At the elections of 12 Apr and 10 May 69 for the Social and Political Council there were 179 candidates for the 120 seats. 87% of the electorate voted. There were 624 candidates for the 360 seats of the four specialized councils.

The first elections to be held on the 'delegate' principle, as outlined in the new Constitution, took place between March and May 1974. In early May elections were held to the two Chambers of the new Assembly of the Federation. Subsequent elections were held in May 1978. All candidates were either chosen or screened by the socialist Alliance of the Working People of Yugoslavia, the official Communist organization.

6 POLITICAL PARTIES

ALBANIA

ALBANIAN PARTY OF LABOUR

Founded 1941, present name adopted in 1948. Communist; the only recognized party in the state. Its First Secretary throughout the 1970s was the long-serving Enver Hoxha.

AUSTRIA

SOCIAL DEMOCRATIC PARTY 1889

Socialist social and economic aims, supported political union with Germany. After World War II, changed its name to the *Austrian Socialist Party* (*SPO*), no longer pan-German.

CHRISTIAN SOCIALIST PARTY 1892

Conservative with strong clerical Roman Catholic influence. Politically divided with one section monarchist and the other pan-German. In 1945 it was reformed as the *Austrian People's Party* (*OVP*) with a conservative Christian-Democrat programme.

ALL-GERMANY PARTY 1917

Developed out of the German National Club and some sections of the old National Democratic Party. Politically centre, committed to union with Germany. Dissolved by World War II.

COMMUNIST PARTY (KPO) 1918

Communist programme includes committal to strict neutrality. Major strength is in the trade unions.

AUSTRIAN LIBERAL PARTY (FPO) 1955

Partially succeeds the previous Independent League dissolved in 1956. Programme of moderate social reform and inter-Europe co-operation.

DEMOCRATIC PROGRESSIVE PARTY (DPF) 1965

Centre party, formed as a balance between the OVP and SPO.

BELGIUM

CATHOLIC PARTY

This, with the Liberal Party, was one of the main parties of the nineteenth century. It was divided on the French-Flemish language question, and had clearly defined left and right wings but was mainly conservative and clerical. It survived until 1945, when it was reformed as the *Christian Socialist Party* (*PSC*) which is now undenominational and has a Christian-Democrat moderate reform programme.
Membership 1980, 200 000.

LIBERAL PARTY

The other main party of the nineteenth century, less influential since. It had a moderate social and religious policy. In 1961 it was succeeded by the *Party for Liberty and Progress* (*PLP*). This is anti-federalist and concerned specially with farmers and industrial workers.

BELGIAN SOCIALIST PARTY (PSB) 1885

Founded as Parti Ouvrier Belge. Orthodox socialist programme. Split from the Flemish wing in 1979.

FRONT PARTY 1918

Founded to divide Belgium by setting up a separate Flemish state. Modern counterpart is the *People's Union*, Flemish nationalist party founded in 1954.

FRONT DEMOCRATIQUE DES FRANCOPHONES

Front composed of several small Walloon parties.

FLEMISH PARTY

The Vlaamske Blok was founded in 1979.

PEOPLE'S UNION (VOLKSUNIE)

Flemish Nationalist Party, founded in 1954, aiming at a Federal structure for the country.

BULGARIA

COMMUNIST PARTY 1918

Dominant party of the Fatherland Front organization which claims 800 000 members, Founded from a splinter group of the moderate left *Social Democratic Party* (1893).

AGRARIANS' UNION 1899

Founded to protect farming and related industries. Main body continued as Stamboulinsky's party when Draghyeff's party broke away in 1919 as a more moderate group, defending parliamentary methods in politics.

DEMOCRATIC PARTY 1895

Founded as a group to reconcile differing parties with a centre policy. In 1906 the *Radical Party* split off, in support of co-operatives, radical tax reforms and a federation of Balkan states.

NATIONAL LIBERAL PARTY 1920

United three small parties to rebuild post-war Bulgaria and gain a revision of the peace treaty. Stambouloff's *National Liberal Party* broke away in 1925.

PARTY OF THE DEMOCRATIC ENTENTE 1923

Moderate reform party committed to peace and strengthening of the law and the economy.

CYPRUS

Since the division of the island, political parties have polarised as follows:

GREEK

These include AKEL (Progressive Party of the Working People, successor to the Communist Party), the Democratic Party (f. 1976, supports UN policy on Cyprus), the Democratic Rally (f. 1976, opposition party) and the socialist EDEK (f. 1969).

TURKISH

These include the socialist Republican Turkish Party, the social democratic Democratic People's Party (f. 1979), the Populist Party (f. 1976) and the government National Unity Party (f. 1976).

CZECHOSLOVAKIA

COMMUNIST PARTY OF CZECHOSLOVAKIA 1921

Incorporated extreme left elements of the former Czech Social Democratic Labour Party, a working-class and mainly anti-communist socialist party, and the Slovak Labour Party.
Membership 1980 *c.* 1 450 000.

CZECH CATHOLIC PEOPLE'S PARTY 1918

Founded from three smaller Catholic parties, with mainly peasant support. The *Slovak Catholic People's Party* seceded from it in 1921.

CZECH NATIONAL DEMOCRATIC PARTY 1917

Developed from the Young Czech Party (liberals), the Radical Party (right-wing), the Moravian Progressive Party and the Realist Party. The bulk of membership of the last two seceded in 1925 to form the National Party of Labour. The party represented big industrial and banking interests and the anti-Socialist bourgeoisie.

NATIONAL PARTY OF LABOUR 1925

Liberal intellectual support. Programme of moderate social reform, its socialist tendencies evolutionary and not revolutionary.

CZECH PEOPLE'S PARTY 1919

Christian party supporting the National Front government.

SLOVAK RECONSTRUCTION PARTY 1948

Developed from the former Slovak Democratic Party. Supports the National Front government.

DENMARK

LIBERAL-DEMOCRATIC PARTY 1870

Support mainly from farmers, and its main aim the dominance of the Folkesting (second chamber) over Landsting (first chamber). Name changed to *Venstre*, a moderate liberal party with support no longer confined to farmers. Programme of free trade and a minimum of state interference.

SOCIAL DEMOCRATIC PARTY 1871

Non-communist socialist party supported mainly by industrial and farm workers.
Membership 1980, *c.* 125 000 members.

CONSERVATIVE PEOPLE'S PARTY 1916

Originally supported by propertied class and concerned to support the authority of the Landsting over the Folkesting. Developed as a party of free initiative, maintaining private property, restricting state action to necessary economic and social intervention.

RADICAL LIBERAL PARTY 1905

Smallholders' party, committed to reduction of armaments, international co-operation through UN, state control of large trusts and monopolies, but encouragement for small private enterprise.
Chairman 1984, T. Møller.

Other parties include the Retsforbund (Single Tax Party), founded 1919, the Communist Party (f. 1919), the Christian People's Party (f. 1970), the left-wing Socialist People's Party (f. 1959) and the Progress Party (f. 1972).

ESTONIA

CHRISTIAN PEOPLE'S PARTY 1918

Formed mainly to introduce religious teaching into the elementary and secondary school. A centre party, slightly to the right.

REFORMIST LABOUR PARTY 1917

Left of centre, formed from the old Radical Socialist Party.

PEOPLE'S PARTY

Right of centre, developed from the old Democratic and Radical-Democratic parties.

FINLAND

SOCIAL DEMOCRATIC PARTY 1899

Constitutional socialist.
Membership 1980, 100 000. Chairman, 1984, A. Saarinen.

CENTRE PARTY 1906

Formed as the Agrarian Union, name changed in 1965. Centre with tendencies to the left, aims to support the interests of smallholders and small farmers.
Membership 1980 c. 300 000. Chairman 1984, I. Virolainen.

FINNISH PEOPLE'S DEMOCRATIC LEAGUE 1944

Union of Communists and left-wing socialists, including the old Socialist Union Party.
Membership 1984, 176 000. Chairman 1984, K. Kivistö.

COMMUNIST PARTY 1918

Established in Moscow in 1917 before becoming active in Finland. It did not become legal in Finland until 1944.
General Secretary 1984, A. Aalto.

NATIONAL COALITION PARTY 1918

Conservative, supporting private enterprise.
Membership 1984, 80 000. Secretary 1984, J. Isotal.

SWEDISH PEOPLE'S PARTY 1906

To protect the interests of the Swedish minority; divided politically, but mainly liberal.
Chairman 1984, P. Stenback.

FRANCE

ACTION FRANÇAISE 1898

Right-wing, nationalist, monarchist, anti-democratic and originally anti-semitic. Supported considerable autonomy for the provinces and a government of ministers responsible only to a king.

ACTION NATIONALE 1918

A combination of the former Action Liberale Populaire (Catholic), the Federation of Democratic Republicans and the Republican Federation. A centre party supporting indirect taxation, the free play of economic laws, decentralized administration and free enterprise.

DEMOCRATIC AND SOCIAL REPUBLICAN PARTY 1901

Founded as Republican Democratic Alliance. Favoured direct taxation, diplomatic relations with the Vatican, but a careful balance between clerical and anti-clerical influences and the separation of church and state.

GAUCHE RADICALE

Moderate socialist party, most active following 1918. Conciliatory in foreign policy.

FEDERATION OF RADICALS AND RADICAL SOCIALISTS POST-1918

Socialist reform party supporting state monopolies, supporting the League of Nations and the full implementation of the Treaty of Versailles.

SOCIALIST PARTY 1905

Amalgamation of the Socialist Party of France (revolutionary) and the French Socialist Party (moderate evolutionary). The union split in 1920 and the resulting party was anti-communist, collectivist in theory but moderate in practice. Moved towards the eventual abolition of private property.

UNION OF DEMOCRATS FOR THE REPUBLIC

Development through several former parties with successive titles:

> Democratic Labour Union
> Union for the New Republic
> Democratic Union for the Fifth Republic
> Union for the Defence of the Republic

The Gaullist Party, which actively supported continuation of Gaullist policy and a more independent role for France in the Western Alliance.

NATIONAL FEDERATION OF INDEPENDENT REPUBLICANS 1962

Liberal policy.

REPUBLICAN RADICAL AND RADICAL-SOCIALIST PARTY

Traditional centre party of the third Republic. Extreme left-wing dissidents broke away in 1956, the remaining body continued with a liberal economic policy, support for NATO and European unity.

UNITED SOCIALIST PARTY 1960

Developed from the Independent Socialist Party, the Union of the Left Socialist Party and the Tribune of Communism dissident section.

DEMOCRATIC CENTRE

Formed from former sections of the Independent and Republican Movement parties. Centre left policy, supported a united Europe and NATO.

Of the parties active in the post-de Gaulle years, there are:

SOCIALIST PARTY (PS) 1971

Proposes planned economy, nationalization of key industries.
Membership, 1984, *c*. 200 000. Subscribed to the United Left programme with the Communists until 1977.

COMMUNIST PARTY (PCF) 1920

Advocates democratic path to socialism.
Membership, 1980, *c*. 700 000. Subscribed to United Left programme with Socialists until 1977.

RASSEMBLEMENT POUR LA REPUBLIQUE (RPR) 1976

A successor of the Gaullist UDR (Union of Democrats for the Republic) following the resignation of Jacques Chirac.

UNION POUR LA DEMOCRATIE FRANCAISE (UDF) 1978

Formed to unite the non-Gaullist 'majority' candidates.

REPUBLICAN PARTY 1977

Part of the UDF (see above).

RADICAL PARTY 1901

Forms part of the UDF (see above).

Among smaller parties are the *Ecologistes* (f. 1977) and on the right-wing *Le Front National* (f. 1972).

FEDERAL REPUBLIC OF GERMANY

CHRISTIAN-DEMOCRATIC UNION (CDU) 1945

Chairman, 1984, Dr H. Kohl. Membership 1984, 682 000.

CHRISTIAN SOCIAL UNION (CSU) – EQUIVALENT BAVARIAN PARTY 1945

United Catholic-Protestant action on Christian principles, supporting maintenance of private property and individual freedom. Moderate conservative. Membership 1984, 169 000. Chairman 1984, Dr F. J. Strauss.

SOCIAL DEMOCRATIC PARTY OF GERMANY (SPD) 1945

Orthodox social-democrat policies, supporting a competitive economy, moderate social policy.
Membership 1984, 1 000 000. Chairman, 1984, W. Brandt.

FREE DEMOCRATIC PARTY (FDP)

Liberal social policies, policy of appeasement in Central Europe.
Membership 1984, 80 000. Chairman 1984, D. G. Genscher.

NATIONAL DEMOCRATIC PARTY OF GERMANY (NPD) 1964

Right-wing, nationalist.
Membership 1984, 15 000. Chairman 1984, M. Mussgnug.

DIE GRUNEN (THE GREENS)

Founded 1980. A left-wing party concentrating on ecological issues, it is anti-Nato, anti-Warsaw Pact and favours smaller economic units.

GERMAN DEMOCRATIC REPUBLIC

SOCIALIST UNITY PARTY OF GERMANY 1946

Founded as a union of the Social Democratic Party and the Communist Party. Communist policy.
Membership 1984, 20m. First Secretary 1984, E. Honecker.

CHRISTIAN DEMOCRAT UNION OF GERMANY 1945

These and six others belong to a National Front and issue a joint manifesto before elections.

GERMANY 1918–45

GERMAN NATIONAL PEOPLE'S PARTY (DNVP) 1918

Conservative, formed from a union of the Free Conservative Party, the Economic Union, the Conservative Party and the Christian Socialists. Aimed at a restoration of German sovereignty and a revision of the Treaty of Versailles. Protection for home industries, anti-Communist, pro-Christian.

NATIONAL PARTY OF GERMAN MODERATES (RDM) 1920

Supported by and concerned for the industrial and commercial middle classes. Anti-Socialist and against state controls.

SOCIAL DEMOCRATIC PARTY OF GERMANY 1875

Republican, democratic. Unqualified support for peace and reconciliation after 1918. Repudiated nationalism, aimed at socialization of large-scale production.

GERMAN DEMOCRATIC PARTY 1918

Formed from the former Progressive People's Party of 1910 and the left-wing of the National Liberal Party. Republican and moderate reformist.

GERMAN COMMUNIST PARTY 1919

Revolutionary communist.

GERMAN CENTRE PARTY 1870

Catholic centre party committed to fulfilling Versailles treaty obligations with a view to reconciliation. Supported the Weimar constitution.

GERMAN PEOPLE'S PARTY 1918

Formed from the right-wing of the former National Liberal Party, Protectionist in trade, nationalist and monarchist in politics.

NATIONAL SOCIALIST GERMAN WORKERS' PARTY 1925

Seceded from the German People's Party. Nationalist, supporting re-armament. Anti-Semitic. Protectionist in trade policy. Committed to social and educational reform, expansion of German sovereignty in Europe.

GREECE

POPULAR PARTY 1920

Parliamentary methods, moderate socialist policies.

LIBERAL-CONSERVATIVE PARTY 1920s

Republican. Aimed at government through a state council.

REPUBLICAN UNION 1920s

Formerly the extreme left of the Liberal Party. Committed to increased industrial production and the welfare of industrial workers. Supported proportional representation.

COMMUNIST PARTY

Supported proportional representation, women's suffrage, confiscation of large properties. Anti-armament.

NATIONAL RADICAL UNION 1956

Concerned with stimulating production and economic stability. Moderate. Chairman, K. Karamanlis.

This and other parties were suspended in 1967 when all political parties ceased to function. Other parties recently formed and then suspended:

> Union of Democratic Left – extreme left-wing.
> Progressive Agrarian Democratic Union – moderate.
> Union of Populist Parties – right-wing, monarchist.
> Centre Union – liberal and progressive coalition.
> Liberal Democratic Centre Party – breakaway group from the CU.

Since the restoration of democracy in Greece, the following major parties have emerged:

PANHELLENIC SOCIALIST MOVEMENT (PASOK) 1974

Left-wing, incorporating Democratic Defence and Panhellenic Liberation Movement resistance organizations. Led by Andreas Papandreou, it favours socialization of the means of production.

DEMOCRATIC CENTRE UNION (EDIK) 1974

A democratic socialist party which combined the Centre Union (f. 1961) and the New Political Forces (f. 1974).

COMMUNIST PARTY OF GREECE (KKE) 1918

The orthodox Moscow-dominated party. It was banned in 1947 and reappeared in 1974.

GREEK COMMUNIST PARTY (KKE-INTERIOR) 1968

A Marxist movement, independent of the 'Moscow-line'. It separated from the pro-Moscow Communist Party of Greece in 1968.

Other parties include the Democratic Socialist Party (f. March 1979 by former EDIK activists), the New Democracy (f. 1974), a moderate pragmatic reform party, the right-wing Progressive Party (f. 1979) and the Liberal Party (f. 1981).

HUNGARY

PARTY OF NATIONAL UNITY 1921

Developed from the Party of Christian Small Landowners and Citizens. Conservative.

CHRISTIAN ECONOMY PARTY 1923

Formed from the former People's Party, Unionist Party, and Christian Socialists. Conservative and legitimist.

SOCIAL DEMOCRATIC PARTY 1984

Extreme left.

HUNGARIAN SOCIAL WORKERS' PARTY 1956

The Communist Party and the Social Democratic Party merged to create the Working People's Party. The name was later changed. Moscow-oriented Communist.
Membership 1979, c. 800 000. First Secretary 1984, J. Kadar.

PATRIOTIC PEOPLE'S FRONT 1954

Replaced the former Hungarian Independent People's Front. Represents the mass organizations such as Trade Unions. Independent Communist.

ICELAND

INDEPENDENCE PARTY (1929)

Amalgamation of Conservative (1924) and Liberal (1925) parties. Aimed at social reform within a capitalist framework and furtherance of national independence, through renunciation of the Act of Union with Denmark.

PROGRESSIVE PARTY 1916

Supports co-operatives, aims at educational and social reform.
Chairman 1984, S. Hermannsson.

SOCIAL DEMOCRATIC PARTY 1916

Moderate evolutionary socialist.
Chairman, 1984, B. Gröndal.

PEOPLE'S ALLIANCE 1956

Formed from sections of the Social Democrats and the Socialist Unity Party. Marxist.
Chairman 1984, L. Joseppson.

IRELAND

CUMAN-NA-GAEDHEAL

Moderate party accepting partition and the Act of Settlement in 1921. Aimed for economic and social stability within the Empire.

FIANNA FAIL 1926

Republican. Successor to those bodies not accepting the Act of Settlement. Neutralist.
President 1984, C. Haughey. General Secretary, S. Brennan.

FINE GAEL 1933

Formed by amalgamating Cuman-na-Gaedheal, the Centre Party and the National Guard Party. Centre.
Leader 1984, Dr Garret Fitzgerald.

LABOUR PARTY 1912

Formed as an organ of the Trades Unions, separated from them in 1930. Socialist.
Chairman 1984, M. Higgins.

SINN FEIN 1905

Formed to end British occupation, and then to end partition and achieve a Democratic Socialist Republic of all Ireland.

Among smaller parties are the Irish Republican Socialist Party, the Communist Party of Ireland (f. 1933) and the Socialist Party (f. 1970).

ITALY

ITALIAN LIBERAL PARTY 1848

Founded by Cavour as a democratic force in the re-unification of Italy. Liberal.
Membership 1980, c. 150 000.

ITALIAN REPUBLICAN PARTY 1897

Founded on the doctrines of Mazzini.

CHRISTIAN DEMOCRAT PARTY 1943

Successor to the pre-Fascist Popular Party, Anti-Communist, moderate social policy.

ITALIAN COMMUNIST PARTY 1921

The largest in Western Europe. Advocates nationalization and land redistribution.
Membership 1980, c. 1 700 000.

ITALIAN SOCIALIST PARTY (PSI) 1966

Founded by a merger of the Italian Socialist Party and the Italian Democratic Socialist Party. The latter broke away in 1969. Centre left, adhering to the Second International.
Secretary General 1984, Bettino Craxi.

UNITED SOCIALIST PARTY (PSU) 1969

Democrat splinter from the United Socialists. Centre party.

ITALIAN SOCIAL MOVEMENT 1946

Extreme right.
Membership 1980, c. 400 000.

UNITED PROLETARIAN ITALIAN SOCIALIST PARTY 1964

Further left than the Italian Socialist Party, from whom it broke away.

NATIONAL FASCIST PARTY 1919

Formed to resist Bolshevism by force. Policies developed as conservative, nationalist, militarist and imperialist. ('Fascismo' = absolute and dictatorial government.) The party of Benito Mussolini.

ITALIAN POPULAR PARTY 1919

Catholic independent party with social-democrat policies.

(All non-fascist parties were dissolved in 1926)

UNITED PARTY 1922

Formed from a section of the old Socialist Party. Revolutionary socialist and reformist.

MASSIMALIST PARTY 1922

Hard-core theoretical socialists remaining after the United Party breakaway.

LATVIA

SOCIAL DEMOCRATIC PARTY
Allied with the Jewish Bund. Moderate.

DEMOCRATIC CENTRE PARTY
Middle-class support, policy left of centre.

FARMERS' UNION
Left-of-centre party to support rural interests.

INDEPENDENT NATIONALISTS
Right-wing, support from the commericial and industrial class.

LIECHTENSTEIN

PROGRESSIVE CITIZENS' PARTY
Chairman 1984, Dr P. Marxer.

FATHERLAND UNION
Secretary, E. Nott.

CHRISTIAN-SOCIALIST PARTY 1962

Chairman 1984, F. Kaiser.

LITHUANIA

Christian Democrats ⎫
Farmers' Union ⎬ Extreme right.
Labour Federation ⎭

Populist Party ⎫
Nationalist Party ⎬ Liberal.

Social Democrats   Left of centre.

LUXEMBOURG

LUXEMBOURG SOCIALIST WORKERS' PARTY 1902

Orthodox socialist policies.
Secretary 1984, R. Goebbels.

COMMUNIST PARTY 1921

Leader 1984, R. Urbany.

CHRISTIAN SOCIALIST PARTY 1914

Dominant party in government since its foundation.
President 1984, J. Santer.

MALTA

NATIONALIST PARTY

Supports the European and Catholic tradition in Malta. Democratic conservative. Pro-Western. The party of Borg Olivier.

MALTA LABOUR PARTY 1920

Socialist. Foreign policy of non-alignment and security through the United Nations. The party of Dom Mintoff.

PROGRESSIVE CONSTITUTIONAL PARTY 1953

Supports association with EEC, close relations with Britain and NATO. The party of Mabel Strickland.

THE NETHERLANDS

ROMAN CATHOLIC STATE PARTY

Influential nineteenth-century party. Policies based on encyclicals: 'Quanta cura', 'Immortale Dei', and 'Rerum Novae'. Right wing.

CATHOLIC PEOPLE'S PARTY (KVP) 1945

Democratic section seceding from the above. Present-day membership open to Protestants.
Membership 1980, 60 000.

ANTI-REVOLUTIONARY PARTY (ARP) 1877

Originally neo-Calvinist, basing policies on the traditional Dutch native character as it was thought to be expressed in Calvinism. Conservative, becoming Christian-Democrat in policies.
Membership 1980, 60 000.

CHRISTIAN-HISTORICAL UNION (CHU) 1908

Seceded from the Anti-Revolutionaries. Protestant, and to the left of the ARP.
Membership 1980, 30 000.

RADICAL POLITICAL PARTY (PPR) 1968

Progressive, pro-environmental, anti-nuclear party. Co-operates with socialist groups.
Membership 1980, 13 000.

PEOPLE'S PARTY FOR FREEDOM AND DEMOCRACY (VVD) 1948

Undenominational. Liberal. Free enterprise and social security within one system.

SOCIAL DEMOCRATIC WORKERS' PARTY

Developed from the previous Socialist Party which it saw as anarchical and non-parliamentary. Moderate left. In 1946 the most active section broke away and formed the Labour Party (q.v.).

LABOUR PARTY (PVDA) 1946

A democratic socialist party, it took many members from the Social Democratic Workers Party.
Membership 1980, 120 000.

208

NORWAY

HØYRE 1884

Conservative. Aimed at a property-owning democracy, private enterprise.

CENTRE PARTY 1920

Moderate democratic party. Formed as Farmers' Party, name changed in 1959.

CHRISTIAN DEMOCRATIC PARTY 1933

Traditional Christian Democrat party.

LIBERAL PARTY (VENSTRE) 1884

Moderate reform party.

WORKERS' PARTY (ARBEIDERPARTIET) 1887

Orthodox evolutionary socialist.
Chairman 1971, T. Bratteli.

SOCIALIST PEOPLE'S PARTY 1961

Broke away from Workers' Party, being farther to the left. Opposed nuclear weapons and the Atlantic alliance. Neutralist. Merged into the Socialist Left Party in 1975.

SOCIALIST LEFT PARTY 1975

A union of the group which had formed the Socialist Electoral League in 1973 *e.g.* the Socialist People's Party, the Democratic Socialists etc.

POLAND

Polish People's Party National Christian Club Christian Democrats	The right wing, Catholic, alliance of Church and State, nationalist, anti-Communist and anti-Socialist.

PEASANTS' UNION 1924

Aimed for the abolition of the senate and universal franchise for men and women.

UNION OF POLISH PEASANT PARTIES 1923

Radical, concerned for small farmers and labourers. Aimed for peasant proprietorship.

RADICAL PEASANTS' PARTY 1918
Bolshevik.

NATIONAL LABOUR PARTY 1905
Workers' reform party, nationalist.

POLISH SOCIALIST PARTY 1892
Orthodox socialist, evolutionary reform party.

POLISH UNITED WORKERS' PARTY 1948
Formed by merging the former Socialist Party and Workers' Party. Communist.
Membership 1979, 3m. First Secretary, E. Gierek.

UNITED PEASANTS' PARTY 1949
Formed from merging the Peasant Party and the Polish Peasant Party. Communist, concerned for small farmers and rural workers.
Membership 1979, 440 000. Chairman, S. Gucwa.

DEMOCRATIC PARTY 1939
Progressive intellectual communist.
Membership 1979, 106 000.

PORTUGAL

MONARCHIST PARTY
Formed to support the claims of former King Manuel or Prince Duarte Nuno.

CATHOLIC PARTY
Conservative.

pre-Salazar

NATIONALIST PARTY
Conservative policy, republican.

REPUBLICAN PARTY
Democratic policy, republican.

POPULAR NATIONAL ACTION
Formerly National Union, the ruling conservative party under the Salazar régime until the revolution.

After the military *coup* of 25 April 74, the following main parties have emerged in Portugal.

SOCIAL DEMOCRATIC PARTY (PSD) 1974

Policies similar to major European Social Democratic parties. The party of Francisco Sá Carneiro. A partner in the Democratic Alliance. Membership *c.* 85 000.

PORTUGUESE COMMUNIST PARTY (PCP) Legalised 1974

Marxist-Leninist. Ultimate goal of a Socialist Portugal. Membership, *c.* 165 000. Led by Secretary-General Alvaro Cunhal. A partner in the United People's Alliance (*q.v.*).

DEMOCRATIC ALLIANCE (AD) 1979

An alliance of the Social Democratic Party (*q.v.*) and the Centre Democratic Party (*q.v.*) to fight the 1979 elections.

CENTRE DEMOCRATIC PARTY (CDS) 1974

Centrist Party, in Christian Democrat tradition. The party of Professor Freitas Do Amaral. Partner in the Democratic Alliance.

UNITED PEOPLES ALLIANCE (APU) 1979

An electoral alliance of two main groupings: the People's Democratic Movement (*q.v.*) and the Portuguese Communist Party (*q.v.*).

PEOPLES DEMOCRATIC MOVEMENT

A partner in the United People's Alliance led by Jose Tengarrinha.

SOCIALIST PARTY (PS) 1973

Democratic socialist. Affiliated to Socialist International. A successor to the earlier Portuguese Socialist Action. Led by Dr Mario Soares. Membership *c.* 100 000.

SPAIN

Prior to the Franco régime, the historic parties included:

CONSTITUTIONAL LIBERAL PARTY 1875

Advocated religious toleration, a bicameral system of government, a constitutional monarchy and universal suffrage. Split into left and right factions in 1903.

REFORMISTS' PARTY 1913

Sovereignty to be vested in the people. Foreign policy for friendship with neighbouring states.

PATRIOTIC UNIONISTS 1924

'Religion, country, monarchy' – party formed and inspired by the Military Directory.

In the Franco régime, there was only one political party, the National Movement. Its adherents were better known as Falangists.

In the post-Franco era. a large number of political parties, both national and regional, have emerged. They include:

POPULAR ALLIANCE (AP) 1976

Centrist party. Part of the Democratic Coalition (CD).

COMMUNIST PARTY OF SPAIN (PCE) 1922

A Euro-Communist party. Secretary-General, Gerardo Iglesias.

SOCIALIST PARTY (PSOE) 1879

Democratic Socialist. Secretary-General, Felipe González Márquez. Affiliated to the Socialist International.

CENTRE DEMOCRATIC UNION (UCD) 1977

A coalition of several centre parties to fight elections.

There are a host of smaller parties and regional parties.

SWEDEN

SOCIAL DEMOCRATIC LABOUR PARTY 1880

Socialist party, economical reform policy, supports United Nations. Membership 1980, *c*. 1m.

PEOPLE'S PARTY 1902

Liberal.

MODERATE UNION PARTY 1904

Conservative, free enterprise and private property.

COMMUNIST PARTY OF THE LEFT (VPK) 1917

Formed as the Left Social Democratic Party of Sweden, renamed the Communist Party in 1921 and renamed again in 1967, Marxist. Membership *c*. 16 000.

CENTRE PARTY 1922

Formed from a coalition of two smaller moderate parties. Developed more progressive social policies.

CHRISTIAN DEMOCRATIC UNION 1964

Orthodox Christian-Democrat policies.

SWEDISH WORKERS' COMMUNIST PARTY 1977

A breakaway group from the VPK, which it regarded as too Euro-Communist.

SWITZERLAND

RADICAL DEMOCRATIC PARTY

Led the movement towards the confederation of 1848. Liberal policies, supports strong central, federal power.

CHRISTIAN DEMOCRATIC PEOPLE'S PARTY OF SWITZERLAND 1912

Formed by parties which had opposed centralization since 1848. Joined also by the Kulturkampf of the Radical Majority Party. Non-sectarian Christian; the most numerous parliamentary group in the Council of States.

SOCIAL DEMOCRATIC PARTY OF SWITZERLAND 1870

Socialist. Its influence dates mainly from the first proportional representation in 1919.

FARMERS', ARTISANS' AND CITIZENS' PARTY 1919

Seceded from the Radical Democrats. Mainly agrarian concerns, liberal social policies. Merged into Swiss Peoples Party, 1971.

LABOUR PARTY 1944

Communist and left-wing socialist; aims to co-ordinate all left-wing influences.

SWISS PEOPLES PARTY 1971

A union of the Democratic Party and the Farmers, Artisans and Citizens Party.

REPUBLICAN MOVEMENT 1917

Founded to maintain Swiss independence. Opposed to UN or EEC entry.

INDEPENDENT PARTY 1936

An opposition party, liberal in social policies.

TURKEY

The National Security Council banned all political parties in September 1980. Prior to this decision the main parties were:

REPUBLICAN PEOPLE'S PARTY 1923

Founded by Kemal Atatürk. Left of centre, favoured a combination of state and private enterprise. The party of Bulent Ecevit.

PROGRESSIVE REPUBLICANS 1924

Liberal policies, free trade programmes. Dissolved for 'being in league with reactionary groups'.

JUSTICE PARTY 1961

Private enterprise party. The party of Süleyman Demirel.

NATIONAL SALVATION PARTY 1972

Right-wing Islamic. The replacement party for the National Order Party (q.v.).

RELIANCE PARTY 1967

Broke away from the Republican People's Party. Belief in political democracy. Policies left of centre. Merged 1973 with the Republican Party.

NATIONAL ORDER PARTY 1969

Extreme right-wing, aimed for the abolition of the Senate. Dissolved 1971, but resurrected 1979.

TURKISH SOCIALIST WORKERS' PARTY 1974

Left wing socialist. Supported nationalization, withdrawal from NATO.

The 1983 elections were contested by the victorious Motherland Party, the Populist Party and the Nationalist Democracy Party. These parties had been allowed to form after May 1983, but under very strict conditions. Thus the military rulers had a veto over which candidates could stand.

USSR

COMMUNIST PARTY OF THE SOVIET UNION 1903

Began as the Bolshevik movement, named the Russian Communist Party in 1917, the All-Union Communist Party of Bolsheviks in 1925, the present name given in 1952.

UNITED KINGDOM

CONSERVATIVE AND UNIONIST PARTY 1886

Formed by merger of the original Tory Party, renamed Conservative, with Liberals who did not accept Home Rule for Ireland. Policy imperialist and protectionist. Current policy free enterprise, EEC membership, and the strengthening of the Commonwealth.
Leader 1984, Mrs M. Thatcher.

LABOUR PARTY 1900

Formed as a federation of trades unions and similar organizations. Socialist economic and social policies, support for UN in foreign relations, opposes EEC membership.
Leader 1984, N. Kinnock.

LIBERAL PARTY 1832

Formed from amalgamation of the old Whig Party, the Radical Party and the Reformers. Originally aimed at free trade, Home Rule for Ireland, reform of the House of Lords and moderate social reform and land reform. Supported the League of Nations and later the United Nations. Supports entry into EEC. Fought 1983 election in alliance with Social Democratic Party (*q.v.*).
Leader 1984, D. Steel.

SOCIAL DEMOCRATIC PARTY 1981

Launched 26 March 1981 by Labour moderates opposed to left-wing movement in the Labour Party. Its four leading figures were Roy Jenkins, David Owen, William Rodgers and Shirley Williams. Leader 1984, David Owen.

CO-OPERATIVE PARTY 1917

Sponsors Labour and Co-operative candidates through a formal agreement of 1926, in which Co-operative parties became eligible for affiliation to Labour parties, and a further agreement of 1946 whereby Co-operative candidates were to run as Co-operative and Labour candidates.

INDEPENDENT LABOUR PARTY 1893

Originally affiliated to the Labour Party until policy differences grew and the parties split in 1932. Its members gradually returned to the Labour Party after 1946.

WELSH NATIONALIST PARTY (PLAID CYMRU) 1925

Campaigns for greater independence for Wales. Gen. Sec. 1984, D. Williams.

SCOTTISH NATIONAL PARTY 1928

Formed as the National Party of Scotland. Merged with the Scottish Party in 1933. Campaigns for independence for Scotland.
National Secretary 1984, N. MacCallum.

COMMUNIST PARTY OF GREAT BRITAIN 1920

Secretary 1984, G. McLennan. Not represented in Parliament since 1950.

ECOLOGY PARTY 1973

The environmentalist party. It has yet to secure representation in Parliament.

NATIONAL FRONT 1974

A nationalist, anti-immigration extreme right grouping.

YUGOSLAVIA

LEAGUE OF COMMUNISTS OF YUGOSLAVIA

The only effective party.
Membership 1980, 1.75m.

National Radical Party — monarchist, centralist and nationalist

Slovenian People's Party — anti-centralist, demanding autonomy for different groups

National Democratic Party — split from the Radicals, centralists but ready to grant autonomy as a concession in some cases

Peasants' Party — originally republican, by 1925 veering towards monarchy. Supported co-operatives and agrarian reform

} pre-1945

7 JUSTICE

ALBANIA

Justice is administered by People's Courts. In 1952 a new penal code was introduced, modelled on Soviet law,but with severer penalties (41 offences carry the death penalty). Minors (14–18 years) are criminally responsible, but may not receive the death penalty. In Sep 66 the Ministry of Justice was incorporated into the Ministry of the Interior. In 1968 tribunals were set up in towns and villages to try minor crimes which had previously been dealt with by district courts.

AUSTRIA

The Supreme Court of Justice (*Oberster Gerichtshof*) in Vienna is the highest court. There are 4 higher provincial courts (*Oberlandesgerichte*), 20 provincial and district courts (*Landes- und Kreisgerichte*) and 205 local courts (*Bezirksgerichte*).

BELGIUM

Judges are appointed for life. There is a court of cassation, 5 courts of appeal, and assize courts for political and criminal cases. There are 26 judicial districts, each with a court of first instance. In each of the 222 cantons is a justice and judge of the peace. There are, besides, various special tribunals. There is trial by jury in assize courts.

BULGARIA

The constitution of 1947 provided for the election (and recall) of the judges by the people and, for the Supreme Court, by the National Assembly, but in 1982 this was amended so that all judges are elected and recalled by the National Assembly. The lower courts include laymen ('assessors') as well as jurists. There are a Supreme Court, 28 provincial (including Sofia) courts and 105 (formerly 103) people's courts.

In June 61 'Comrades' Courts' were set up for the trial of minor offenders by their fellow-workers.

New family and penal codes were approved by the National Assembly in Apr 68. The maximum term of imprisonment is 20 (formerly 15) years except for murder which is punishable by a minimum of 20 years' imprisonment.

The Prosecutor-General, elected by the National Assembly for five years and subordinate to it alone, exercises supreme control over the correct observance of the law by all government bodies, officials and citizens. He appoints and discharges all Prosecutors of every grade. The powers of this office were extended and redefined in 1980 to put greater emphasis on crime prevention and the rights of citizens.

CYPRUS

The administration of justice is exercised by the island's separate and independent Judiciary. Under the 1960 Constitution and subsequent legislation the following judicial institutions exist: The Supreme Court of the Republic, Assize Courts, District Courts, Ecclesiastical Courts, Turkish Family Courts.

The Supreme Court is composed of 5 to 7 Judges one of whom is the President of the Court. The Supreme Court adjudicates exclusively and finally on all constitutional law matters as well as in relation to recourses for annulment of administrative acts, decisions or omission. The Supreme Court is the highest appellate Court in the Republic and has jurisdiction to hear and determine all appeals, civil and criminal, from any other Court. It has exclusive jurisdiction to issue orders in the nature of habeas corpus, mandamus, prohibition, quo warranto and certiorari and in admiralty and certain matrimonial matters.

There is an Assize Court and a District Court for each district. The Assize Courts have unlimited criminal jurisdiction and may order the payment of compensation up to £C800. The District Courts exercise original civil and criminal jurisdiction, the extent of which varies with the composition of the Bench. In civil matters a District Court composed of not less than two judges has unlimited jurisdiction. A President or a Senior District Judge of a District Court sitting alone has jurisdiction up to £3000 and a district Judge sitting alone up to £1000. In criminal matters the jurisdiction of a District Court is exercised by the members sitting singly and is of a summary nature. A President, or a Senior District Judge or a District Judge sitting alone has power to try any offence punishable with imprisonment up to 3 years, or with a fine up to £C500 or with both, and may order the payment of compensation up to £C500.

There is a Supreme Council of Judicature, consisting of the Attorney-

General of the Republic, the President and Judges of the Supreme Court, entrusted with the appointment, promotion, transfers, termination of appointment and disciplinary control over all judicial officers, other than the Judges of the Supreme Court.

CZECHOSLOVAKIA

The criminal and criminal procedure codes date from 1 Jan 62, as amended in Apr 73.

Police powers were strengthened in Jul 74.

There is a Federal Supreme Court and federal military courts, with judges elected by the Federal Assembly. Both republics have Supreme Courts and a network of regional and district courts whose professional judges are elected by the republican National Councils. Lay judges are elected by regional or district local authorities. Local authorities and social organizations may participate in the decision-making of the courts.

DENMARK

The lowest courts of justice are organized in 105 tribunals (*underretter*), where minor cases are dealt with by a single judge. The tribunals at Copenhagen have 29 judges and Aarhus 8 and the other tribunals have 1 to 3. Cases of greater consequence are dealt with by the superior courts (*Landsretterne*); these courts are also courts of appeal for the above-named minor cases. Of superior courts there are two: *Østre Landsret* in Copenhagen with 33 judges. *Vestre Landsret* in Viborg with 20 judges. From these an appeal lies to the Supreme Court (*Højesteret*) in Copenhagen, composed of 15 judges. Judges under 70 years of age can be removed only by judicial sentence.

FINLAND

The lowest courts of justice are the municipal courts in towns and district courts in the country. Municipal courts are held by the burgomaster and at least two members of court, district court by judge and five jurors, the judge alone deciding, unless the jurors unanimously differ from him, when their decision prevails. From these courts an appeal lies to the courts of appeal (*Hovioikeus*) in Turku, Vaasa, Kuopio and Helsinki. The Supreme Court (*Korkein oikeus*) sits in Helsinki. Judges can be removed only by judicial sentence.

Two functionaries, the *Oikeuskansleri* or Chancellor of Justice, and the

Oikeusasiamies, or Solicitor-General, exercise control over the administration of justice. The former acts also as counsel and public prosecutor for the government; while the latter, who is appointed by the parliament, exerts a general control over all courts of law and public administration.

FRANCE

The French judicial system has been reorganized by a number of ordinances and decrees dated 22 Dec 1958.

Before this reform, the lowest courts were those of the Justices of Peace (*juges de paix*), one in each *canton*, who tried less important civil cases. The Tribunals of First Instance (*Tribunaux de Première Instance* or *Tribunaux Civils*), one in each *arrondissement*, dealt with more important civil cases and served as Tribunals of Appeal for the Justices of Peace, when their decisions were susceptible of appeal.

Since 2 Mar 59, 467 *tribunaux d'instance* (ten in overseas departments), under a single judge each and with increased material and territorial jurisdiction, have replaced the cantonal justices of the peace; and 178 *tribunaux de grande instance* (six in overseas departments) have taken the place of the 357 *tribunaux de première instance*.

The *tribunaux de grande instance* usually have a collegiate composition: however a law dated 10 July 70 has allowed them to administer justice under a single judge in some civil cases.

All petty offences (*contraventions*) are disposed of in the Police Courts (*Tribunaux de Police*) presided over by the *Juge d'Instance*. The Correctional Courts pronounce upon all graver offences (*délits*), including cases involving imprisonment up to five years. They have no jury, and consist of three judges who administer both criminal and civil justice. In all cases of a *délit* or a *crime* the preliminary inquiry is made in secrecy by an examining magistrate (*juge d'instruction*), who either dismisses the case or sends it for trial before a court where a public prosecutor (*Procureur*) endeavours to prove the charge.

The Conciliation Boards (*Conseils de Prud'hommes*) composed of an equal number of employers and employees deal with small trade and industrial disputes. Commercial litigation goes to the Commercial Courts (*Tribunaux de Commerce*) composed of tradesmen and manufacturers elected for two years.

When the decisions of any of these Tribunals are susceptible of appeal, the cases go to the Courts of Appeal (*Cours d'Appel*). There are 31 Courts of Appeal (3 in overseas departments), composed each of a president and a variable number of members.

The Courts of Assizes (*Cours d'Assises*), composed each of a president, assisted by two other magistrates who are members of the Courts of Appeal, and by a jury of nine people, sit in every *département*, when called upon to try very important criminal cases. The decisions of the Courts of Appeal and the Courts of Assizes are final; however, the Court of Cassation (*Cour de Cassation*) had discretion to verify if the law had been correctly interpreted and if the rules of procedure have been followed exactly. The Court of Cassation may annul any judgment, and the cases have to be tried again by a Court of Appeal or a Court of Assizes.

A State Security Court has been established by 2 laws dated 15 Jan 63. It is usually composed of three civilian judges, including the president, and two judges of general or field officer rank, and has jurisdiction to deal with subversion in peace-time.

The French penal institutions have been reorganized by the procedural code which came into force on 2 Mar 59 and was modified by a law dated 17 July 70. They consist of: (1) *maisons d'arrêt* and *de correction*, where persons awaiting trial as well as those condemned to short periods of imprisonment are kept; (2) central prisons (*maisons centrales*) for those sentenced to long imprisonment; (3) special establishments, namely (a) schools for young adults, (b) hostels for old and disabled offenders, (c) hospitals for the sick and psychopaths, (d) institutions for recidivists. Special attention is being paid to classified treatment and the rehabilitation and vocational re-education of prisoners, including work in open-air and semi-free establishments.

Juvenile delinquents go before special judges and courts; they are sent to public or private institutions of supervision and re-education.

GERMANY

A uniform system of law courts existed throughout Germany, though, with the exception of the *Reichsgericht*, all courts were directly subject to the State in which they exercised jurisdiction, and not to the central Government.

After April 1935 all courts became organs of central Government. The Nazi concept of justice was defined as 'Right is that which is useful to the nation.'

The lowest courts of first instance were the *Amtsgerichte*, competent to try petty civil and criminal cases, with the exception of capital cases which fell within the jurisdiction of the Court of Assizes, or the *Reichsgericht*. Cases relating to property in which the amount involved did not exceed 500 marks were usually tried by a single judge. In the trial of more serious criminal cases the judge was assisted by two assessors (laymen), to whom on the request of the public prosecutor a professional magistrate might further be added (*Schöffengericht*). The *Amtsgerichte* dealt also with guardianships, estates and official records. The *Landgerichte* contained both civil and criminal chambers. The former, consisting of three judges, were competent to deal in first instance with all civil cases in as far as they had not been referred to the *Amtsgerichte*, especially with divorces, and also exercised a revisory jurisdiction over the

Amtsgerichte. For trying commercial cases there were further commercial chambers, consisting of one judge and two laymen. The criminal chamber heard appeals from the *Amtsgerichte* in criminal cases; if the appeal was from the decision of a single magistrate it was heard by one judge with two lay assessors (small chamber); if from a decision of the *Schöffengericht*, by three judges and two laymen (large chamber). For the trial of capital cases, the *Landgerichte* were transformed into *Schwurgerichte*, consisting of three judges and six laymen. The *Amtsgerichte* and *Landgerichte* had as superior court the *Oberlandesgerichte*. There were twenty-seven such courts in Germany. The *Oberlandesgerichte* contained criminal and civil senates consisting of three judges. They exercised appellate jurisdiction over the *Landgerichte* in civil cases, and over the 'small chambers' (and in some cases over the 'large chambers') in criminal cases. The supreme court was the *Reichsgericht*, which sat at Leipzig. This court exercised an appellate jurisdiction over all inferior courts, and also an original and final jurisdiction in cases of treason.

A law promulgated in July 1935 established the novel principle in criminal law that the courts should punish offences not punishable under the Criminal Code if they were deserving of punishment 'according to the underlying idea of a penal code or according to healthy public sentiment'.

Special courts existed for all civil disputes arising from the relationship between employers and employed. Qualified judges were appointed to these judicial bodies and they were attended by representatives of employers and employed.

There were 206 Sterilization Courts, composed of 1 judge and 2 medical men, in 1934, and 56 344 persons were sterilized.

GERMAN DEMOCRATIC REPUBLIC

The judicial system of German Democratic Republic was instituted following World War II. The principles on which the judicial system functions are embodied in the constitution. Judges are elected by the people's representative bodies or by the citizens directly. State Prosecuting Counsels are nominated by the Prosecutor-General. Jurisdiction is exercised by the Supreme Court, by the *Bezirke* Courts and by the *Kreis* Courts. All courts decide on the appointment of one presiding and two assistant magistrates. The Assistant Magistrates in the first instance are jurors (lay magistrates from all classes of society); the Labour Law Tribunal of the Supreme Court appoints two official judges and three lay magistrates.

Judges are independent and subject only to the constitution and the Legislature. A judge can be recalled only if he has committed a breach of the law, grossly neglected his duties or been convicted by a court.

Lay magistrates are elected for a period of four years after nomination by the democratic parties and organizations. Magistrates of the *Kreis* Courts are directly elected by the people; Magistrates of the *Bezirke* Courts, by the *Bezirkstag*; Magistrates of the Labour Law Tribunal of the Supreme Court, by the *Volkshammer*. All are equally authorized Judges.

Attached to the *Volkshammer* is a Constitutional and Legislature Commission in which all parties are represented according to their numbers. In addition there are on the Commission three members of the Supreme Court as well as three State Law Teachers who may not be members of the *Volkshammer*. All members of the Constitutional and Legislature Commission are appointed by the *Volkshammer*.

On 14 Jan 68 the whole judicial and penal system was reformed; the most important reform being the introduction of a new criminal code to replace the German Criminal Code of 1871.

FEDERAL REPUBLIC OF GERMANY

Justice is administered by the federal court and by the courts of the Länder. In criminal procedures, civil cases and procedures of non-contentious jurisdiction the courts on the Land level are the local courts (*Amtsgerichte*), the regional courts (*Landgerichte*) and the courts of appeal (*Oberlandesgerichte*). On the federal level decisions regarding these matters are taken by the Federal Court (*Bundesgerichtshof*) at Karlsruhe. In labour law disputes the courts of the first and second instance are the labour courts and the Land labour courts and in the third instance, the Federal Labour Court (*Bundesarbeitsgericht*) at Kassel. Disputes about public law in matters of social security, unemployment insurance, maintenance of war victims and similar cases are dealt with in the first and second instances by the social courts and the Land social courts and in the third instance by the Federal Social Court (*Bundessozialgericht*) at Kassel. In most tax matters the finance courts of the Länder are competent and in the second instance, the Federal Finance Court (*Bundesfinanzhof*) at Munich. Other controversies of public law in non-constitutional matters are decided in the first and second instance by the administrative and the higher administrative courts (*Oberverwaltungsgerichte*) of the Länder, and in the third instance by the Federal Administrative Court (*Bundesverwaltungsgericht*) at Berlin.

For the inquiry into maritime accidents the admiralty courts (*Seeämter*) are competent on the Land level and in the second instance the Federal Admiralty Court (*Bundesoberseeamt*) at Hamburg.

The constitutional courts of the Länder decide on constitutional questions. The Federal Constitutional Court (*Bundesverfassungsgericht*) as the supreme German court decided such questions as loss of basic rights, unconstitutional character of political parties, validity of laws, charges against judges and complaints regarding violations of basic rights by the public force. The death sentence is abolished.

GREECE

Under the 1975 Constitution, judges are appointed for life by the President of the Republic, after consultation with the judicial council. Judges enjoy personal and functional independence. There are three divisions of the courts – administrative, civil, and criminal – and they must not give decisions which are contrary to the Constitution. Final jurisdiction lies with a Special Supreme Tribunal.

Some laws, passed before the 1975 Constitution came into force, and which are not contrary to it, remain in force.

HUNGARY

The administration of justice is the responsibility of the Procurator-General, who is elected by parliament for a term of six years. Civil and criminal cases fall under the jurisdiction of the district courts, county courts and the Supreme Court in Budapest. Criminal proceedings are dealt with by district courts through three-member councils and by county courts and the Supreme Court in five-member councils.

District courts act only as courts of first instance; county courts as either courts of first instance or of appeal. The Supreme Court acts normally as an appeal court, but may act as a court of first instance in cases submitted to it by the Public Prosecutor. All courts, when acting as courts of first instance, consist of one professional judge and two people's assessors, and, as courts of appeal, of three professional judges. Local government Executive Committees may try petty offences.

District or county judges and assessors are elected by the district or county councils, all members of the Supreme Court by Parliament.

There are also military courts of the first instance. Military cases of the second instance go before the Supreme Court.

Judges are appointed for life, subject to removal for disciplinary reasons.

ICELAND

The courts consist of courts of first instance, exercising jurisdiction on a district level, and the Supreme Court, a national court of appeal.

There were 33 judicial districts in 1984. Each has one court of ordinary jurisdiction for civil cases and another for criminal cases, as well as a Sheriff's Court, a Probate Court and a Court of Auctions. However, one district, being divided for purposes of criminal law and law enforcement, has an additional Criminal Court and Sheriff's Court, making 34 in all. The urban districts also have a Maritime and Commercial Court. Other special courts are of less importance.

There are no intermediate courts of appeal, but these existed on a regional level prior to 1920, at which time the Supreme Court was established in its current form.

Appeal to the Supreme Court may be made from all other courts except the High Court of State, the decisions of which are not subject to judicial review. The Labour Court and the Ecclesiastical Court also constitute an exception. As to the Labour Court, only questions of procedure can be appealed to the Supreme Court. As regards the Ecclesiastical Court, its decisions are subject to appeal to the Synodal Court, which thus replaces the Supreme Court as the court of last resort.

Generally, unanimity of opinion in a court of more than one judge is not required for a valid decision, the issue being conclusively decided by a majority of votes. Dissenting opinions will be recorded and published in the same manner as the majority opinion.

Juries are not used within the judicial system.

In most judicial districts there is only one permanent judge and some judges serve in two districts. On the other hand, 5 judicial districts have more than one permanent judge. Outside the capital of Reykjavik the same judge sits in all the courts of his jurisdiction. In Reykjavik the judges are appointed either to the Town Court, the Criminal Court or the Sheriff's Court, the judges of the latter court sitting also in the Probate Court and the Court of Auctions.

IRELAND

The Constitution provides that justice shall be administered in public in Courts established by law by judges appointed by the President on the advice of the Government. The jurisdiction and organization of the Courts are dealt with in the Courts (Establishment and Constitution) Act, 1961, the Courts (Supplemental Provisions) Acts, 1961–81. These Courts consist of Courts of First Instance and a Court of Final Appeal, called the Supreme Court. The Courts of First Instance are the High Court with full original jurisdiction and the Circuit and the District Courts with local and limited jurisdiction. A judge may not be removed from office except for stated misbehaviour or incapacity and then only on resolutions passed by both Houses of the *Oireachtas*. Judges of the Supreme, High and Circuit Courts are appointed from among practising barristers. Judges of the District Court (called District Justices) may be appointed from among practising barristers or practising solicitors.

The Supreme Court, which consists of the Chief Justice (who is *ex officio* an additional judge of the High Court) and 5 ordinary judges, has appellate jurisdiction from all decisions of the High Court. The President may, after consultation with the Council of State, refer a Bill, which has been passed by both Houses of the *Oireachtas* (other than a money bill and certain other bills), to the Supreme Court for a decision on the question as to whether such Bill or any provision thereof is repugnant to the Constitution.

The High Court, which consists of a President (who is *ex officio* an additional Judge of the Supreme Court) and 15 ordinary judges, has full original jurisdiction in and power to determine all matters and questions, whether of law or fact, civil or criminal. In all cases in which questions arise concerning the validity of any law having regard to the provisions of the Constitution, the High Court alone exercises original jurisdiction. The High Court on Circuit acts as an appeal court from the Circuit Court.

The Court of Criminal Appeal consists of the Chief Justice or an ordinary judge of the Supreme Court, together with either 2 ordinary judges of the High Court or the President and one ordinary judge of the High Court. It deals with appeals by persons convicted on indictment where the appellant obtains a certificate from the trial judge that the case is a fit one for appeal, or, in case such certificate is refused, where the court itself, on appeal from such refusal, grants leave to appeal. The decision of the Court of Criminal Appeal is final, unless that court or the Director of Public Prosecutions certifies that the decision involves a point of law of exceptional public importance, in which case an appeal is taken to the Supreme Court.

The High Court execising criminal jurisdiction is known as the Central Criminal Court. It consists of a judge or judges of the High Court, nominated by the President of the High Court. The Court sits in Dublin and tries criminal cases which are outside the jurisdiction of the Circuit Court or which may be sent forward to it for trial from the Circuit Court on the application of the Director of Public Prosecution.

ITALY

Italy has 1 court of cassation, in Rome, and is divided for the administration of justice into 23 appeal court districts (and 3 detached sections), subdivided into 159 tribunal districts, and these again into *mandamenti* each with its own magistracy (*Pretura*), 899 in all. There are also 85 first degree assize courts and 26 assize courts of appeal. For civil business, besides the magistracy above mentioned, *Conciliatori* have jurisdiction in petty plaints.

LIECHTENSTEIN

Jurisdiction in civil and criminal cases is exercised in the name of the Prince in first instance by the Lower Court, in second instance by the High Court, and in third and final instance by the Supreme Court. All these courts sit in Vaduz.

In matters of civil law all rulings of the Lower Court are made by summary procedure, i.e. by judges sitting alone (there are at present seven in office). In criminal cases a single judge of the Lower Court, sitting in the first instance, handles only those misdemeanours and felonies punishable by a maximum sentence of six months' imprisonment or a fine. In all other cases, misdemeanours are tried before the *Schöffengericht* (bench of three: one judge and two lay assessors). Felonies which cannot be dealt with by the simplified procedure are tried before the Criminal Court (bench of five). Juvenile cases are treated in the Juvenile Court (bench of three).

The High Court and the Supreme Court are corporate judicial bodies. While the business of the High Court is divided between two benches, the Supreme Court has the same composition for all its rulings in civil and criminal cases. Both the High Court and the Supreme Court have a bench of five.

All judges whether they sit singly or as members of a bench, are, within the lawful limits of their activity and in judicial procedure, independent of any influence by the administration.

LUXEMBOURG

The courts are entrusted by the Constitution with the exercise of judicial power. The Constitution applies to them the principle of the separation of powers by making them independent in performing their functions, restricting their sphere of activity, defining their limits of jurisdiction and providing for a number of procedural guarantees.

The courts of the Justices of the Peace are the lowest; they are at Luxembourg City, Esch-sur-Alzette and Dickirch. They deal with minor civil, commercial and criminal cases. There are two judicial districts of Luxembourg and Diekirch. The district courts deal with civil, commercial and criminal cases. The Superior Court of Justice includes both a court of appeal, hearing decisions made by district courts, and a *Cour de Cassation*. The Court of Assizes, which falls within the jurisdiction of the Superior Court, hears criminal cases. There is no jury system. A defendant is acquitted if fewer than four of the six judges finds him guilty. The highest administrative court is the *Comité du Contentieux du Conseil d'Etat*. Matters of social administration such as social insurance are dealt with by special tribunals. The administration

227

of the judiciary and the supervision of judicial police investigations is the responsibility of the *Procureur général*.

Judges are appointed for life by the Grand Duke, and are not removable except by judicial sentence.

MALTA

Civil law has generally evolved from Roman law. Public law and some commercial and maritime affairs are influenced by English law.

There is a Constitutional Court, a Court of Appeal and a Criminal Court of Appeal, together with a Civil Court, a Criminal Court, a Commercial Court and Court of Judicial Police including a Juvenile Court.

THE NETHERLANDS

Justice is administered by the High Court of the Netherlands (Court of Cassation), by 5 courts of justice (Courts of Appeal), by 19 district courts and by 62 cantonal courts; trial by jury is unknown. The Cantonal Court, which deals with minor offences, is formed by a single judge; the more serious cases are tried by the district courts, formed as a rule by three judges (in some cases one judge is sufficient); the courts of appeal are constituted of three and the High Court of five judges. All judges are appointed for life by the Sovereign (the judges of the High Court from a list prepared by the Second Chamber of the States-General). They can be removed only by a decision of the High Court.

Juvenile courts were set up in 1922. The juvenile court is formed by a single judge specially appointed to try children's civil cases, at the same time charged with the administration of justice for criminal actions committed by young persons who are between 12 and 18 (in special cases up to 21) years old, unless imprisonment of 6 months or more ought to be inflicted; such cases are tried by three judges.

NORWAY

The judicature is common to civil and criminal cases. The same professional judges, who are legally educated, preside over both kinds of cases. These judges are as such state officials. The participation of lay judges and jurors, both summoned for the individual case, varies according to the kind of court and kind of case.

The ordinary Court of First Instance (*Herredsrett* and *Byrett*) is in criminal cases composed of one professional judge and two lay judges, chosen by ballot from a panel elected by the district council. In civil cases two lay judges may participate. The ordinary Court of First Instance is in general competent in all kinds of cases, with the exception of criminal cases where the maximum penalty prescribed in the Criminal Code for the offence in question exceeds five years' imprisonment. Altogether there are 98 ordinary courts of first instance.

In every community there is a Conciliation Council (*Forliksråd*) composed of three lay persons elected by the district council. A civil lawsuit usually begins with mediation in the council which also has judicial authority in minor civil cases.

The ordinary Courts of Second Instance (*Lagmannsrett*), of which there are five, are composed of three professional judges. Additionally, in civil cases two or four lay judges may be summoned. In criminal cases a jury of ten lay persons is summoned to determine whether the defendant is guilty according to the charge. In civil cases, the Court of Second Instance is an ordinary court of appeal. In criminal cases in which the lower court does not have judicial authority, it is itself the court of first instance. In other criminal cases it is an appeal court as far as the appeal is based on an attack against the lower court's assessment of the facts when determining the guilt of the defendant. An appeal based on any other alleged mistakes is brought directly before the Supreme Court.

The Supreme Court (*Høyesterett*) is the court of last resort. There are eighteen Supreme Court judges. Each individual case is heard by five judges. Some major cases are determined in plenary session. The Supreme Court may in general examine every aspect of the case and the handling of it by the lower courts. However, in criminal cases the Court may not overrule the lower court's assessment of the facts as far as the guilt of the defendant is concerned.

The Court of Impeachment (*Riksretten*) is composed of five judges of the Supreme Court and ten members of parliament.

All serious offences are prosecuted by the state. The public prosecution authority (*påtalemyndigheten*) consists of the Attorney-General (*Riksadvokaten*), eighteen district attorneys (*statsadvokater*) and legally qualified officers of the ordinary police force. Counsel for the defence is in general provided for by the state.

POLAND

The legal system was reorganized in 1950. A new penal code was adopted in 1969. Espionage and treason carry the severest penalties and severer punishment is provided for 'serious crimes'. For minor crimes there is more provision for probation sentences and fines. Previous jurisprudence was based on a penal code of 1932 supplemented by the Concise Penal Code of 1946.

There exist the following courts: The Supreme Court: voivodship, district and special courts. Judges and lay assessors are elected. The State Council elects the judges of the Supreme Court for a term of five years and appoints the Prosecutor-General. The office of the Prosecutor-General is separate from the judiciary.

Family courts were established in 1977 for cases involving divorce and domestic relations.

PORTUGAL

Portuguese law distinguishes civil (including commercial) and penal, labour, administrative and fiscal law, each branch having its lower courts, courts of appeal and the Supreme Court.

The Republic is divided for civil and penal cases into 216 *comarcas*; in every *comarca* there is a lower court. In the *comarca* of Lisbon there are 39 lower courts (22 for criminal procedure and 17 for civil or commercial cases); in the *comarca* of Oporto there are 21 lower courts (12 for criminal and 9 for civil or commercial cases); at Coimbra, Setúbal, Sintra and Vila Nova de Gaia there are four courts; at Amanda, Braga, Cascais, Funchal, Guimarães, Leiria, Lovres, Matosinhos, Oeiras Santarém and Viseu there are three courts; 19 comarcas have two courts each. There are 4 courts of appeal (*Tribunal de Relação*) at Lisbon, Coimbra, Evora and Oporto, and a Supreme Court in Lisbon (*Supremo Tribunal de Justiça*).

Capital punishment was abolished under the 1976 Constitution.

ROMANIA

Justice is administered by the Supreme Court, the 40 district courts and lower courts. People's assessors (elected for four years) participate in all court trials, collaborating with the judges. The Procurator-General exercises 'supreme supervisory power to ensure the observance of the law' by all authorities, central and local, and all citizens. The Procurator's Office and its organs are independent of any organs of justice or administration, and only responsible to the Grand National Assembly (which appoints the Procurator-General for four years) and, between its sessions, to the State Council. Since 1968 the Ministry of the Interior has been responsible only for 'ordinary' police work. State security is the responsibility of a new, separate State Security Council. A new penal code came into force on 1 Jan 69. It is based on 'the rule of law' and is aimed at preventing illegal trials. The death penalty is retained for 'specially serious offences' (treason, some classes of murder, theft of state property having serious consequences).

SPAIN

Justice is administered by *Tribunales* and *Juzgados* (Tribunals and Courts), which conjointly form the *Poder Judicial* (Judicial Power). Judges and magistrates cannot be removed, suspended or transferred except as set forth by law. The Constitution of 1978 has established a new organ, the *Consejo General del Poder Judicial* (General Council of the Judicial Power), formed by magistrates, judges, attorneys and lawyers, governing the Judicial Power in full independence from the other two powers of the State, the Legislative (Cortes) and the Executive (President of the Government and his Cabinet). The territorial organization of justice is being gradually changed, adapting it to the new map of the country in Autonomous Communities.

The Judicature is composed of the *Tribunal Supremo* (Supreme High Court); 16 *Audiencias Territoriales* (Division High Courts); 50 *Audiencias Provinciales* (Provincial High Courts); 518 *Juzgados de Primera Instancia* (Courts of First Instance), 742 *Juzgados de Distrito* (District Courts) and 7532 *Juzgados Municipales y de paz* (Municipal and Peace Courts, Court of Lowest Jurisdiction held by Justices of the Peace).

The *Tribunal Supremo* consists of a President (appointed by the King, on proposal from the *Consejo General del Poder Judicial*) and various judges distributed among six chambers; one for trying civil matters, three for administrative purposes, one for criminal trials and one for social matters. The *Tribunal Supremo* has disciplinary faculties; is court of cassation in all criminal trials; for administrative purposes decides in first and second instance disputes arising between private individuals and the State, and in social matters resolves in the last instance all cases involving over 100 000 pesetas.

The *Audiencias Territoriales* have power to try in second instance sentences passed by judges in civil matters.

The *Audiencias Provinciales* try and pass sentence in first instance on all cases filed for delinquency. The jury system, re-established by the art. 125 of the Constitution, had not been applied by Jan 84, pending its parliamentary regulation.

The *Juzgados Municipales* try small civil cases and petty offences. The *Juzgados Comarcales* deal with the same charges, but their jurisdiction embraces larger districts.

Military cases are tried by the *Tribunal Supremo de Justicia Militar* but its sentences can now pass to the (civil) *Tribunal Supremo*, as final cassation instance.

The *Tribunal Constitucional* (Constitutional Court) has power to solve conflicts between the State and the Autonomous Communities, to determine if legislation passed by the Cortes is contrary to the Constitution and to protect constitutional rights of the individuals violated by any authority. Its 12 members are appointed by the King in the following way: 4, on proposal of the Congress of Deputies; 4, on proposal of the Senate; 2, on proposal of the *Consejo General del Poder Judicial*; and 2, on proposal of the Cabinet.

The death penalty was abolished in 1978 by the Constitution (art. 15). Divorce was allowed from July 81.

SWEDEN

The administration of justice is entirely independent of the government. The *Justitiekansler*, or Chancellor of Justice (a royal appointment) and the *Justitieombudsmän* (Judicial Commissioners appointed by the Diet), exercise a control over the administration. In 1968 a reform was carried through which meant that the offices of the former *Justitieombudsmän* (Ombudsman for civil affairs) and the *Militeombudsmän* (Ombudsman for military affairs) were turned into one sole institution with three Ombudsmen, each styled *Justitieombudsmän*. They exert a general supervision over all courts of law, the civil service, military laws and the military service.

The *Riksånlagaren* (a royal appointment) is the chief public prosecutor.

The kingdom has a Supreme Court of Judicature and is divided into 6 high-court districts and 135 district-court divisions.

These district courts (or courts of first instance) deal with both civil and criminal cases. More serious criminal cases are generally tried by a judge and a jury (*nämnd*) of seven to nine members; in minor criminal cases the jury is reduced to three; petty cases are tried by the judge alone. In larger towns civil cases are tried as a rule by three to four judges or in minor cases by one judge. In rural districts and small towns civil cases are tried in the same way as criminal cases.

In trials by jury the judge decides the case except when the whole jury – or at least seven members if the jury consists of more than seven – differs from him, when the decision of the jury prevails.

Persons of poor or moderate means may be provided with the services of lawyers in civil and criminal proceedings from special state-aided legal aid centres, and may also be granted costs for their proceedings. Moreover, the community may bear the cost of free legal advice to poor persons by private lawyers in cases not brought before a court.

SWITZERLAND

The Federal Tribunal (*Bundes-Gericht*), which sits at Lausanne consists of 26–28 members, with 11–13 supplementary judges, appointed by the Federal Assembly for six years and eligible for re-election; the president and vice-president serve for two years and cannot be re-elected. The Tribunal has original and final jurisdiction in suits between the Confederation and cantons; between cantons and cantons; between the Confederation or cantons and corporations or individuals, the value in dispute being not less than 8000 francs; between parties who refer their case to it, the value in dispute being at least 20 000 francs; in such suits as the constitution or legislation of cantons places within its authority; and in many classes of railway suits. It is a court of appeal against decisions of other federal authorities, and of cantonal authorities applying federal laws. The Tribunal also tries persons accused of treason or other offences against the Confederation. For this purpose, it is divided into four chambers: Chamber of Accusation, Criminal Chamber (*Cour d'Assises*), Federal Penal Court and Court of Cassation. The jurors who serve in the Assize Courts are elected by the people, and are paid 70 francs a day when serving.

On 3 July 38 the Swiss electorate accepted a new federal penal code, to take the place of the separate cantonal penal codes. The new code, which abolished capital punishment, came into force on 1 Jan 42.

By federal law of 5 Oct 50 several articles of the penal code concerning crime against the independence of the state have been amended with a view to reinforcing the security of the state.

TURKEY

The unified legal system consists of: (1) justices of the peace (single judges with limited but summary penal and civil jurisdiction); (2) courts of first instance (single judges, dealing with cases outside the jurisdiction of (3) and (4): (3) central criminal courts (a president and two judges, dealing with cases where the crime is punishable by imprisonment over five years): (4) commercial courts (three judges).

The Court of Cassation sits at Ankara.

The Council of State is the highest administration tribunal; it consists of five chambers. Its 31 judges are nominated from among high-ranking personalities in politics, economy, law, the army, etc. The Military Court of Cassation in Ankara is the highest military tribunal.

The Constitutional Court, set up under the 1961 constitution, can review and annul legislation and try the President of the Republic, Ministers and senior judges. It consists of 15 regular and 5 alternate members.

233

The Civil Code and the Code of Obligations have been adapted from the corresponding Swiss codes. The Penal Code is largely based upon the Italian Penal Code, and the Code of Civil Procedure closely resembles that of the Canton of Neuchâtel. The Commercial Code is based on the German.

UNION OF SOVIET SOCIALIST REPUBLICS

The basis of the judiciary system is the same throughout the Soviet Union, but the constituent republics have the right to introduce modifications and to make their own rules for the application of the code of laws. The Supreme Court of the USSR is the chief court and supervising organ for all constituent republics and is elected by the Supreme Soviet of the USSR for five years. Supreme Courts of the Union and Autonomous Republics are elected by the Supreme Soviets of these republics, and Territorial, Regional and Area Courts by the respective Soviets, each for a term of five years. At the lowest level are the People's Courts, which are elected directly by the population.

Court proceedings are conducted in the local language with full interpreting facilities as required. All cases are heard in public, unless otherwise provided for by law, and the accused is guaranteed the right of defence.

Laws establishing common principles of criminal legislation, criminal responsibility for state and military crimes, judicial and criminal procedure and military tribunals were adopted by the Supreme Soviet on 25 Dec 58 for the courts both of the USSR and the constituent Republics.

The Law Courts are divided into People's Courts and higher courts. The People's Courts consist of the People's Judge and two Assessors, and their function is to examine, as the first instance, most of the civil and criminal cases, except the more important ones, some of which are tried at the Regional Court, and those of the highest importance at the Supreme Court. The regional Courts supervise the activities of the People's Courts and also act as Courts of Appeal from the decisions of the People's Court. Special chambers of the higher courts deal with offences committed in the Army and the public transport services.

People's Judges and rota-lists of assessors are elected directly by the citizens of each constituency: judges for five years, assessors for two and a half, they must be over 25 years of age. Should a judge be found not to perform his duties conscientiously and in accordance with the mandate of the people, he may be recalled by his electors.

The People's Assessors are called upon for duty for two weeks in a year. The People's Assessors for the Regional Court must have had at least two years' experience in public or trade-union work. The list of Assessors for the Supreme Court is drawn up by the Supreme Soviet of the Republic.

The Labour Session of the People's Court supervises the regulations relating to the working conditions and the protection of labour and gives decisions on conflicts arising between managements and employees, or the violation of regulations.

Disputes between state institutions must be referred to an arbitration commission. Disputes between Soviet state institutions and foreign business firms may be referred by agreement to a Foreign Trade Arbitration Commission of the All-Union Chamber of Commerce.

The Procurator-General of the USSR is appointed for five years by the Supreme Soviet. All procurators of the republics, autonomous republics and autonomous regions are appointed by the Procurator-General of the USSR for a term of five years. The procurators supervise the correct application of the law by all state organs, and have special responsibility for the observance of the law in places of detention. The procurators of the Union republics are subordinate to the Procurator-General of the USSR, whose duty it is to see that acts of all institutions of the USSR are legal, that the law is correctly interpreted and uniformly applied; he has to participate in important cases in the capacity of State Prosecutor.

Capital punishment was abolished on 26 May 47, but was restored on 12 Jan 50 for treason, espionage and sabotage, on 7 May 54 for certain categories of murder, in Dec 58 for terrorism and banditry, on 7 May 61 for embezzlement of public property, counterfeiting and attack on prison warders and, in particular circumstances, for attacks on the police and public order volunteers and for rape (15 Feb 62) and for accepting bribes (20 Feb 62).

In view of criminal abuses, extending over many years, discovered in the security system, the powers of administrative trial and exile previously vested in the security authorities (MVD) were abolished in 1953; accelerated procedures for trial on charges of high treason, espionage, wrecking, etc., by the Supreme Court were abolished in 1955; and extensive powers of protection of persons under arrest or serving prison terms were vested in the Procurator-General's Office (1955). Supervisory commissions, composed of representatives of trade unions, youth organizations and local authorities, were set up in 1956 to inspect places of detention.

Further reforms of the civil and criminal codes were decreed on 25 Dec 58. Thereby the age of criminal responsibility has been raised from 14 to 16 years; deportation, banishment and deprivation of citizenship have been abolished; a presumption of innocence is not accepted, but the burden of proof of guilt has been placed upon the prosecutor; secret trials and the charge of 'enemy of the people' have been abolished. Articles 70 and 100 of the Criminal Code, which deal with 'anti-Soviet agitation and propaganda' and 'crimes against the system of administration' respectively, have, however, been widely used against political dissidents in more recent years.

235

UNITED KINGDOM

Although the United Kingdom is a unitary state, it does not have a single body of law applicable universally within it limits. Scotland has its own distinctive legal system and law courts, and although a single Parliament exists for Great Britain since 1707, common opinions on broader issues, and a common final court of appeal in civil cases have resulted in substantial identity on many points, differences in legal procedure and practice remain. In Northern Ireland on the other hand, the structure of the courts and legal procedure and practice have closely resembled those of England and Wales for centuries but, as Northern Ireland has its own parliament with defined powers (as well as being represented in the parliament at Westminster), its enacted law derives in certain spheres from a different source and may differ in substance from that which operates in England and Wales. However, a large volume of modern legislation, particularly in the social field, applies throughout the United Kingdom. A feature common to all systems of law in the United Kingdom (which differentiates them from some continental systems) is that there is no complete code, although the Law Commission is working on the codification of certain branches of law. The sources of law in all the systems include legislation and unwritten or 'common' law.

Legislation includes some 3000 Acts of Parliament and delegated or subordinate legislation made by ministers and others under powers conferred by parliament, Acts of Parliament being absolutely binding on all courts of the United Kingdom, and taking precedence over any other source of law. The common law of England originated in the customs of the realm and was built up by decisions of the courts. A supplementary system of law, known as 'equity', came into being during the Middle Ages to provide and enforce more effective protection for existing legal rights. It was administered by a separate court and later became a separate body of legal rules. In 1875 the courts of equity were fused with the courts of common law, so that all courts now apply both systems but, where they conflict, equity prevails. In Scotland the basis of common law, which largely depends on the canon law of Rome, helped by continental commentators, is embodied in the writings of certain seventeenth-, eighteenth- and early nineteenth-century lawyers who, between them, described systematically almost the whole field of private and criminal law as existing in their times. Broadly speaking, the principles enunciated by these lawyers, together with the many judicial decisions which have followed and developed from those principles, form the body of Scots non-statutory law. Scotland has never had a separate system of equity – equitable principles having always permeated the ordinary rules of law. A feature common to the legal systems of the United Kingdom is the distinction made between the criminal law and the civil law. Criminal law is concerned with wrongs against

236

the community as a whole; civil law is concerned with the rights, duties and obligations of individual members of the community between themselves.

YUGOSLAVIA

There are county tribunals, district courts, the Supreme Court of the Autonomous Province of Vojvodina, Supreme Courts of the constituent republics and the Supreme Court of the Socialist Federal Republic of Yugoslavia. In county tribunals and district courts the judicial functions are exercised by professional judges and by lay assessors constituted into collegia. There are no assessors at the supreme courts.

All judges are elected by the social-political communities in their jurisdiction. The judges exercise their functions in accordance with the legal provisions enacted since the liberation of the country.

The constituent republics enact their own criminal legislation, but offences concerning state security and the administration are dealt with at federal level.

8 DEFENCE AND TREATIES

PRINCIPAL EUROPEAN ARMED CONFLICTS
1918–84

RUSSIAN CIVIL WAR. *June 1918–November 1920*

Civil War between Soviet Communists and White Russian forces, with intervention by outside powers on behalf of the anti-Communists. The first landing of British forces took place at Murmansk in June 18, and further French and British troops landed at Archangel in Aug 18; Japan and the United States also sent troops. The Civil War effectively ended when White Russian forces under General Wrangel evacuated the Crimea in Nov 20.

RUSSO-POLISH WAR. *April 1919–October 1920*

Invasion by Polish forces of territory occupied by the Soviet Union as the German army withdrew at the end of World War I, in the hope of establishing a Soviet-Polish frontier which would give Poland possession of all the areas it traditionally claimed. After a Soviet counter-attack had been defeated, an armistice was signed on 12 Oct 20, and a settlement was reached in the treaty of Riga (18 Mar 21).

GRECO-TURKISH WAR. *January 1921–October 1922*

Greek invasion of Asian Turkey (Anatolia). This was repelled by the Turkish republican forces, and the Armistice of Mudanya (11 Oct 22) ended the fighting. By the Treaty of Lausanne (24 July 23), Greece renounced any claim to territory in Asia Minor, whilst Turkey surrendered all claims to territories of the Ottoman empire occupied by non-Turks.

SPANISH CIVIL WAR. *July 1936–March 1939*

A revolt by military leaders in Spanish Morocco against the civilian government led to general civil war. Unofficial military assistance was given by Germany, Italy, Portugal and the USSR; in all, 40 000 foreign volunteers including 2000 British, fought in the International Brigade on the Republican side. The civil war ended when General Franco's Nationalist forces entered Madrid on 28 Mar 39.

WORLD WAR II (EUROPE). *September 1939 – May 1945*

German forces invaded Poland on 1 Sep 39, which led Britain and France to declare war on Germany on 3 Sep. The Germans invaded the Low Countries on 10 May 40, and France was compelled to sign an armistice on 22 June, the British army being evacuated from Dunkirk. Italy declared war on Britain and France on 10 June 40. Breaking the Nazi-Soviet Pact of Aug 39, Hitler invaded Russia on 22 June 41. Allied forces drove Italian and German armies out of North Africa and invaded Italy in 1943. The invasion of Normandy was launched on 6 June 44, and Germany was forced to accept unconditional surrender on 7 May 45.

RUSSO-FINNISH WAR. *November 1939 – March 1940*

Soviet forces invaded Finland following Finnish rejection of demands for territorial concessions. The war was ended by the Treaty of Moscow (12 Mar 40), in which the Finns surrendered to Russia the south-eastern part of the country.

GREEK CIVIL WAR. *1946 – 1949*

Civil war between Communist partisan forces and the civilian government. The likelihood of a Communist victory was reduced by the break between Yugoslavia and the Communist bloc in 1948, which led to the closing of one stretch of Greece's northern frontier to the rebels. The Greek Communist broadcasting station announced the end of open hostilities on 16 Oct 49.

GERMAN DEMOCRATIC REPUBLIC UPRISING. *June 1953*

Demonstrations in East Berlin and other cities of the German Democratic Republic against Russian domination began on 17 June 53, but were suppressed by Soviet armed forces.

HUNGARIAN UPRISING. *October 1956*

Student demonstrations on 23 Oct 56 led to a general uprising against the civil government and Soviet occupying power. On 27 Oct Soviet troops were forced to evacuate Budapest, but reinforcements arrived to surround the capital, and after ten days' fighting the uprising was suppressed.

INVASION OF CZECHOSLOVAKIA. *August 1968*

During the night of 20–21 Aug, Soviet troops and Warsaw Pact forces from Poland, Hungary, German Democratic Republic and Bulgaria occupied Prague and other leading cities to reverse the liberalizing reforms of the Czechoslovakian government. Though the Czechoslovakian armed forces were ordered to offer no resistance, there were extensive civilian demonstrations against the occupying forces.

239

TURKISH INVASION OF CYPRUS. *July–August 1974*

On 15 July 74 a *coup* was staged by men of the Greek ruling junta for the overthrow of President Makarios and fighting between Greek and Turkish Cypriots led to a Turkish invasion of Cyprus on 20 July. A cease-fire on 22 July was followed by peace talks between Britain, Greece and Turkey at Geneva, but there was renewed fighting 14–16 Aug. Turkey was left in control of the northern two-fifths of the island.

PRINCIPAL ARMED CONFLICTS (OUTSIDE EUROPE) IN WHICH EUROPEAN POWERS PARTICIPATED 1918–84

ABYSSINIAN WAR. *October 1935–July 1936*

Italy invaded Abyssinia on 3 Oct 35. Addis Ababa was captured on 5 May 36, and the Emperor Haile Selassie was forced into exile in Britain. The League of Nations imposed sanctions on Italy, but these proved ineffective; they were lifted in July 36.

WORLD WAR II (ASIA). *December 1941–August 1945*

Japan attacked the American base at Pearl Harbor on 7 Dec 41, and within six months the Japanese were masters of South-east Asia and Burma. The Allied counter-offensive culminated in the dropping of the first atomic bombs on Hiroshima and Nagasaki in Aug 45. On 15 Aug 45 the Emperor of Japan broadcast to the nation to cease fighting. The principal European powers involved in the conflict were Britain and the Netherlands; the Soviet Union also declared war on Japan on 8 Aug 45.

FIRST VIETNAM WAR. *December 1946–July 1954*

The war between the French colonial government and Communist forces led by Ho Chi Minh began with attacks on French garrisons by Vietminh troops throughout Vietnam on 19 Dec 46. The French army was defeated at Dien Bien Phu in May 54, and the war was ended by the Geneva Agreement of 21 July 54, which divided Vietnam into the area north of the 17th parallel and an independent South Vietnam.

MALAYAN EMERGENCY. *June 1948–July 1960*

Insurgency by Communist forces, eventually suppressed by British and Malayan troops. The State of Emergency was ended on 31 July 60. British troops were also involved in the 'confrontation' with Indonesia after the creation of the Malaysia Federation on 16 Sep 63. An agreement was reached ending confrontation on 1 June 66.

KOREAN WAR. *June 1950–July 1953*

The invasion of South Korea by North Korea on 25 June 50 led to intervention by United Nations forces following an emergency session of the Security Council. The advance of the United Nations forces into North Korea on 1 Oct 50 led to the entry of the Chinese into the war. An armistice was signed at Panmunjon on 27 July 53. The European powers which contributed to the United Nations force were Britain, France, Turkey, Belgium, Luxembourg, the Netherlands and Greece.

ALGERIAN REVOLUTIONARY WAR. *October 1954–March 1962*

The uprising by the FLN (Front de Libération Nationale) against the French colonial government began during the night of 31 Oct–1 Nov 54. A cease-fire agreement was signed on 18 Mar 62, and after a referendum the independence of Algeria was recognized on 3 July 62.

SUEZ WAR. *October–November 1956*

The Israeli army attacked Egypt on 29 Oct 56. The rejection of a British and French ultimatum by Egypt resulted in a combined British and French attack on Egypt on 31 Oct. Hostilities ended at midnight on 6–7 Nov following the call for a cease-fire by the United Nations.

PORTUGAL'S WARS IN AFRICA. *1961–75*

The struggle for independence against colonial rule in Portugal's African colonies began with an uprising in Angola in 1961 and spread to Guinea-Bissau and Mozambique. The conflicts put a growing strain on Portugal and by 1974 her forces had suffered some 11 000 dead and 30 000 wounded. Following the overthrow of the Portuguese government by a *coup d'état* in Apr 74, independence was rapidly granted to Angola (11 Nov 75), Guinea-Bissau (10 Sep 74) and Mozambique (25 Jun 75).

SOVIET INVASION OF AFGHANISTAN. *December 1979*

The instability of the Soviet-backed régime and growing resistance to its reforms led to a full-scale Russian invasion of Afghanistan on 27 Dec 79. A new government under Babrak Karmal was installed, but a considerable Soviet military presence had to be maintained in the country to combat the Mujaheddin guerrillas.

FALKLANDS CONFLICT. *April–June 1982*

On 2 Apr 82 Argentinian forces invaded East Falkland to assert Argentina's longstanding claim to sovereignty over the Falkland Islands. The first warships of the British Task Force sailed for the South Atlantic 3 days later. British troops established a beachhead at San Carlos on East Falkland on 21 May and Argentinian forces surrendered on 14 Jun.

WORLD WAR I
EUROPEAN BELLIGERENTS

	Population (in millions)	Total mobilized (in thousands)	Soldiers killed or died of wounds (in thousands)
Austria-Hungary	47	7 800	1 200
Belgium	7	267	14
Britain	41	8 904	908
Bulgaria	4	560	87
France	39	8 410	1 363
Germany	63	11 000	1 774
Italy	33	5 615	560
Romania	7	750	336
Russia	150	12 000	1 700
Serbia	3	707	45
Turkey	26	2 850	325

Source: Quincy Wright, *A Study of War*, The University of Chicago Press, 1942: second edition, 1965.

WORLD WAR II
PRINCIPAL EUROPEAN BELLIGERENTS

	Population (in millions)	Total mobilized (in thousands)	Soldiers killed or died of wounds (in thousands)	Civilians killed (in thousands)
Belgium	8	625	8	101
Britain	48	5896	557	61
Bulgaria	7	450	10	..
Czechoslovakia	15	150	10	490
Denmark	4	25	4	..
Finland	4	500	79	..
France	39	5000	202	108
Germany	71	10 200	3250	500
Greece	6	414	73	400
Hungary	9	350	147	..
Italy	44	3100	149	783
Netherlands	9	410	7	242
Norway	3	75	2	2
Poland	35	1000	64	2000
Romania	14	1136	520	—
Soviet Union	175	22 000	7500	7500
Yugoslavia	15	3741	410	1275

Source: Quincy Wright. *A Study of War*. University of Chicago Press, 1942: second edition, 1965.

EUROPEAN ARMED FORCES 1983–4

	Population	Army	Navy	Air Force	Para-military	Estimated Reservists	Defence Expenditure US$m. in 1982
Albania	2 800 000	30 000	3200	7200	12 500	155 000	194
Austria	7 584 000	45 400	–	4600	3000	1 097 000	787
Belgium	9 900 000	70 000	4500	20 500	16 200	178 900	2 799
Britain	55 965 000	159 100	71 700	89 800	–	280 700	24 200
Bulgaria	8 990 000	120 000	8500	33 800	172 500	795 000	1287
Czechoslovakia	15 500 000	148 000	–	56 500	131 000	230 000	3774
Denmark	5 120 000	17 500	5800	7400	–	156 200	1122
Finland	4 840 000	34 900	2500	3000	4100	700 000	809
France	54 270 000	311 200	68 000	100 400	93 100	457 000	21 969
Germany (GDR)	16 760 000	116 000	14 000	37 000	411 500	385 000	6163
Germany (FRG)	61 600 000	335 500	36 400	105 900	20 000	750 000	28 453
Greece	9 900 000	142 000	19 500	23 500	29 000	404 000	2574
Hungary	10 760 000	84 000	–	21 000	75 000	143 000	1318
Ireland	3 443 000	13 431	963	837	–	38 000	207
Italy	57 400 000	258 000	44 500	70 600	206 600	794 000	8924
Luxembourg	365 100	720	–	–	500	–	41
Netherlands	14 250 000	67 000	17 350	17 500	8700	176 500	4468
Norway	4 100 000	24 175	8850	9860	–	248 000	1680
Poland	36 500 000	230 000	22 000	88 000	635 000	500 000	6254
Portugal	10 000 000	41 000	13 000	9500	37 300	90 000	778
Romania	22 650 000	150 000	7500	32 000	1 590 000	565 000	1297
Soviet Union	271 800 000	1 800 000	46 000	365 000	80 450 000	25 000 000	23 000[1]
Spain	38 300 000	260 000	54 000	33 000	105 000	1 085 000	4529
Sweden	8 330 000	48 500	10 000	9500	500 500	735 000	3042
Switzerland	6 468 000	580 000[2]	–	45 000[2]	–	605 000	2036
Turkey	47 000 000	470 000	46 000	53 000	125 000	836 000	2755
Yugoslavia	22 650 000	191 000	12 000	36 700	3–5 000 000	500 000	2319

[1] Official budget.   [2] On mobilization.   Source: *Military Balance 1983–84*

PEACE TREATIES ARISING FROM WORLD WAR I 1918–23

TREATY OF BREST-LITOVSK. *3 March 1918*

The Soviet Union surrendered the Baltic Provinces and Russian Poland to the Central Powers, recognized the independence of Finland and the Ukraine, and ceded to Turkey the districts of Kars, Ardahan and Batum. The Treaty was formally invalidated by the Armistice in the West on 11 Nov 18.

TREATY OF VERSAILLES. *28 June 1919*

The peace treaty between Germany and the Allied Powers, Germany surrendered territory to Belgium, Denmark, Poland and Czechoslovakia; Alsace-Lorraine was ceded to France. Germany also surrendered all her overseas territories. The Rhineland was declared a demilitarized zone, with Allied occupation for fifteen years from when the Treaty came into effect on 10 Jan 20. Severe restrictions were placed on the German Armed Forces; the army was limited to 100 000 men. The union of Germany and Austria was forbidden. The Treaty declared Germany's responsibility for causing the war, and made Germany liable for the payment of Reparations. The Treaty also contained the Covenant of the League of Nations.

TREATY OF ST. GERMAIN. *10 September 1919*

The peace treaty between the Austrian Republic and the Allied Powers. By the settlement Austria lost territory to Italy, Yugoslavia, Czechoslovakia, Poland and Romania. Hungary was recognized as an independent state, and the union of Austria and Germany was forbidden. The Austrian army was limited to 30 000 men, and the Republic was made liable for the payment of Reparations.

TREATY OF NEUILLY. *27 November 1919*

The peace treaty between Bulgaria and the Allied Powers. Bulgaria lost Western Thrace to Greece, and territory to Yugoslavia. The Bulgarian army was limited to 20 000 men, and Bulgaria was made liable for Reparations.

TREATY OF TRIANON. *4 June 1920*

The peace treaty between Hungary and the Allied Powers. Hungary surrendered territory to Romania, Czechoslovakia, Yugoslavia, Poland, Italy and the Austrian Republic, to a total of about two-thirds of its pre-war lands. The Hungarian army was limited to 35 000 and Hungary was made liable for Reparations.

TREATY OF SÈVRES. *10 August 1920*

The peace treaty made with Ottoman Turkey, but never ratified by the Turks.

TREATY OF LAUSANNE. *24 July 1923*

Treaty made necessary by Turkey's refusal to accept the treaty of Sèvres. Turkey surrendered its claims to territories of the Ottoman Empire occupied by non-Turks, whilst retaining Constantinople and Eastern Thrace in Europe. The Greeks surrendered Smyrna, but were confirmed in possession of all the Aegean Islands except Imbros and Tenedos which were returned to Turkey. Turkey recognized the annexation of Cyprus by Britain and of the Dodecanese by Italy. The Bosphorus and the Dardanelles were declared to be demilitarized. (By the Montreux Convention of 20 July 36 Turkey was permitted to re-fortify the Straits.)

TREATIES, AGREEMENTS AND ALLIANCES BETWEEN EUROPEAN COUNTRIES 1918–84

3 Mar 18	Treaty of Brest-Litovsk	Russia and the Central Powers
Aug 19	Franco-Belgian Military Convention	
28 June 19	Treaty of Versailles	Germany and the Allied Powers
10 Sep 19	Treaty of St Germain	Austrian Republic and the Allied Powers
27 Nov 19	Treaty of Neuilly	Bulgaria and the Allied Powers
4 June 20	Treaty of Trianon	Hungary and the Allied Powers
10 Aug 20	Treaty of Sèvres	Turkey and the Allied Powers (not ratified by Turkey)
19 Feb 21	Franco-Polish Treaty	
3 Mar 21	Polish-Romanian Treaty	
18 Mar 21	Treaty of Riga	Poland and the Soviet Union
16 Apr 22	Treaty of Rapallo	Russia and Germany
31 Aug 22	Little Entente	Czechoslovakia, Yugoslavia and Romania
24 July 23	Treaty of Lausanne	
1 Dec 25	Locarno Treaties	France, Belgium, Germany; guaranteed by Britain and Italy
24 Apr 26	Soviet-German Neutrality Pact	
25 July 32	Polish-Soviet Treaty	
26 Jan 34	Polish-German Pact	
2 May 35	Franco-Russian Alliance	
20 July 36	Montreux Convention	Turkey permitted to re-fortify the Straits
25 Nov 36	Anti-Comintern Pact	Germany and Japan; signed by Italy 6 Nov 37
2 Jan 37	Anglo-Italian Gentleman's Agreement	
29 Sep 38	Munich Agreement	Britain, France, Germany, Italy
22 May 39	Pact of Steel	Germany and Italy
23 Aug 39	Nazi-Soviet Pact	
25 Aug 39	Polish-British Treaty	
19 Oct 39	British-French-Turkish Agreement	
12 Mar 40	Treaty of Moscow	Ended war between Finland and Soviet Union
27 Sep 40	Tripartite Pact	Germany, Italy, Japan
26 May 42	Anglo-Soviet Treaty	
12 Dec 43	Soviet-Czech Pact	
10 Dec 44	Franco-Soviet Treaty	
21 Apr 45	Soviet-Polish Pact	
4 Mar 47	Dunkirk Treaty	Britain and France
10 Mar 47	Polish-Czech Pact	
16 Dec 47	Bulgarian-Albanian Pact	

16 Jan 48	Bulgarian-Romanian Pact	
24 Jan 48	Hungarian-Romanian Pact	
4 Feb 48	Soviet-Romanian Pact	
18 Feb 48	Soviet-Hungarian Pact	
17 Mar 48	Brussels Treaty	Britain, France, Benelux
18 Mar 48	Soviet-Bulgarian Pact	
5 Apr 48	Soviet-Finnish Pact	
23 Apr 48	Bulgarian-Czech Pact	
9 June 48	Polish-Hungarian Pact	
18 June 48	Bulgarian-Hungarian Pact	
21 July 48	Romanian-Czech Pact	
21 Jan 49	Polish-Romanian Pact	
4 Apr 49	North Atlantic Treaty	
16 Apr 49	Hungarian-Czech Pact	
9 Aug 54	Balkan Pact	Greece, Turkey, Yugoslavia
24 Feb 55	Baghdad Pact	Turkey and Iraq; Britain 5 Apr 55; Pakistan 23 Sep 55
5 May 55	London and Paris Agreements	
13 May 55	Warsaw Pact	
15 May 55	Austrian State Treaty	
22 Jan 63	Franco-Federal German Treaty	
27 Nov 63	Soviet-Czech Pact	
12 June 64	Soviet-Democratic German Pact	
8 Apr 65	Soviet-Polish Pact	
1 Mar 67	Polish-Czech Treaty	
15 Mar 67	Polish-Democratic German Treaty	
17 Mar 67	Democratic German-Czech Treaty	
13 May 67	Soviet-Bulgarian Pact	
18 May 67	Hungarian-Democratic German Pact	
6 Apr 67	Polish-Bulgarian Pact	
7 Sep 67	Soviet-Hungarian Pact	
7 Sep 67	Bulgarian-Democratic German Pact	
26 Apr 68	Bulgarian-Czech Pact	
16 May 68	Polish-Hungarian Pact	
10 July 69	Bulgarian-Hungarian Pact	
20 Mar 70	Soviet-Czech Pact	
7 July 70	Soviet-Romanian Pact	
12 Aug 70	Soviet-Federal German Treaty	
12 Nov 70	Polish-Romanian Treaty	
7 Dec 70	Polish-Federal German Treaty	
26 Mar 72	British-Maltese Agreement	Seven-year agreement on bases
21 Dec 72	Federal German-Democratic German Treaty	Normalization of relations
11 Dec 73	Czech-Federal German Treaty	
14 June 75	Portuguese-Romanian Treaty	
7 Oct 75	Soviet-Democratic German Treaty	
10 Nov 75	Treaty of Osimo	
24 Mar 77	Democratic German-Hungarian Treaty	
28 May 77	Democratic German-Polish Treaty	
14 Sep 77	Democratic German-Bulgarian Treaty	
3 Oct 77	Democratic German-Czech Treaty	
20 June 83	Soviet-Finnish Treaty	Renewed for 20 years

OUTLINE OF PRINCIPAL EUROPEAN DEFENCE TREATIES AND AGREEMENTS 1918–84

FRANCO-BELGIAN MILITARY CONVENTION. *August 1920*

The abrogation of treaties for the neutralization of Belgium was confirmed in a treaty signed by Britain, France and Belgium on 22 May 26. Belgium announced its return to neutrality in Oct 36 after the remilitarization of the Rhineland (7 Mar 36), thereby preventing the vital co-ordination of strategic planning with France prior to World War II.

FRANCO-POLISH TREATY. *19 February 1921*

Provided for mutual defence against unprovoked aggression. Poland concluded a similar treaty with Romania on 3 Mar 21.

TREATY OF RAPALLO. *16 April 1922*

Germany and Soviet Russia re-established diplomatic relations, renounced financial claims on either side, and pledged economic co-operation. The Treaty was reaffirmed by the German-Soviet Neutrality Pact of 24 April 26.

THE LITTLE ENTENTE. *31 August 1922*

Bilateral agreements between Yugoslavia, Czechoslovakia and Romania were consolidated into a single treaty in Aug 22, and further strengthened in May 29. The object of the Little Entente was the maintenance of the *status quo* in Central Europe.

LOCARNO TREATIES. *1 December 1925*

The signatories, France, Germany and Belgium, recognized the inviolability of the Franco-German and Belgo-German frontiers, and the existence of the demilitarized zone of the Rhineland; this was guaranteed by Britain and Italy. Franco-Polish and Franco-Czech Treaties of Mutual Guarantee were also signed, and action under these treaties was not to be regarded as aggression against Germany. The treaty was violated on 7 Mar 36 when Hitler sent troops into the Rhineland.

POLISH-SOVIET TREATY. *25 July 1932*

A non-aggression treaty, valid for five years. It was prolonged for ten years in Dec 34 after the signing of a Polish-German Treaty.

POLISH-GERMAN TREATY. *26 January 1934*

A non-aggression treaty, valid for ten years; repudiated by Hitler on 28 Apr 39.

FRANCO-RUSSIAN ALLIANCE. *2 May 1935*

Provided for mutual aid in the event of unprovoked aggression.

ANGLO-GERMAN NAVAL AGREEMENT. *18 June 1935*

Limited the German navy to 35% of the British, with submarines at 45% or equality in the event of danger from Russia.

ANTI-COMINTERN PACT. *25 November 1936*

Signed by Germany and Japan to oppose the spread of communism. Italy joined the Pact on 6 Nov 37.

ANGLO-ITALIAN 'GENTLEMAN'S AGREEMENT'. *2 January 1937*

An agreement to maintain the *status quo* in the Mediterranean.

MUNICH AGREEMENT. *29 September 1938*

An agreement reached by Britain, France, Italy and Germany, by which territorial concessions were to be made to Germany, Poland and Hungary at the expense of Czechoslovakia. The rump of Czechoslovakia was to be guaranteed against unprovoked aggression, but German control was extended to the rest of Czechoslovakia in Mar 39.

THE PACT OF STEEL. *22 May 1939*

The formal treaty of alliance between Italy and Germany. Prior to this Mussolini had announced the existence of the 'Rome-Berlin Axis' in a speech at Milan on 1 Nov 36.

NAZI-SOVIET PACT. *23 August 1939*

The Soviet Union agreed to remain neutral if Germany was involved in a war. The Pact was broken when Hitler invaded Russia on 22 June 41.

BRITISH-POLISH TREATY. *25 August 1939*

A mutual assistance treaty, subsequent to the Franco-British guarantee against aggression given to Poland on 31 Mar 39.

BRITISH-FRENCH-TURKISH AGREEMENT. *19 October 1939*

A mutual assistance treaty. Turkey, however, remained neutral until 1 Mar 45, and signed a treaty of non-aggression with Germany in June 41.

TRIPARTITE PACT. *27 September 1940*

Germany, Italy and Japan undertook to assist each other if one of them was attacked by a power not already in the war. The Pact was signed by Hungary, Romania, Slovakia, Bulgaria and Yugoslavia 1940–41.

ANGLO-SOVIET TREATY. *26 May 1942*

A treaty of alliance and mutual assistance, valid for twenty years. The treaty was abrogated by the Soviet Union on 7 May 55 as a result of the ratification of the London and Paris Agreements by the British government.

FRANCO-SOVIET TREATY. *10 December 1944*

A treaty of alliance and mutual assistance, valid for twenty years. The Treaty was abrogated by the Soviet Union on 7 May 55 as a result of the ratification of the London and Paris Agreements by the French government.

DUNKIRK TREATY. *4 March 1947*

Treaty of alliance between Britain and France, valid for fifty years.

BRUSSELS TREATY. *17 March 1948*

An agreement signed by France, Britain and the Benelux countries for mutual aid in military, economic and social matters.

NORTH ATLANTIC TREATY. *4 April 1949*

Collective Security treaty signed by Belgium, Britain, Canada, Denmark, France, Iceland, Italy, Luxembourg, the Netherlands, Norway, Portugal, and the United States. Greece and Turkey joined NATO in Feb 52, and the Federal Republic of Germany in May 55.

BALKAN PACT. *9 August 1954*

A treaty of alliance, political co-operation and mutual assistance signed by Greece, Turkey and Yugoslavia, and valid for twenty years.

BAGHDAD PACT. *24 February 1955*

A mutual assistance treaty signed by Turkey and Iraq. Britain joined the Pact on 5 Apr 55, and Pakistan on 23 Sep 55.

LONDON AND PARIS AGREEMENTS. *5 May 1955*

The occupation régime in West Germany was ended, and the German Federal Republic attained full sovereignty and independence. The Federal Republic became a member of NATO, and of the Western European Union, the expanded Brussels Treaty Organization which came into being on 5 May.

WARSAW PACT. *13 May 1955*

A treaty of friendship, co-operation and mutual assistance signed by the Soviet Union, Poland, Czechoslovakia, German Democratic Republic, Hungary, Romania, Bulgaria and Albania. The Treaty also provided for the creation of a unified command for all the countries.

AUSTRIAN STATE TREATY. *15 May 1955*

Signed by the Soviet Union, Britain, France and the United States, the treaty re-established Austria as a sovereign, independent and neutral state.

FRANCO-WEST GERMAN TREATY. *22 January 1963*

Treaty of co-operation, providing for co-ordination of the two countries' policies in foreign affairs, defence, information and cultural affairs.

SOVIET-FEDERAL GERMANY TREATY. *12 August 1970*

A treaty renouncing the use of force.

POLISH-FEDERAL GERMAN TREATY. *7 December 1970*

An agreement that the existing boundary line on the Oder and the West Neisse constitutes the western frontier of Poland, and renouncing the use of force for the settlement of disputes.

TREATY OF OSIMO. *10 November 1975*

A treaty between Italy and Yugoslavia in which the two countries accepted border changes around Trieste slightly in favour of Italy, that national minorities were to be protected and there was to be greater economic co-operation.

9 DEPENDENCIES

Zaïre, formerly Belgian Congo and then Congo (Kinshasa). Until the middle of the nineteenth century the territory drained by the Congo River was practically unknown. When Stanley reached the mouth of the Congo in 1877, King Leopold II of the Belgians recognized the immense possibilities of the Congo Basin and took the lead in exploring and exploiting it. The Berlin Conference of 1884–85 recognized King Leopold II as the sovereign head of the Congo Free State.

The annexation of the state to Belgium was provided for by treaty of 28 Nov 07, which was approved by the chambers of the Belgian Legislature in Aug and Sep and by the King on 18 Oct 08. The law of 18 Oct 08, called the Colonial Charter (last amended in 1959), provided for the government of the Belgian Congo, until the country became independent on 30 June 60.

The departure of the Belgian administrators, teachers, doctors, etc., on the day of independence left a vacuum which speedily resulted in complete chaos. Neither Joseph Kasavubu, the leader of the Abako Party, who on 24 June 60 had been elected head of state, nor Patrice Lumumba, leader of the Congo National Movement, who was the prime minister of an all-party coalition government, could establish his authority. Personal, tribal and regional rivalries led to the breakaway of Katanga province under premier Moïse Tshombe. Lumumba found his main support in the Oriental and Kivu provinces. Early in July the *Force Publique* mutinied and removed all Belgian officers. Lumumba called for intervention by the UN as well as the USSR. The Secretary-General dispatched a military force of about 20 000, composed of contingents of African and Asian countries. Lumumba was kidnapped by Katanga tribesmen and, in early Feb 61, murdered; his place was taken by Antoine Gizenga, who set up a government in Stanleyville.

On 15 Aug 61 the UN recognized the government of Cyrille Adoula as the central government. UN forces, chiefly Irish and Ethiopians, in mid-Sep invaded Katanga.

On 15 Jan 62 the forces of Gizenga in Stanleyville surrendered to those of the central government, and on 16 Jan Adoula dismissed Gizenga. UN forces, chiefly Ethiopians and Indians, again invaded Katanga in Dec 62 and by the end of Jan 63 had occupied all key towns; Tshombe left the country. The UN troops left the Congo by 30 June 64.

The Gizenga faction started a fresh rebellion and after the capture of

Albertville (19 June) and Stanleyville (5 Aug) proclaimed a People's Republic on 7 Sep 64. Government troops, Belgian paratroopers and a mercenary contingent captured Stanleyville on 24 Nov after the rebels had massacred thousands of black and white civilians. The last rebel strongholds were captured at the end of Apr 65.

DENMARK

The Faroe Islands, Faerøerne. The islands were first colonized in the ninth century and were Norwegian possessions until 1380 and subsequently belonged to Denmark. They were occupied by British troops in World War II. In Sep 46 they voted for independence from Denmark but now return two members to the *Folketing*. Home rule was granted in 1948. Population 1980, 13 757.

Greenland, Grønland. From 1261 to 1953 Greenland was a Danish colony. On 5 June 53 Greenland became an integral part of the Danish Realm with the same rights as other counties in Denmark, returning two members to the *Folketing*, and with a democratically elected council (*landsråd*). A Danish-American agreement for the common defence of Greenland was signed on 27 Apr 51.

Iceland, Island. The first settlers came to Iceland in 874. Between 930 and 1264 Iceland was an independent republic, but by the 'Old Treaty' of 1263 the country recognized the rule of the King of Norway. In 1381 Iceland, together with Norway, came under the rule of the Danish kings, but when Norway was separated from Denmark in 1814, Iceland remained under the rule of Denmark. Since 1 Dec 18 it has been acknowledged as a sovereign state. It was united with Denmark only through the common sovereign until it was proclaimed an independent republic on 17 June 44.

FRANCE

The French Community, La Communauté. The constitution of the Fifth Republic 'offers to the overseas territories which manifest their will to adhere to it new institutions based on the common ideal of liberty, equality and fraternity and conceived with a view to their democratic evolution'. The territories were offered three solutions: they could keep their status; they could become overseas *départements*; they could become, singly or in groups, member states of the Community (Art. 76).

According to the amendment of the constitution adopted on 4 June 60, member-states of the Community could become independent and sovereign republics without ceasing to belong to the Community. The 12 African and Malagasy members availed themselves of this *loi constitutionnelle* and became independent by the transfer of 'common powers' (*compétences communes*).

The territorial structure of the Community and affiliated states was as follows:

I. FRENCH REPUBLIC

   A. Metropolitan Departments

   B. Overseas Departments:

   (i) Martinique; (ii) Guadeloupe; (iii) Réunion; (iv) Guiana.

   C. Overseas Territories:

   (i) French Polynesia; (ii) New Caledonia; (iii) French Territory of the Afars and the Issas; (iv) Comoro Archipelago; (v) Saint-Pierre and Miquelon; (vi) Southern and Antarctic Territories; (vii) Wallis and Futuna Islands.

II. MEMBER STATES

   1. French Republic; 2. Central African Republic; 3. Republic of Congo; 4. Republic of Gabon; 5. Madagascar; 6. Republic of Senegal; 7. Republic of Chad.

These countries concluded formal 'Community participation agreements'.

III. 'Special relations' or 'special links' were established by agreements between France and the other Franc zone countries and the following states:

   1. Republic of Ivory Coast; 2. Republic of Dahomey; 3. Republic of Upper Volta; 4. Islamic Republic of Mauritania; 5. Republic of Niger; 6. Federal Republic of Cameroun.

IV. Co-operation in certain fields was established by special agreements between France and the Republic of Mali.

V. Co-operation was established between France and the Togo Republic by a convention signed on 10 July 63.

VI. The states listed under II, 2–7, III, 1–3, 5 and 6, and V are the members of the Organisation *Commune Africaine et Malgache*.

VII. Other regional organizations:

   1. The Customs and Economic Union of Central Africa, comprising the Central African Republic, Congo, Gabon, Chad and Cameroun; the common external tariff, effective from 1 July 62, did not apply to the countries listed under II and III;

   2. The entente of Ivory Coast, Dahomey, Upper Volta, Niger;

3. The customs union of Senegal, Mali, Ivory Coast, Dahomey, Upper Volta, Niger and Mauritania;
4. The West-African monetary union of Senegal, Mauritania, Ivory Coast, Upper Volta, Niger, Dahomey and Togo.

VIII. Relations between France and Algeria (comprising the former Algerian and Sahara Departments) are governed by the Évian agreements of 19 Mar 62 and subsequent agreements.

IX. The Anglo-French Condominium of the New Hebrides is administered according to the London Protocol of 6 Aug 14.

Algeria. Algeria was annexed by France in 1885 and became a department of France. French policy was to integrate Algeria completely into France itself but this was not acceptable to the French settlers, *colons*.

On 1 Nov 54 the National Liberation Front (FLN), founded 5 Aug 51, went over to open warfare against the French administration and armed forces. In Sep 58 a free Algerian government was formed in Cairo with Ferhat Abbas as provisional president.

A referendum was held in Metropolitan France and Algeria on 6–8 Jan 61 to decide on Algerian self-determination as proposed by President de Gaulle. His proposals were approved by 15 200 073 against 4 996 474 votes in Metropolitan France, and by 1 749 969 against 767 546 votes in Algeria. In Metropolitan France 20.2m. out of 27.2m. registered voters went to the polls; in Algeria 2.5m. out of 4.5m. registered voters.

Long delayed by the terrorism, in Metropolitan France as well as Algeria, of a secret organization (OAS) led by anti-Gaullist officers, a cease-fire agreement was concluded between the French government and the representatives of the Algerian Nationalists on 18 Mar 62; but OAS terror acts continued for some months. On 7 Apr a provisional executive of 12 members was set up, under the chairmanship of Abderrhaman Farès.

On 8 Apr 62 a referendum in Metropolitan France approved the Algerian settlement with 17 505 473 (90.7%), against 1 794 553 (9.3%) and 1 102 477 invalid votes; 6 580 772 voters abstained. On 1 July 62, 5 975 581 Algerians voted in favour of, 16 534 against the settlement.

Morocco. From 1912 to 1956 Morocco was divided into a French protectorate (established by the Treaty of Fez concluded between France and the Sultan on 30 Mar 12), a Spanish protectorate (established by the Franco-Spanish convention of 27 Nov 12) and the international zone of Tangier (set up by France, Spain and Britain on 18 Dec 23).

On 2 Mar 56 France and the Sultan terminated the Treaty of Fez; on 7 Apr 56 Spain relinquished her protectorate, and on 29 Oct 56 France, Spain, Britain, Italy, USA, Belgium, the Netherlands, Sweden and Portugal abolished the international status of the Tangier Zone.

Indo-China, Cambodia. Attacked on either side by the Vietnamese and the Thai from the fifteenth century on, Cambodia was saved from annihilation by the establishment of a French protectorate in 1863. Thailand eventually recognized the protectorate and renounced all claims to suzerainty in exchange for Cambodia's north-western provinces of Battambang and Siem Reap, which were, however, returned under a Franco-Thai convention of 1907, confirmed in the Franco-Thai treaty of 1937. In 1904 the province of Stung Treng, formerly administered as part of Laos, was attached to Cambodia.

A nationalist movement began in the 1930s, and anti-French feeling strengthened in 1940–41, when the French submitted to Japanese demands for bases in Cambodia and allowed Thailand to annex Cambodian territory. On 9 Mar 45 the Japanese suppressed the French administration and the treaties between France and Cambodia were denounced by King Norodom Sihanouk, who proclaimed Cambodia's independence. British troops occupied Phnom Penh in Oct 45, and the re-establishment of French authority was followed by a Franco-Cambodian *modus vivendi* of 7 Jan 46, which promised a constitution embodying a constitutional monarchy. Elections for a National Consultative Assembly were held on 1 Sep 46, and a Franco-Thai agreement of 17 Nov 46 ensured the return to Cambodia of the provinces annexed by Thailand in 1941.

In 1949 Cambodia was granted independence as an Associate State of the French Union. The transfer of the French military powers to the Cambodian government on 9 Nov 53 is considered in Cambodia as the attainment of sovereign independence. In Jan 55 Cambodia became financially and economically independent, both of France and the other two former Associate States of French Indo-China, Vietnam and Laos.

Laos. In 1893 Laos became a French protectorate and in 1907 acquired its present frontiers. In 1945 French authority was suppressed by the Japanese. When the Japanese withdrew in 1945 an independence movement known as *Lao Issara* (Free Laos) set up a government under Prince Phetsarath, the Viceroy of Luang Prabang. This government collapsed with the return of the French in 1946 and the leaders of the movement fled to Thailand.

Under a new constitution of 1947 Laos became a constitutional monarchy under the Luang Prabang dynasty, and in 1949 became an independent sovereign state within the French Union.

Vietnam, French interest in Vietnam started in the late sixteenth century with the arrival of French and Portuguese missionaries. The most notable of these was Alexander of Rhodes, who, in the following century, romanized Vietnamese writing. At the end of the eighteenth century a French bishop and several soldiers of fortune helped to establish the Emperor Gia-Long (with whom Louis XVI had signed a treaty in 1787) as ruler of a unified Vietnam, known then as the Empire of Annam.

An expedition sent by Napoleon III in 1858 to avenge the death of some French missionaries led in 1862 to the cession to France of part of Cochin-China, and thence, by a series of treaties between 1874 and 1884, to the establishment of French protectorates over Tonkin and Annam, and to the formation of the French colony of Cochin-China. By a Sino-French treaty of 1885 the Empire of Annam (including Tonkin) ceased to be a tributary to China. Cambodia had become a French protectorate in 1863, and in 1899, after the extension of French protection to Laos in 1893, the Indo-Chinese Union was proclaimed.

In 1940 Vietnam was occupied by the Japanese and used as a military base for the invasion of Malaya. During the occupation there was considerable underground activity among nationalist, revolutionary and Communist organizations. In 1941 a nominally nationalist coalition of such organizations, known as the Vietminh League, was founded by the Communists.

On 9 Mar 45 the Japanese interned the French authorities and proclaimed the 'independence' of Indo-China. In Aug 45 they allowed the Vietminh movement to seize power, dethrone Bao Dai, the Emperor of Annam, and establish a republic known as Vietnam, including Tonkin, Annam and Cochin-China with Hanoi as capital. In Sep 45 the French re-established themselves in Cochin-China and on 6 Mar 46, after a cease-fire in the sporadic fighting between the French forces and the Vietminh had been arranged, a preliminary convention was signed in Hanoi between the French High Commissioner and President Ho Chi Minh by which France recognized 'the Democratic Republic of Vietnam' as a 'Free State within the Indo-Chinese Federation'. Subsequent conferences convened in the same year at Dalat and Fontainebleau to draft a definitive agreement broke down chiefly over the question of whether or not Cochin-China should be included in the new republic. On 19 Dec 46 Vietminh forces made a surprise attack on Hanoi, the signal for hostilities which were to last for nearly eight years.

An agreement signed by the Emperor Bao Dai on behalf of Vietnam on 8 Mar 49 recognized the independence of Vietnam within the French Union. and certain sovereign powers were forthwith transferred to Vietnam. Others remained partly under French control until Sep 54. The remainder connected with services in which Cambodia, France, Laos and Vietnam had a common interest were regulated by the Pau conventions of Dec 50. These conventions were abrogated by the Paris agreements of 29 Dec 54, which completed the transfer of sovereignty to Vietnam. Supreme authority in the military field remained with the French until the departure of the last French C.-in-C. in Apr 56. Treaties of independence and association were initiated by representatives of the French and Vietnamese governments on 4 June 54.

In 1974 Mayotte voted against becoming independent with the rest of the

Comoro Archipelago (an Overseas Territory). Comoros therefore became an independent state on 6 July 75; Mayotte remained a dependency, and in 1976 was given the status of *collectivité territoriale* an intermediate status between Overseas Territory and Overseas Department.

In July 76 Saint-Pierre and Miquelon, an Overseas Territory, became an Overseas Department.

On 27 June 77 the French Territory of the Afars and Issas, an Overseas Territory, became independent as the Republic of Djibouti.

ITALY

Ethiopia. In 1936 Ethiopia was conquered by the Italians, who were in turn defeated by the Allied forces in 1941 when the Emperor returned.

The former Italian colony of Eritrea, from 1941 under British military administration, was in accordance with a resolution of the General Assembly of the United Nations, dated 2 Dec 50, handed over to Ethiopia on 15 Sep 52. Eritrea thereby became an autonomous unit within the federation of Ethiopia and Eritrea, under the Ethiopian Crown. This federation became a unitary state on 14 Nov 62 when Eritrea was fully integrated with Ethiopia.

Somalia. The Somali Republic came into being on 1 July 60 as a result of the merger of the British Somaliland Protectorate, which became independent on 26 June 60, and the Italian Trusteeship Territory of Somalia.

THE NETHERLANDS

Netherlands Antilles, De Nederlandse Antillen. Since Dec 54, the Netherlands Antilles have been fully autonomous in internal affairs, and constitutionally equal with the Netherlands and Surinam. The Sovereign of the Kingdom of the Netherlands is head of the Government of the Netherlands Antilles and is represented by a Governor. Population 1980, 265 000.

Netherlands East Indies. From 1602 the Netherlands East India Company conquered the Netherlands East Indies, and ruled them until the dissolution of the company in 1798. Thereafter the Netherlands government ruled the colony from 1816 to 1945.

Company and unconditional sovereignty was transferred to the Republic of the United States of Indonesia on 27 Dec 49, except for the western part of New Guinea, the status of which was to be determined through negotiations between Indonesia and the Netherlands within one year after the transfer of sovereignty. A union was created to regulate the relationship between the two countries. A settlement of the New Guinea (West Irian) question was, however, delayed until 15 Aug 62, when, through the good offices of the UN, an agreement was concluded for the transfer of the territory to Indonesia on 1 May 63.

Suriname, Dutch Guiana. At the peace of Breda (1667) between Great Britain and the United Netherlands, Suriname was assigned to the Netherlands in exchange for the colony of New Netherland in North America, and this was confirmed by the Treaty of Westminster of Feb 1674. Since then Suriname has been twice in British possession, 1799–1802 (when it was restored to the Batavian Republic at the peace of Amiens) and 1804–16, when it was returned to the Kingdom of the Netherlands according to the convention of London of 13 Aug 14, confirmed at the peace of Paris of 20 Nov 15. Suriname became fully independent on 25 Nov 75.

NORWAY

Svalbard. The main islands of the archipelago are Spitsbergen (formerly Vestspitsbergen), Nordaustlandet, Edgeøya, Barentsøya, Prins Karls Forland, Bjørnøya, Hopen, Kong Karls Land, Kvitøya, and many small islands.

The archipelago was probably discovered by Norsemen in 1194 and rediscovered by the Dutch navigator Barents in 1596. In the seventeenth century the very lucrative whale-hunting caused rival Dutch, British and Danish-Norwegian claims to sovereignty and quarrels about the hunting-places. But when in the eighteenth century the whale-hunting ended, the question of the sovereignty of Svalbard lost its actuality; it was again raised in the twentieth century, owing to the discovery and exploitation of coalfields. By a treaty, signed on 9 Feb 20 in Paris, Norway's sovereignty over the archipelago was recognized. On 14 Aug 25 the archipelago was officially incorporated in Norway. Population 1981, 3 910.

Jan Mayen. The island was possibly discovered by Henry Hudson in 1608, and it was first named Hudson's Tutches (Touches). It was again and again rediscovered and renamed. Its present name derives from the Dutch whaling captain Jan Jacobsz May, who indisputably discovered the island in 1614. It was uninhabited, but occasionally visited by seal hunters and trappers, until 1921 when Norway established a radio and meteorological station. On 8 May 29 Jan Mayen was officially proclaimed as incorporated in the Kingdom of Norway. Its relation to Norway was finally settled by law of 27 Feb 30.

Bouvet Island, Bouvetøya. This uninhabited island was discovered in 1739 by a French naval officer, Jean Baptiste Lozier Bouvet, but no flag was hoisted until, in 1825, Capt. Norris raised the Union Jack. In 1928 Britain waived its claim to the island in favour of Norway, which in Dec 27 had occupied it. A law of 27 Feb 30 declared Bouvetøya a Norwegian dependency.

Peter I Island, Peter I øy. This uninhabited island was sighted in 1821 by the Russian explorer, Admiral von Bellingshausen. The first landing was made in 1929 by a Norwegian expedition which hoisted the Norwegian flag. On 1 May 31 Peter I Island was placed under Norwegian sovereignty, and on 24 Mar 33 it was incorporated in Norway as a dependency.

Queen Maud Land, Dronning Maud Land. On 14 Jan 39 the Norwegian cabinet placed that part of the Antarctic Continent from the border of Falkland Islands dependencies in the west to the border of the Australian Antarctic Dependency in the east (between 20°W. and 45°E.) under Norwegian sovereignty. The territory had been explored only by Norwegians and hitherto been ownerless. Since 1949 expeditions from various countries have explored the area. In 1957 Dronning Maud Land was given the status of a Norwegian dependency.

PORTUGAL

On 11 June 51 the status of the Portuguese overseas possessions was changed from 'colonies' to 'overseas territories'. Each one has a Governor and enjoys financial and administrative autonomy. Their budgets are under approval of the Minister for the Overseas Territories. They are not allowed to contract public loans in foreign countries. Under the Organic Law for Overseas Territories, of May 72, the overseas provinces were given greater autonomy 'without affecting the unity of the nation'. Angola and Moçambique were designated States instead of overseas provinces.

On 6 Sep 61 all Africans were given full Portuguese citizenship, thereby achieving the same status as the inhabitants of Portuguese India and the other provinces.

All customs duties between Portugal and the overseas provinces were abolished with effect from 1 Jan 64.

Cape Verde Islands. The Cape Verde Islands were discovered in 1460 by Diogo Gomes, the first settlers arriving in 1462. In 1587 its administration was unified under a governor. The territory consists of ten islands and five islets which were administered by a Governor, whose seat was at Praia, the capital.

The islands are divided into two groups, named Barlavento (windward) and Sotavento (leeward), the prevailing wind being north-east. The former is constituted by the islands of São Vicente, Santo Antão, São Nicolau, Santa Luzia, Sal and Boa Vista, and the small islands named Branco and Raso. The latter is constituted by the islands of Santiago, Maio, Fogo and Brava, and the small islands named Rei and Rombo. São Vicente is an oiling station which supplies all navigation to South America. The total area is 4033 sq. km. (1557 sq. miles). The population (census, 1970) was 272 071. The islands became independent on 5 July 75.

Portuguese Guinea. Portuguese Guinea, on the coast of Guinea, was discovered in 1446 by Nuno Tristão. It became a separate colony in 1879. It is bounded by the limits fixed by the convention of 12 May 86 with France, and is bounded by Senegal in the north and by Guinea in the east and south. It includes the adjacent archipelago of Bijagoz, with the island of Bolama. The capital is, since 1942, Bissau. Area is 36 125 sq. km. (13 948 sq. miles); population (census, 1970), 487 448. The dependency became an independent state, as Guinea-Bissau, on 10 Sep 74.

São Tomé e Principe. The Islands of S. Tomé and Principe, which are about 125 miles off the coast of Africa, in the Gulf of Guinea, were discovered in 1471 by Pedro Escobar and João Gomes, and after 1522 constituted a province under a Governor. The province also includes the islands of Pedras Tinhosas and Rolas; the fort of St Jean Baptiste d'Ajudã on the coast was annexed by the Dahomey Republic on 1 Aug 61. Area of the islands 964 sq. km (372 sq. miles). According to the census of 1970 the population of the islands was 73 811. The islands became independent on 12 July 75.

Angola. Angola, with a coastline of over 1000 miles, is separated from the Congo by the boundaries assigned by the convention of 12 May 86; from Zaïre by those fixed by the convention of 22 July 27; from Rhodesia in accordance with the convention of 11 June 91, and from South-West Africa in accordance with that of 30 Dec 86. The Congo region was discovered by the Portuguese in 1482, and the first settlers arrived there in 1491. Luanda was founded in 1575. It was taken by the Dutch in 1641 and occupied by them until 1648. The area is 1 246 700 sq. km. (481 351 sq. miles). By a decree of 20 Oct 54 it is divided into 13 districts. The important towns are S. Paulo de Luanda (capital), Benguela, Moçâmedes, Lobito, Sá da Bandeira, Malange and Huambo (Novo Lisboa) the future capital. The population at census, 1970, was 5 673 046, of whom 300 000 are white. Angola became independent on 11 Nov 75.

Moçambique. MoÇambique was discovered by Vasco da Gama's fleet on 1 Mar 1498, and was first colonized in 1505. The frontier with British Central and South Africa was fixed between Great Britain and Portugal in June 1891. The border with Tanganyika, according to agreements of 1886 and 1890, ran from Cape Delgado at 10° 40′ S. Lat. until it meets the courses of the Rovuma, which it follows to the point of its confluence with the 'Msinje, the boundary thence to Lake Nyasa being the parallel of latitude of this point. The Treaty of Versailles, 1919, allotted to Portugal the original Portuguese territory south of the Rovuma, known as the 'Kionga Triangle' (formerly part of German East Africa).

Moçambique, with an area of 784 961 sq. km. (303 070 sq. miles) was administered by the state, since 19 July 42, when the state took over the territory of Manica and Sofala, which was incorporated as a fourth district of the province, with Beira as its capital. Lourenço Marques is the capital of the province. As established by decree of 20 Oct 54, the province was divided into nine districts: Lourenço Marques, Gaza, Inhambane, Manica and Sofala, Tete, Zambézia, Moçambique, Cabo Delgado, Niassa.

There was a government council composed of officials and elected representatives of the commercial, industrial and agricultural classes, and also an executive council. The population, according to the census of 1970, was 8 233 034. Mozambique became independent on 25 July 75.

Macao. Macao, in China, situated on a peninsula of the same name at the mouth of the Canton River, which came into possession of the Portuguese in 1557, forms with the two small adjacent islands of Taipa and Colôane a province, divided into two wards, each having its own administrator. The boundaries have not yet been definitely agreed upon; at present Portugal holds the territory in virtue of the treaty with China of 1 Dec 1887. The area of the province is 16 sq. km. (6 sq. miles). The population, according to the census of 1981, is 276 673; the steady influx of Chinese refugees is creating serious social and economic difficulties while Chinese communists cause sporadic political unrest.

Timor. Portuguese Timor was under Portuguese administration from 1586. It consisted of the eastern portion of the island of that name in the Malay Archipelago, with the territory of Ambeno and the neighbouring islands of Pulo Cambing and Pulo Jako, a total area of 14 925 sq. km. By a treaty of Apr 1859, ratified 18 Aug 1860, the island was divided between Portugal and Holland; by convention of 1 Oct 04, ratified in 1908, the boundaries were straightened and settled. The territory, formerly administratively joined to Macao, was in 1896 (confirmed in 1926) made an independent province. Population in 1970, 610 541. On 7 Dec 75, during a civil war, the province was invaded by Indonesian forces. On 17 July 76 it became an Indonesian province and was renamed Loro Sae.

Portuguese India, Estado da India, was under Portuguese rule 1505–1961. It consisted of Goa, containing the capital, Goa, together with the islands of Angediva, São Jorge and Morcegos, on the Malabar coast; Damão, with the territories of Dadrá and Nagar-Haveli, on the Gulf of Cambis; and Diu, with the continental territories of Gogola and Simbor, on the coast of Gujerat.

Indian troops invaded Goa, Damão and Diu without declaration of war on 18–19 Dec 61 and forcibly incorporated the Portuguese territory in the Indian Union.

SPAIN

In Jan 58 the territory of 'Spanish West Africa' was divided into the provinces of Ifni and Spanish Sahara; both were under the jurisdiction of the commanding officer of the Canary Islands. The province of Ifni was returned to Morocco on 30 June 69.

The Province of Spanish Sahara consisted of two districts: Sekia El Hamra (82 000 sq. km.) and Rio de Oro (184 000 sq. km.). Area 266 000 sq. km. (102 680 sq. miles). The population consisted of some 10 000 Spanish civilians, about 15 000 Spanish soldiers and perhaps 30 000–50 000 nomadic Saharans. The capital is El Aaiún (population, 4000–5000). The strip between 27° 40′ N. and Wad Draa was ceded by Spain to Morocco on 10 Apr 58. Strong pressure was brought, in 1970, by Morocco, Mauritania and Algeria for a referendum to be conducted by Spain in the province. In 1975, Spain, Morocco and Mauritania reached agreement on the transfer of power over Western Sahara to Morocco and Mauritania. The Spanish province ceased to exist on 31 Dec 75, and the country was partitioned by Morocco and Mauritania. A Saharan nationalist party claims the independence of the country from Spain.

Equatorial Guinea, Territorios Españoles del Golfo de Guinea. The territory was ceded to Spain by Portugal in 1777. Spain leased it to Britain in 1827, and began to administer it in 1855, as a colony. In 1959 it was turned into two provinces, comparable to the Spanish metropolitan provinces, and called Fernando Poo and Rio Muni. In 1964 a degree of self-government was achieved, and independence followed on 12 Oct 68.

UNITED KINGDOM

The Commonwealth is a free association of the United Kingdom, Canada, Australia, New Zealand, India, Sri Lanka, Ghana, Nigeria, Cyprus, Sierra Leone, Jamaica, Trinidad and Tobago, Uganda, Kenya, Malaysia, Tanzania,

Malawi, Malta, Zambia, The Gambia, Singapore, Guyana, Botswana, Lesotho, Barbados, Mauritius, Swaziland, Tonga, Fiji, Western Samoa, Nauru, Bangladesh, Bahamas and their dependent territories.

Up to July 25 the affairs of all the British Empire, apart from the United Kingdom and India, were dealt with by the Colonial Office. From that date a new secretaryship of state, for Dominion Affairs, became responsible for the relations between the United Kingdom and all the independent members of the Commonwealth.

In July 47 the designations of the Secretary of State for Dominion Affairs and the Dominions Office were altered to 'Secretary of State for Commonwealth Relations' and 'Commonwealth Relations Office'. The following month, on the independence of India and Pakistan, the India Office ceased to exist and the staff were transferred to the Commonwealth Relations Office, which then became responsible for relations with India and Pakistan.

The Colonial Office was merged with the Commonwealth Relations Office on 1 Aug 66 to form the Commonwealth Office, and the post of Secretary of State for Commonwealth Relations became Secretary of State for Commonwealth Affairs. The post of Secretary of State for the Colonies was retained until 6 Jan 67. The Commonwealth Office was merged with the Foreign Office on 17 Oct 68.

The Secretary of State for Foreign and Commonwealth Affairs is now responsible for relations with the independent members of the Commonwealth, with the Associated States, with the protected state of Brunei and for the administration of the UK dependent territories, in addition to his responsibilities for relations with foreign countries.

On 18 Apr 49, when the Republic of Ireland Act 1948 came into force, Southern Ireland ceased to be a member of the Commonwealth.

The Imperial Conference of 1926 defined Great Britain and the Dominions, as they were then called, as 'autonomous communities within the British Empire, equal in status, in no way subordinate one to another in any aspect of their domestic or foreign affairs, though united by a common allegiance to the Crown, and freely associated as members of the British Commonwealth of Nations'. On 11 Dec 31 the Statute of Westminster, which by legal enactment recognized the status of the Dominions as defined in 1926, became law. Each of the Dominions, which then included Canada, Australia, New Zealand, South Africa and Newfoundland (which in 1949 became a Canadian Province) had signified approval of the provisions of the Statute.

India and Pakistan became independent on 15 Aug 47; Ceylon, now Sri Lanka, on 4 Feb 48; Ghana (formerly the Gold Coast) on 6 Mar 57; the Federation of Malaya on 31 Aug 57 (renamed the Federation of Malaysia on 16 Sep 63, including from that date North Borneo, Sarawak and Singapore until 9 Aug 65 when Singapore became a separate independent state); Nigeria on 1 Oct 60; Cyprus on 16 Aug 60; Sierra Leone on 27 Apr 61; Tanganyika on

9 Dec 61 (renamed United Republic of Tanzania on 26 Apr 64 when she joined with Zanzibar, which had become independent on 10 Dec 63); Jamaica on 6 Aug 62; Trinidad and Tobago on 31 Aug 62; Uganda on 9 Oct 62; Western Samoa on 1 Jan 62; Kenya on 12 Dec 63; Malawi (formerly Nyasaland) on 6 July 64; Malta on 21 Sep 64; Zambia (formerly Northern Rhodesia) on 24 Oct 64; The Gambia on 18 Feb 65; Guyana (formerly British Guiana) on 26 May 66; Botswana (formerly Bechuanaland) on 30 Sep 66; Lesotho (formerly Basutoland) on 4 Oct 66; Barbados on 30 Nov 66; Mauritius on 12 Mar 68; Swaziland on 6 Sep 68; Nauru on 31 Jan 68; Tonga on 4 June 70; Fiji on 10 Oct 70; Bangladesh on 4 Feb 72; Bahamas on 10 July 73; Papua New Guinea on 16 Sep 75; Seychelles on 29 June 76; Solomon Islands on 7 July 78; Tuvalu on 1 Oct 78; Kiribati on 12 July 79; Zimbabwe on 18 Apr 80; Vanuatu on 30 July 80; Belize on 21 Sep 81; Brunei on 31 Dec 83. The Maldives became independent in 68, but did not join the Commonwealth until 1982. All became members of the Commonwealth on independence, except Cyprus, Western Samoa and Bangladesh which joined on 13 Mar 61, 28 Aug 70 and 18 Apr 72 respectively.

India became a republic on 26 Jan 50, Ghana on 29 June 60, Cyprus on 16 Aug 60, Tanganyika on 9 Dec 62, Nigeria on 1 Oct 63, Kenya on 12 Dec 63, Tanzania (on the unification of Tanganyika and Zanzibar) on 26 Apr 64, Zambia on 24 Oct 64, Singapore on 9 Aug 65, Malawi on 6 July 66, Botswana on 30 Sep 66, Uganda on 8 Sep 67, Nauru on 31 Jan 68, Guyana on 23 Feb 70, The Gambia on 24 Apr 70, Sierra Leone on 19 Apr 71, Ceylon as the Republic of Sri Lanka on 22 May 72, Seychelles on independence, Dominica on independence, Kiribati on independence, Zimbabwe on independence, Vanuatu on independence, Maldives on independence. They accept the Queen as the symbol of the free association of its independent member nations and as such Head of the Commonwealth.

On 4 Jan 48 Burma became an independent republic outside the Commonwealth.

South Africa withdrew from the Commonwealth on becoming a republic on 31 May 61.

To cater for the special circumstances of small states (Nauru, Tuvalu, St Vincent and the Grenadines, Maldives) a 'special membership' of the Commonwealth has been devised in close consultation with their governments.

They have the right to participate in all functional activities of the Commonwealth and to receive appropriate documentation in relation to them as well as the right to participate in non-Governmental Commonwealth organizations. They are not represented at meetings of Commonwealth Heads of Government, but may attend Commonwealth meetings at ministerial or official level in such fields as education, medical co-operation, finance and other functional and technical areas as their governments desire, and are eligible for Commonwealth technical assistance.

Pakistan withdrew from the Commonwealth on 30 Jan 72.

Territories dependent on the United Kingdom comprise dependent territories (properly so-called), a protectorate, a protected state and a Condominium. A dependent territory is a territory belonging by settlement, conquest or annexation to the British Crown. A protectorate is a territory not formally annexed but in which, by treaty, grant and other lawful means the Crown has power and jurisdiction. A protected state is a territory under a ruler which enjoys Her Majesty's protection, over whose foreign affairs she exercises control, but in respect of whose internal affairs she does not exercise jurisdiction.

United Kingdom dependencies administered through the Foreign and Commonwealth Office comprise in the Far East: Hong Kong (dependent territory); in the Indian Ocean: British Indian Ocean Territory; in the Mediterranean: Gibraltar; in the Atlantic Ocean: Bermuda, Falkland Islands and dependencies, South Georgia and South Sandwich Islands, British Antarctic Territory, St Helena and dependencies of Ascension and Tristan da Cunha; in the Caribbean: Montserrat, British Virgin Islands, Cayman Islands, Turks and Caicos Islands, Anguilla; in the Western Pacific: Pitcairn.

The island of Anguilla, although technically still a part of the State of St Christopher-Nevis-Anguilla, came under the direct administration of the United Kingdom through the Anguilla Act of 1971, and was formally separated from St Christopher-Nevis in 1980. The islands of Antigua, St Christopher-Nevis-Anguilla, Dominica, Grenada and St Lucia had entered a new form of relationship with Britain in 1967, as associated states. St Vincent became an associated state in 1969. Each had control of its own internal affairs, with the right to amend the constitution and the right to end the associated status if it so wished. Grenada became independent on 7 Feb 74, Dominica on 3 Nov 78, St Lucia on 22 Feb 79, St Vincent and the Grenadines on 27 Oct 79, Antigua and Barbuda on 1 Nov 81 and St Christopher-Nevis on 19 Sep 83.

The Island of Anguilla, although technically a part of the State of Saint Christopher-Nevis-Anguilla, through the Anguilla Act of 1971 and the Anguilla (Administration) Order 1971, come under the direct administration of the United Kingdom and by the Anguilla Act 1980 *de jure* a separate dependency of the United Kingdom. Provision is thereby made for Her Majesty's Commissioner to administer the Island in consultation with the Anguilla council.

While constitutional responsibility to parliament for the government of the dependent territories rests with the Secretary of State for Foreign and Commonwealth Affairs, the administration of the territories is carried out by the governments of the territories themselves.

A protected state is a territory under a ruler which enjoys Her Majesty's protection, over whose foreign affairs she exercises control but in respect of

265

whose internal affairs she does not exercise jurisdiction. Brunei is a protected state. Under the 1959 Agreement, as amended Nov 71 the UK remains responsible for the external affairs of Brunei, while Brunei has full responsibility for all internal matters. The two governments would consult together about measures to be taken separately and jointly in the event of any external threat to the State of Brunei.

Commonwealth Secretariat. In the communiqué issued at the end of the Commonwealth Prime Ministers' Conference in July 64, instructions were given for the preparation of proposals for the establishment of a Commonwealth Secretariat. These proposals were approved at the Commonwealth Prime Ministers' Conference in June 65, and the first Secretary-General, Arnold Smith (Canada), took up his duties on 17 Aug 65.

The following territories were dependencies or protectorates of Britain, and did not become members of the Commonwealth when they became independent:

Aden, held by Britain as a colony since 1939, and its associated territory as a protectorate, became independent on 30 Nov 67 (as the Southern Yemen People's Republic) and later changed its name to the People's Democratic Republic of Yemen.

Bahrain had been under British protection by treaty since 1882, and became independent on 15 Aug 71.

British Somaliland had been under British protection since 1887, and became independent on 26 June 60; on 1 July 60 it joined the former Italian Trusteeship Territory of Somalia as the Somali Republic.

Burma was annexed, by provinces, to British India between 1824 and 1886; the Indian Province of Burma was formed in 1852. Burma was separated from India in 1937 and became independent on 4 Jan 48.

Egypt became a British protectorate in 1914, having been occupied in 1882. The protectorate ended on 28 Feb 22 and Egypt became an independent kingdom.

Iraq came under British control in 1916 when it was part of the Ottoman Empire allied with Germany during World War I. It became a kingdom under British mandate in 1921 and an independent state on 3 Oct 32.

Palestine was administered by Britain under a League of Nations mandate, 1922–48.

Sudan was an Anglo-Egyptian condominium from 1899 until independence on 1 Jan 56.

Transjordan was administered by Britain under a League of Nations mandate 1922–28, and full independence as a kingdom (Jordan) was achieved on 22 Mar 46.

10 POPULATION[1]

ALBANIA

	Population	Area	Density
1924	831 877	27 529	30.2
1930	1 003 124	27 529	36.4
1947	1 150 000	28 748	40.0
1960	1 626 315	28 748	56.6
1967	1 964 730	28 748	68.3
1970	2 135 600	28 748	74.2
1979	2 590 600	28 748	90.0

AUSTRIA

	Population	Area	Density
1910	7 529 935	101 010	74.5
1920	6 428 336	83 792	76.7
1923	6 534 481	83 835	77.9
1934	6 760 233	83 835	80.6
1951	6 933 905	83 850	82.7
1961	7 073 807	83 850	84.4
1971	7 456 403	83 850	88.9
1981	7 555 338	83 853	90.0

BELGIUM

	Population	Area	Density
1910	7 423 784	29 456	252.0
1920	7 465 782	30 437	245.3
1930	8 092 004	30 437	265.9
1940	8 294 674	30 497	272.0
1947	8 512 195	30 497	279.1
1961	9 189 741	30 513	301.2
1970	9 690 991	30 513	317.6
1980	9 863 374	30 519	323.2

[1] area in sq. km.

BULGARIA

	Population	Area	Density
1910	4 337 516	87 146	49.8
1921	4 909 700	103 188	47.6
1926	5 478 741	103 188	53.1
1934	6 077 939	103 146	58.9
1946	7 022 206	110 841	63.3
1956	7 629 254	110 911	68.8
1965	8 227 866	110 911	74.2
1970	8 467 300	110 911	76.3
1975	8 727 771	110 911	78.5
1981	8 890 002	110 911	80.2

CYPRUS

	Population	Area	Density
1931	347 959	9251	37.6
1946	450 114	9251	48.7
1956	528 879	9251	57.2
1960	573 566	9251	62.0
1970	633 000	9251	68.4
1981	637 100	9251	68.9

CZECHOSLOVAKIA

	Population	Area	Density
1921	13 613 172	140 490	96.9
1930	14 729 536	140 490	104.8
1947	12 164 661	127 827	95.2
1961	13 745 577	127 870	107.5
1970	14 445 301	127 870	112.9
1980	15 276 799	127 871	119.0

DENMARK

	Population	Area	Density
1911	2 775 076	40 357	68.8
1921	3 289 195	44 403	74.1
1930	3 550 656	42 931	82.7
1935	3 706 349	42 931	86.3
1950	4 281 275	42 931	99.7
1960	4 585 256	43 069	106.5
1971	4 950 048	43 069	115.0
1981	5 123 989	43 080	119.0

ESTONIA

	Population	Area	Density
1922	1 110 538	47 549	23.4
1934	1 126 413	47 549	23.7
1939	1 134 000	47 549	23.8

FINLAND

	Population	Area	Density
1910	3 115 197	343 209	9.1
1920	3 364 807	343 209	9.8
1930	3 667 067	343 405	10.7
1942 (est.)	3 887 217	343 405	11.3
1950	4 029 803	305 475	13.2
1960	4 446 222	305 475	14.6
1970	4 707 000	305 475	15.4
1980	4 787 778	305 475	15.7

FRANCE

	Population	Area	Density
1911 (excluding Alsace-Lorraine)	39 601 509	536 464	73.8
1921 (including Alsace-Lorraine)	39 209 518	550 986	71.1
1931	41 834 923	550 986	76.0
1946	40 506 639	550 986	73.5
1954	42 777 174	551 601	77.6
1962	46 519 997	551 601	84.3
1968	49 778 540	551 601	90.2
1972	51 500 000	551 601	93.3
1975	52 655 802	551 601	97.0
1982	54 257 000	551 601	99.7

GERMANY (to 1940)

	Population	Area	Density
1910 (including Alsace-Lorraine)	64 925 993	540 740	120.1
1925 (after reduction at Versailles)	62 410 619	468 728	133.1
1933 (including Waldeck and Saarland)	66 030 491	470 600	140.3
1939 (including Austria and Sudetenland)	79 576 758	583 265	136.4

FEDERAL REPUBLIC OF GERMANY

	Population	Area	Density
1950	47 695 672	245 317	194.4
1971	61 502 500	248 593	247.4
1982	61 713 000	248 687	248.2

GERMAN DEMOCRATIC REPUBLIC

	Population	Area	Density
1947	19 102 000	108 173	176.6
1950	17 313 734	108 173	160.1
1964	17 003 655	108 173	157.2
1971	17 042 363	108 178	157.5
1980	16 737 200	108 177	154.0

GIBRALTAR

	Population	Area	Density
1911	19 586	6.5	3013.0
1921	17 160	6.5	2640.0
1931	17 613	6.5	2709.0
1951	23 232	6.5	3574.0
1961	24 075	6.5	3704.0
1968	26 007	6.5	4001.0
1970	26 833	6.5	4127.0
1981	30 522	6.5	4692.0

GREECE

	Population	Area	Density
1913	4 821 300	108 606	44.4
1920	5 536 375	108 606	51.0
1928	6 204 684	130 199	47.7
1940	7 347 002	132 561	55.4
1951	7 403 599	132 727	55.8
1961	8 388 553	131 944	63.6
1971	8 745 084	131 944	66.3
1981	9 706 687	131 986	73.5

HUNGARY

	Population	Area	Density
1910 (including Croatia and Slavonia)	20 886 787	324 773	64.3
1920	7 980 143	92 916	85.9
1931	8 688 349	92 916	93.5
1941	14 670 000	92 916	157.9
1960	9 961 044	93 030	107.0
1970	10 314 152	93 030	110.9
1980	10 710 000	93 032	115.0

ICELAND

	Population	Area	Density
1910	85 183	102 968	0.83
1920	94 679	102 846	0.92
1930	108 870	102 846	1.05
1940	121 618	102 846	1.18
1950	144 263	102 846	1.40
1960	177 292	102 819	1.72
1971	207 174	102 819	2.01
1981	231 958	102 819	2.27

IRELAND

	Population	Area	Density
1921	3 096 000	68 893	44.9
1936	2 968 420	68 893	43.1
1946	2 955 107	68 893	42.9
1956	2 898 264	68 893	42.1
1961	2 818 341	68 893	40.9
1971	2 971 230	68 893	43.1
1981	3 443 405	68 895	50.0

ITALY

	Population	Area	Density
1911	35 441 918	286 324	123.8
1921	37 143 102	305 573	121.5
1931	40 309 621	310 057	130.0
1936	42 024 584	310 189	135.4
1951	46 737 629	301 023	155.3
1961	50 463 762	301 225	167.5
1970	54 418 831	301 225	180.7
1981	56 243 935	301 245	187.0

LATVIA

	Population	Area	Density
1920	1 503 193	51 945	28.9
1935	1 950 502	51 945	37.5
1939	1 994 506	51 945	38.4

LIECHTENSTEIN

	Population	Area	Density
1930	10 213	160	63.8
1960	16 628	160	103.9
1970	21 350	160	133.4
1981	26 130	160	163.3

LITHUANIA

	Population	Area	Density
1923	2 168 971	59 463	36.5
1940	2 879 070	66 119	43.5

LUXEMBOURG

	Population	Area	Density
1916	263 824	2586	102.0
1950	298 578	2586	115.4
1970	339 848	2586	131.4
1980	365 100	2586	141.2

MALTA

	Population	Area	Density
1911	211 864	305.6	693.3
1921	213 024	305.6	697.1
1931	244 002	316.0	772.2
1948	306 996	316.0	971.5
1957	319 620	316.0	1011.4
1967	314 216	316.0	994.4
1971	322 072	316.0	1019.2
1981	319 936	316.0	1011.5

THE NETHERLANDS

	Population	Area	Density
	Population	*Area*	*Density*
1911	6 022 452	32 758	183.8
1920	6 865 314	32 587	210.7
1930	7 935 565	32 580	243.6
1938	8 728 569	32 924	265.1
1947	9 625 499	33 328	288.8
1960	11 556 008	33 612	343.8
1970	13 119 430	33 686	389.4
1980	14 091 014	33 938	415.0

NORWAY

	Population	*Area*	*Density*
1910	2 391 782	321 496	7.4
1920	2 649 775	323 658	8.2
1930	2 814 194	322 683	8.7
1946	3 156 950	323 917	9.7
1950	3 278 546	323 917	10.1
1960	3 591 234	323 917	11.1
1970	3 866 468	323 878	12.6
1980	4 091 142	323 895	12.6

POLAND

	Population	*Area*	*Density*
1921	27 092 025	380 266	71.2
1931	31 948 027	388 396	82.3
1950	24 976 926	311 732	80.1
1960	29 776 000	312 700	95.2
1970	32 670 000	312 700	104.5
1978	35 032 000	312 683	112.0

PORTUGAL

	Population	*Area*	*Density*
1920	6 032 991	89 329	67.5
1930	6 360 347	89 329	71.2
1940	7 722 152	89 329	86.4
1950	8 441 312	91 709	92.0
1960	8 889 392	91 641	97.0
1970	8 668 267	91 641	94.5
1981	9 803 400	91 631	107.0

273

ROMANIA

	Population	Area	Density
1920	17 393 149	316 710	54.9
1930	18 025 037	316 710	56.9
1941	13 551 756	195 198	69.4
1948	15 872 624	237 428	66.9
1956	17 489 794	237 428	73.7
1966	19 103 163	237 428	80.5
1970	20 140 000	237 428	84.8
1975	21 559 910	237 428	89.9
1980	22 200 000	237 428	92.5

SPAIN

	Population	Area	Density
1910	19 588 688	504 488	38.8
1920	21 303 162	504 488	42.2
1930	23 563 867	509 212	46.3
1940	25 877 971	492 229	52.5
1950	27 976 755	503 061	55.6
1960	30 430 698	503 545	60.4
1970	33 823 918	503 545	67.1
1981	37 746 260	504 750	74.0

SWEDEN

	Population	Area	Density
1910	5 522 403	447 749	12.3
1920	5 904 489	448 161	13.2
1930	6 141 571	448 992	13.7
1940	6 370 538	449 101	14.2
1950	7 041 829	449 206	15.7
1960	7 495 129	449 793	16.7
1965	7 766 424	449 793	17.3
1970	9 076 903	449 793	20.1
1975	8 208 442	411 615	20.0
1980	8 317 937	411 615	20.0

SWITZERLAND

	Population	Area	Density
1910	3 741 971	41 378	90.4
1920	3 880 320	41 378	93.8
1930	4 066 400	41 288	98.5
1941	4 265 703	41 288	103.3
1950	4 714 992	41 288	114.2
1960	5 429 061	41 288	131.5
1970	6 269 783	41 288	151.8
1980	6 365 960	41 288	154.0

TURKEY

	Population	Area	Density
1927	13 648 270	762 537	17.9
1935	16 158 018	762 537	21.2
1940	17 820 950	762 537	23.4
1950	20 936 524	767 119	27.3
1960	27 754 820	767 119	36.2
1965	31 391 421	767 119	40.9
1970	35 666 549	767 119	46.5
1980	44 737 000	767 119	58.3

USSR

	Population	Area	Density
1920	135 710 423	24 900 000	5.4
1926	147 013 609	21 300 000	6.9
1939	170 467 186	21 200 000	8.0
1959	208 826 000	22 400 000	9.3
1970	241 748 000	22 400 000	10.8
1979	262 436 000	22 400 000	11.7

UNITED KINGDOM

	Population	Area	Density
1921	43 176 521	243 363	177.8
1931	44 937 444	243 363	185.1
1951	49 012 362	243 363	201.4
1961	51 435 567	243 363	211.4
1971	55 347 000	243 363	227.8
1981	55 775 650	243 363	229.2

YUGOSLAVIA

	Population	Area	Density
1921	12 017 323	248 987	48.3
1931	13 934 039	247 495	56.3
1953	16 927 275	256 393	66.0
1961	18 549 291	255 804	72.5
1970	20 529 000	255 804	80.3
1981	22 427 585	255 804	87.7

INDEX

Most of the chapters in this book run in alphabetical sequence and for this reason we have not attempted to produce a completely detailed index. The main aim has been to allow the reader to locate the country by page for any major subject included in this work.